# Family Matters

# Family Matters

## Adoption and Foster Care in Children's Literature

Ruth Lyn Meese

**LIBRARIES UNLIMITED**

*An Imprint of ABC-CLIO, LLC*

A B C ⬤ C L I O

Santa Barbara, California • Denver, Colorado • Oxford, England

Copyright 2010 by Ruth Lyn Meese

All rights reserved. No part of this publication may be reproduced, stored in a
retrieval system, or transmitted, in any form or by any means, electronic, mechanical,
photocopying, recording, or otherwise, except for the inclusion of brief quotations in a
review, without prior permission in writing from the publisher.

**Library of Congress Cataloging-in-Publication Data**

Meese, Ruth Lyn.
  Family matters : adoption and foster care in children's literature / Ruth Lyn Meese.
     p. cm.
  Includes bibliographical references and index.
    ISBN 978–1–59158–782–8 (hard copy (paper) : alk. paper) — ISBN 978–1–59158–783–5 (ebook)
1.  Adoption—Study and teaching (Primary)—United States. 2.  Adopted children—Education—United States.
3.  Foster children—Education—United States. 4.  Adoption—Juvenile literature—Bibliography. 5.  Foster
children—Juvenile literature—Bibliography. 6.  Adoption in literature—Bibliography. I. Title.
HV875.55.M42   2010
372.83—dc22            2009040750

14  13  12  11  10      1  2  3  4  5

This book is also available on the World Wide Web as an eBook.
Visit www.abc-clio.com for details.

ABC-CLIO, LLC
130 Cremona Drive, P.O. Box 1911
Santa Barbara, California 93116-1911

This book is printed on acid-free paper ∞

Manufactured in the United States of America

*This book is dedicated to the two most influential people in my life, my husband, James W. Windle, and my daughter, Katie Svetlana Windlemeese. You are my daily inspiration and I love you both deeply.*

# Contents

# *Preface*

Family structures have obviously changed through the past 25 years. Families are more diverse than ever before, and many children live with other than biological family members. Teachers today will no doubt have in their classrooms children who have been adopted or placed into foster care. Just as family members help children and youth understand and deal with issues related to foster care or adoption, teachers, too, have a tremendous impact on a child's understanding of self. The teacher, however, may be influenced by the daily news, books, movies, Web sites, or magazines, just like other Americans. Teachers may not possess the knowledge, skills, or attitudes needed to choose lesson plans, language, or activities offering a positive, sensitive, and accurate picture of children living in alternative family structures. Instead, they may unknowingly use language, materials, and lessons that foster stereotypes or provoke questions or teasing of children who have been adopted or placed into foster care.

Because teachers are trained to choose "quality" literature for use in the classroom, for example, they may automatically assume that award-winning books or stories such as those winning Caldecott or Newbery Medals or Honors or those on the Children's Notable List are the "best" books when planning lessons. Unfortunately, few Caldecott or Newbery books include themes associated with foster care or adoption, and those that do may not all accurately represent children and youth currently living in such alternative family arrangements. Furthermore, teachers may be unaware of other literature that does accurately portray adoption and foster care or they may not know how to judge books and stories dealing with these themes.

This book will provide teachers with guidelines for evaluating K–8 literature containing adoption or foster care themes. In addition, the book covers developmental issues related to adoption and foster care for children in grades K–8, and suggestions for positive language, healthy discussions, and sensitive assignments are included. Finally, books and stories not included on the award-winning book lists are also reviewed. The purpose of this book, then, is to help teachers provide youngsters with accurate information and sensitive responses so that all children, no matter their living arrangements, will feel safe and valued in the classroom and know that their family matters!

# *Acknowledgments*

Completing a book is always a group rather than a solo effort. For this reason, I would like to thank the following individuals for their support and advice throughout this process. First, I would like to thank the editor at Libraries Unlimited, Ms. Sharon Coatney, Emma Bailey, Kathy Breit, and the reviewers for their helpful feedback and comments. Second, I must give my Library Media colleagues, Dr. Audrey Church, Ms. Frances Reeve, and Ms. Cindy Schmidt, a huge thank you for their technical assistance and suggestions regarding databases. Finally, I owe my family and colleagues thanks for their patience with me during my research and writing. Thank you all!

*Ruth Lyn Meese*

# CHAPTER 1

## *All Kinds of Families*

Teachers are well aware of diversity in their schools. Gender, race or ethnicity, and religious beliefs are each acknowledged by teachers as important areas of diversity they must consider. As they get acquainted with their students each year, teachers also inevitably notice differences among their families. Katrina lives at home with both of her biological parents and her two siblings. Larry and his younger sister live with their mother and grandmother. Luis lives with his aunt and his married stepsister, while Shakira lives with her mother, her stepfather, two stepbrothers, and one half sister. Lisa lives with her parents who adopted her from Russia at age five, and Diego lives with his foster parents. Although these children come from diverse family backgrounds, all are cared for and nurtured by their families. Differences in family makeup are simply another form of diversity for which teachers must be prepared.

To say that children in schools today come from all kinds of families is almost cliché, yet children do indeed come from diverse family structures. As teachers well know, not all children live with both biological parents in the home. According to the U.S. Census Bureau (Kreider, 2007), large shifts occurred in the United States between 1970 and 1990 in children's living arrangements. The proportion of children living only with their biological mother doubled from 11 to 22 percent during those two decades; however, since 1990 this change has remained relatively stable. In the 2007 current population survey (Edwards, 2008), 73.7 million children under the age of 18 lived in the United States. Of those, 67.8 percent, or approximately 50 million children, lived with two married parents (e.g., two biological parents or one biological and one stepparent), 25.8 percent lived with only one parent, 3.5 percent lived with no parent present, and 2.9 percent lived with two unmarried partners in the same household.

U.S. Census Bureau reports thus indicate what teachers have already noticed: their students come from different types of family arrangements. These may reflect the results of marriage, divorce, economic circumstances, or the remarriage of their parents (Kreider, 2007). Although about 94 percent of children live with at least one biological parent, most (88 percent) of those living with only one parent remain with their mother. Another 8 percent of children live with at least one stepparent, most often a stepfather. In addition, the number of parents in a household varies by race or ethnicity, with 87 percent of Asian children living with two parents as compared with 78 percent of White non-Hispanic children and 38 percent of Black children. Also, one-third of all children today are born to unmarried mothers. These children may be raised in single-parent families or be raised in part by stepparents or others, including relatives and nonrelatives, who contribute to the family income and the child's development.

For example, about 6.5 million children (9 percent of all children) in 2004 lived with at least one grandparent present in the household. This percentage varied by race and ethnicity with 14 percent of Black children, 12 percent of Hispanic children, and 6 percent of White non-Hispanic children living with a grandparent. In addition, Kreider (2007) reported that 1.6 million of those children living with grandparents had no parent present in the home. More than half (56 percent) of all children not living with their parents lived with grandparents. These children were also more likely to be living in poverty than children with no grandparents in the home (22 percent and 17 percent, respectively). Kreider (2007) indicates that grandparents are the most frequently mentioned relatives used by parents as care providers for children under the age of 5, and recent estimates suggest that 4.5 million children in the United States today are primarily being raised by their grandparents (AARP, 2000).

Like grandparents, siblings also contribute to the well-being and development of their brothers and sisters. The majority of children (79 percent) in schools today have at least one sibling and most of these live with their siblings at home (Kreider, 2007). Among children under age 18, 12 percent have at least one half-sibling, a brother or sister with whom they share one biological parent, living with them. For 17 percent of all children (12.2 million), a blended family containing stepchildren, stepparents, half-siblings, or stepsiblings constitutes the normal family structure.

Of course, not all children live with their parents or with biological relatives. Among children living with no parent in the home, 783,000 were cared for by foster parents in 2007 (AFCARS, 2008). Although 287,000 children left foster care during 2007, another 293,000 children entered foster care during that same year. Unfortunately, 130,000 children in foster care were *waiting* to be adopted, but only 51,000 children who left foster care were *actually* adopted from the foster care system in 2007. In addition, over 20,000 children are adopted by U.S. citizens each year from other countries, with more than 200,000 foreign-born children of intercountry adoption currently living in the United States (U.S. Citizenship and Immigration Services, 2008). The number of domestic infant adoptions, babies born in the United States and subsequently adopted by parents in the United States, is not officially counted but is estimated to be between 13,000 and 14,000 infants per year (Hamilton, Ventura, Martin, & Sutton, 2004). As a matter of fact, about one in every 25 households now contains a child who has been adopted by someone other than a stepparent, including children adopted through foster care or through an intercountry or domestic adoption.

## UNDERSTANDING FOSTER CARE AND ADOPTION

Approximately one million children each year obtain their families through foster care or adoption, but because these children are not living with biological parents, their family situations may be misunderstood by peers and teachers or viewed as "inferior" to living with biological family. Although attitudes are changing, some Americans still harbor misperceptions or fears regarding adoption (Harris Interactive, 2002). Thus, teachers must help their students understand that families are made up of people who love and care for each other and that families can be created in many different ways. Adoption and foster care are simply two ways in which loving families are formed.

Children are placed in foster care or available for adoption for numerous reasons, but none of these reasons are related to things the children themselves have done. All have biological parents whose circumstances prevent them from providing appropriate care to their offspring. Children may be voluntarily or involuntarily placed into foster care. Some children are placed in foster care by court order (i.e., an involuntary placement) due to abuse or neglect by the parent or by someone else in the home.

In other cases, such as substance abuse, the court may determine that in the best interest of the child he or she is in need of supervision by someone other than the parent(s). Sometimes parents are temporarily unable to care for their child due to serious medical or emotional conditions or to extreme financial difficulty. Although the child has experienced no abuse or neglect, parents might sign a voluntary placement agreement permitting the child's temporary removal from the home. The training, remuneration, and support offered to foster parents varies from state to state, but all are expected to provide a safe and nurturing home environment for the children placed in their care. In addition, the goal of foster care placement is to plan and prepare for a permanent home for the child including a return to biological family members, finding parents through adoption, or helping older children obtain independent living skills and emancipation. The difficulty for children in foster care, of course, is that the foster care family, no matter how loving, may only be a temporary placement for the child.

Similarly, children are placed for adoption for many different reasons. Some children are adopted by their foster care parents or others when a return to biological parents is not safe or feasible. Many others are adopted by a stepparent following the remarriage of a biological parent. Other children are born to young or unmarried mothers who do not have the skills or the emotional and financial stability to raise a child. These mothers make an adoption plan to ensure their baby will have mature, loving, and responsible parents. In addition, many other children are adopted from other countries by U.S. citizens due to war, poverty, famine, or social upheaval abroad.

Parents who adopt must complete a home study, according to the requirements of their state, through which they must demonstrate the emotional, physical, and financial ability to parent. This process might also entail group or individual sessions on behavior management or the impact of adoption on the child's identity, on other family members, and on members of the adoption triad (i.e., biological parents, parents, and child). In addition, parents who adopt children from other countries must also meet the requirements of that country's adoption law and adopt through an agency licensed both in their home state and in the country of their child's birth. Intercountry adoptions may necessitate additional preparation sessions be provided to parents, such as information about the language or culture of the child or information about the health and development of children from the country of origin before and after adoption.

## The Changing Nature of Adoption and Foster Care in the United States

Differences in family structure are more openly accepted today than in the past, yet adoption and foster care are still not as well understood or freely acknowledged as other forms of family diversity. Some current misunderstandings regarding adoption and foster care are rooted in history and the secrecy and stigma once attached to families living outside the "normal" biological unit. In fact, the earliest forms of foster care and adoption in the United States were not designed with the best interests of the child in mind but rather were conducted as "business" arrangements of benefit to the adults involved (Askeland, 2006). In Colonial America, impoverished and orphaned children were often placed involuntarily by local authorities to work with farmers or business owners or in homes, or they were sold as apprentices. Whereas in England, legitimate "bloodlines" were the only recognized forms of kinship for inheritance, some of the colonies did permit a semilegal status through adoption. Not until 1851, however, did the first state, Massachusetts, pass an adoption law.

Although orphanages existed in the United States before the Revolutionary War, increasing immigration, industrialization, and sweeping epidemics led to the construction of large-scale orphanages, foundling homes, or hospitals in the 1830s (Askeland, 2006). By the mid-1800s, many of these orphanages were operated as charitable missions with most of the children living there as a result of parents too poor or ill to care for them. In the early 1850s, Charles Loring Brace and the Children's Aid Society began relocating children from large urban areas to families in the West, believing that relocating children was preferable to life in a large institution even when the child still had living parents or other biological relatives. According to Holt (2006), these so-called *orphan trains* were conducted as social contracts in which all parties understood that the child was to become a legitimate and loved member of the receiving family. Many placements through the orphan trains did result in loving families for children, yet the Children's Aid Society entrusted the screening of potential placements with local authorities. Some children became servants or workers rather than family members; thus by the end of the 1800s, child advocates, social workers, reformers, and state laws all contributed to a distinction between foster care and adoption and led to the end of "placing out" through the orphan trains (Holt, 2006).

With the Great Depression, the number of children in orphanages in the United States had increased to 144,000 by the middle of the 1930s (Creagh, 2006). Similarly, the number of children living in newly created foster care arrangements grew to an all-time high during the Depression years. By the 1930s state adoption laws and a growing interest in adoption as a way to create a family resulted in 17,000 adoptions in 1937 and 50,000 by 1945. Moreover, following World War II, parents increasingly began to adopt children orphaned in other countries as a result of war. Pearl S. Buck, for example, focused attention on transracial, intercountry adoption when she adopted several children from Korea in the 1950s and also helped other parents adopt through her agency "Welcome House." With the Civil Rights Movement of the 1960s, the Supreme Court ruling in *Roe v. Wade* in 1973, and the changing attitudes toward women and sexual freedom, the number of infants available for adoption in the United States plummeted throughout the 1970s. Prospective parents began increasingly to seek infants and older children through intercountry adoption rather than waiting for the domestic adoption of a newborn child. With the widely publicized plight of children in orphanages in Romania, the media attention focused on girls abandoned in China, and the dissolution of the Soviet Union, the 1990s and early 2000s witnessed increasing numbers of parents forming their families through adoptions in Eastern Europe and China.

The predominant wisdom in the early to mid 1900s was one of protecting the child from knowledge about his or her adoption; therefore, adoptions were "closed" arrangements in which no member of the adoption triad (i.e., birth parents, parents, child) was provided with information. Adoption seemed shrouded in secrecy and was to be avoided in conversation (Carp, 1998). During the latter half of the 1900s, however, the "child saving" or protective efforts of the 1800s and the tendency to surround adoption in a veil of secrets, gave way to the right of the child to know his or her biological roots (Satz & Askeland, 2006). Although adoption records may still be closed in specific states or countries from which a child was adopted, current best practices encourage parents to help children understand their adoption story as early as possible, revisiting the story with increasing complexity as children grow and ask additional questions. According to Satz and Askeland (2006), adoption from the 1970s until the present has been characterized by several "movements":

- The *search movement or adoption rights movement* in which biological parents seek to open records and find their offspring or, similarly, the person who has been adopted seeks to open records to find his or her biological roots;

- The *open adoption movement* in which the birth parents and parents may meet and remain in contact with one another after the adoption has been finalized; and,

- The *intercountry or international adoption movement* characterized by parents traveling to countries such as Guatemala, Russia, or China to adopt their children.

Each of these movements, however, has engendered controversy. Opening records, for example, may help parents and their children determine important medical and genetic information. Opening records may also help children who have been adopted experience a sense of "closure" about the past or a more well-defined identity. On the other hand, opening records may violate the right to privacy for all parties concerned. Similarly, not all individuals who are adopted want to meet or contact their biological families and not all birth parents desire contact with their children who have been placed for adoption. Open adoption, legal in about 20 states, raises concern by parents that biological family members may attempt to interfere with family life, and others (Melosh, 2002) maintain that the benefits of full disclosure of information and ongoing contact are outweighed by evidence that in an open adoption birth mothers may seek little contact with the child, leading to the child experiencing continued feelings of rejection and guilt. Finally, international adoptions are perceived by some to be unjust exploitation of struggling countries by wealthy, White Americans who remove poor or minority children from their cultural or ethnic heritage. Certainly with media coverage of celebrities adopting children from struggling nations seemingly without following the legal processes required of others, or with news stories asserting that parents of these nations are offering their children for a price, adoption could easily be misconstrued as exploitation. Others, however, view intercountry adoption as a loving and far more humane alternative for children than remaining in an orphanage or on the streets (Bartholet, 2006). Despite such controversy, international adoptions have not only increased over the past decade but have also focused attention on the success of transracial or interracial adoptions. Today, more than ever before, adoption is becoming a visible way in the United States to form a family.

## Current Perceptions of Adoption and Foster Care

Pertman (2000) suggests that adoption is transforming the face of America, causing American communities to become more multiracial and multiethnic than ever. He suggests that adoption not only mirrors changes in our society but also contributes to these changes. Television and magazines today give visible testimony to people who have been adopted (e.g., Gerald Ford, Steve Jobs, Faith Hill, Dave Thomas) and to those who have adopted their children (e.g., Steven Spielberg, Tom Cruise, Angelina Jolie). Yet, how do Americans really view adoption today?

In a recent survey conducted on behalf of the Dave Thomas Foundation for Adoption and the Evan B. Donaldson Adoption Institute, four out of ten American adults (81.5 million people) said they had considered adopting a child at some point in their lives, with almost half of all people between the ages of 35 and 54 indicating they had considered this option (Harris Interactive, 2002). No differences in responses occurred across education or income levels. In addition, 65 percent of adults responding to the survey stated they had experience with adoption through their own families or through friends, and two-thirds of all Americans indicated a favorable opinion about adoption. Females were more likely to consider adopting a child than males and Hispanic individuals were more likely to entertain adoption than African American or White individuals. African American adults were, however, more favorable to adoption through the foster care system than were others. Other indicators of strong support for adoption included:

- 78 percent of Americans think the country should be doing more to encourage adoption;
- 95 percent think that adoptive parents should receive the same maternity and paternity benefits from employers as biological parents;
- Three-fourths (75 percent) of Americans believe adoptive parents are likely to love their adopted children just as much as children born to them;
- Over 80 percent think that parents get as much or more satisfaction from raising their adopted children as from raising their biological children; and,
- Americans also have very positive opinions about adoptive parents. They are seen as lucky by 94 percent of Americans (Harris Interactive, 2002, p. 6).

Nevertheless, some Americans still hold misperceptions about adoption. For example, with the few extremely rare cases vividly sensationalized by the media, 82 percent of Americans fear that birth parents might attempt to regain custody of a child after adoption. Others believe that children who have been adopted, especially those adopted through foster care, will have behavioral or adjustment problems; yet, most children who have been adopted have no more difficulty with school work, behavior, substance use, or adjustment than biological children. Others fear that the cost of adoption is prohibitive, despite the federal adoption tax credit. While most Americans believe that international adoptions are easier to finalize than domestic adoptions, 47 percent also believe that children of intercountry adoptions are more likely to have medical or emotional difficulties than children adopted domestically (Harris Interactive, 2002). Interestingly, both intercountry and foster care adoptions have increased over the past decades regardless of lingering concern over medical and emotional risk factors for children in these groups.

Citizens are also divided regarding their opinions about open adoption, the search by and for biological parents, and interracial adoption. About 21 percent believe open adoptions are a "good idea" in *most* cases, 47 percent believe open adoption may be a "good idea" in *some* cases, 21 percent say it is a "good idea" in *only a few* cases, and 10 percent believe open adoption is *never* a "good idea." Similarly, while most Americans believe that for the adopted child to seek out birth parents is both good for the child and for the parents (68 percent and 60 percent, respectively), only 49 percent believe this is appropriate for the birth parents to initiate. Finally, Americans perceive opposition to interracial adoptions, with the opposition higher among African Americans and people 55 years of age and older (Harris Interactive, 2002).

## THE IMPACT OF ADOPTION AND FOSTER CARE ON THE CHILD

When children enter school, they begin to develop an awareness of their differences from peers. Children view themselves as "taller" or "shorter" than others, or they see themselves as wearing the same or different types of clothing as their friends. Physical differences, such as hair color, gender, and race, are quickly noticed by children in the early grades. Over time, children also begin to compare other attributes, noting who is the "fastest" or the "smartest" in the class. Similarly, children begin to notice family membership and ask questions that may be difficult to answer for children in foster care or children who have been adopted. The answers to these questions may also be difficult for peers to understand. Strong emotions such as anger, fear, guilt, shame, or a sense of loss may be generated by any mention of adoption or foster care; therefore, teachers must examine their own attitudes and stereotypes and prepare to assist children through the feelings engendered when questions or comments arise.

Coping with strong emotions and feelings of loss are, of course, not unique to children who have been adopted or placed in foster care. Brodzinsky, Schechter, and Henig (1992), for example, state that many children suffer the loss of a parent through divorce or death. These losses, however, are less complicated and different from those of adoption or foster care. Divorce is relatively common today and is at least potentially reversible. Parents do remarry and noncustodial parents are frequently permitted to visit. In addition, children have a store of memories from before the divorce, which ultimately may help them to adjust to their new parent and new family situation. Similarly, when a child loses his or her parent through death, the experience is less common than that of divorce, but it is one that is universally understood by adults and children alike. The child has a history of memories to help him or her cope with the loss, and family rituals and support systems are available to help the child weather emotions related to the loss of the parent. On the other hand, children who have been adopted or placed in foster care find themselves in a less common and less well-understood situation than children who have lost parents through divorce or death. Children who have been adopted or placed into foster care may fantasize about reunions with their biological family; yet, they may have little history with or information about this family. Extended birth family, genetic heritage, cultural and national origins all may be removed from the child, sometimes creating a feeling of impermanence or loss of self. The biological family lingers "ghostlike" in the imagination, and the child's sense of loss may not be seen or acknowledged by others, making it difficult for children to deal with their loss.

Of course individual children respond to adoption and foster care in different ways. Some children seem barely interested in their family circumstances while others are sensitive to any difference between their own families and those of their friends. In addition, children who are placed in homes through adoption and foster care may not see the broader picture and, instead, may focus only on their own personal situations. Children who have not been adopted or placed outside their biological homes may simply be curious and ask probing questions such as *"Where are your **real** parents?"* or *"When are you going back to your home town?"* or *"Why don't you look like your mother and dad?"* Both children who have and have not been removed from biological family members must be guided to understand adoption and foster care according to their developmental levels.

Brodzinsky, Smith, and Brodzinsky (1998) and Brodzinsky, Schechter, and Henig (1992) describe the developmental tasks of individuals who have been adopted. They suggest that children who have been adopted have the same developmental tasks as typical youngsters of the same age, but that they have *additional* tasks due to their adoption, which may impact them to varying degrees across the life span. (See Table 1.1.) For example, they state that preschoolers are just learning their adoption story

**Table 1.1**
**Developmental Characteristics and Adoption Tasks across the Grade Levels**

| Grade Levels | Typical Developmental Characteristics | Additional Tasks Resulting from Adoption |
|---|---|---|
| Preschool through Grade 2 | Curious and seeking autonomy | Learning one's adoption story |
| | Egocentric (e.g., only has self viewpoint) | Beginning to note some differences from others, particularly when differences are physical as in transracial adoptions |
| | Developing cognitive, motor, and social skills | |
| | Safety and security in home | |
| Grades 3–5 | Acceptance by peers is important | Understanding full meaning of adoption (i.e., to gain a family means a loss of a family) |
| | Mastery of skills is important to self-esteem (May be self-conscious) | Thoughts and feelings about birth mother and birth family (e.g., abandonment, grief, guilt) |
| | Developing abstract thought processes | Feelings of being different |
| | | Coping with peer reactions, questions, and comments |
| Grades 6–8 | Developing an identity | Integrating adoption into identity |
| | Need for sense of belonging | Thoughts and feelings about birth family and heritage (e.g., genetics, thoughts about search or where I belong) |
| | Understands and can take multiple perspectives on issues | Perceptions of family lost versus reality of family gained |
| | | Coping with peer reactions |

from their parents. They receive information and ask questions but have little understanding of what adoption actually means. Six- to 12-year-olds are mastering the meaning of adoption and coming to terms with adoption loss, thinking about their birth parents, and coping with perceived differences associated with their adoption. As children enter and progress through adolescence, they begin to integrate adoption into their identity. Feelings of loss and questions about their birth family and birth heritage, however, may continue. Teachers who are aware of the impact of adoption or foster care across the grade levels may be in a better position to help their students understand one another. They can focus on the developmental *commonalities* among children, such as developing one's "identity," rather than on their differences.

Preschoolers are egocentric and focus on their own families and their own stories. Youngsters who have been adopted may readily repeat parts of their adoption story to peers and to teachers; however, they may not fully understand the facts. For example, children might gleefully tell others "*Mommy and Daddy got me on an airplane*" or "*I've got two mommies.*" These stories precipitate reactions from peers who mistakenly believe that their friend was born on an airplane or who respond with the statement "*No, you **can't** have two mommies.*" Preschoolers are also likely to ask parents questions such as "*Why doesn't Mia look like you?*" when they notice obvious physical differences between parents and children. At this level the teacher can convey to all children in the classroom that people come from all kinds of families, that families are made up of people who love each other and care for each other, and that all kinds of families are "okay."

As children grow, they begin to master their world and become more concerned about differences. The child in kindergarten through the second or third grade begins to understand the nature of birth and biological connections among family members. Children who have been adopted or who are in foster care may listen to a peer provide details about the day he or she was born. Peers might describe the time of their birth, unusual stories about their mother's trip to the hospital, or what family members said or did. Children at this age lose their first teeth, leading some to say when they grew their first tooth as a baby or to share baby pictures of themselves with or without teeth! The child who has been adopted or who has lived in foster care for a long period of time may have only limited or no information regarding his or her birth, and the child who has been adopted from another country may feel even more that he or she is different from others. Baby pictures and details about birth history are often nonexistent for these children; therefore, children not living with biological parents find it difficult to respond to such conversations because they seem to magnify differences from their friends. They may be adjusting to a new family through adoption or worrying about whether or not they will stay with their current foster care family. A growing understanding regarding the difference between most families and their own families leads to anxiety at this stage. Teachers must affirm for children at this level that families are permanent. They can also continue to convey the message that all kinds of families are okay and all provide love and care for their members.

By grades 3–5, upper elementary-aged children are more self-conscious and often actively resist being different from peers. At this level, too, they are beginning to develop more complex thinking skills. Children start to realize that gaining a family also means they have lost one. Children begin to think about their birth mother or birth father, birth siblings, or extended family members. They may also wonder about their country or culture if they were not born in the United States. Children who have been adopted or who have been placed in foster care may question whether something they did led to their removal from their birth family. They may spend time grieving about their loss, daydreaming about what their birth mother might be like, and wondering whether or not their birth mother ever thinks about them. These children may wonder about the choices made by their birth mother and come up with simple solutions, still unable to envision the complexity of her decision. For example, children might think: "If she was too poor to care for me, why didn't she get a job?" or "If she was alone and didn't have anyone to help care for a baby, why didn't she get married, or ask her parents for help?" or "If she didn't know how to care for a baby, why didn't someone teach her?" (Brodzinky, Smith, & Brodzinsky, 1998, p. 29). Similarly, questions or comments that make them feel different, or reactions from others who do not seem to understand, may well be resented. Children who have not been adopted might wonder why any mother would not raise her child. They might wonder what caused their friend to be removed from his or her first family, and they might be scared that this might happen to them. Peers might also worry that their friend will be "sent back" or they might be saddened to think that a child may never know his or her first mother.

Mixed feelings such as these abound in the upper elementary grades. Emotions for children who have been adopted or placed in foster care include sadness over their loss, feelings of anger, rejection, or abandonment, fear that they have no control over their circumstances, shame that their birth family or country was unable to care for them, worry that their birth family may not be well, guilt that they are in good homes, and love for their parents and siblings. So too children who have not been adopted may feel guilt, anxiety, fear, or sadness when they contemplate how their friend is no longer with his or her biological family. At this level, teachers can provide accurate information about adoption and foster care. They can also affirm that conflicting emotions are normal for children at this age and that each person's family is unique.

By grades 6–8, children are seeking to belong and are beginning to develop their identity as an individual independent from their parents. Questions about medical history and genetics may haunt children who have no contact with biological family members but who are simultaneously transforming into adults they see in the mirror. At this age, children think about where they belong, who they look like, and what they will be when they grow up. Although children from 11 to 14 or 15 may be wondering about their birth family, they may not want to talk openly about their adoption or foster care placement. Mention of adoption or foster care might make children of this age feel that they stand out from their peers in undesirable ways. Instead, they might fantasize about the birth family, contrast their existing family with what "might have been," and brood about their situation and loss silently. Confrontations at home may well result in statements such as *"My birth mother wouldn't be so mean . . . she would let me go to that party!"* In addition, children may begin to understand the complex nature of adult circumstances and decision making, yet still pronounce judgment on parents who would "lose" their child to adoption or foster care. Children who have been adopted or placed in foster care may reanalyze existing information, seeking answers to missing pieces of their puzzle and worrying that they may unknowingly develop difficulties they envision their birth parents to have portrayed. According to Schoettle (2003), middle and junior high school students may also be confronted by questions outside of the classroom, in the hallways and on the school bus, that intensify their own self-doubts and that would make anyone uncomfortable including:

- *Were you a mistake?*
- *Is your real mother a prostitute?*
- *How can you be sure what you will look like when you get older?*
- *Do you think you might end up marrying your real brother and never know it?*
- *How much did your parents pay for you?* (p. 21)

Children in the middle and junior high school years are particularly vulnerable to misinformation and sensationalism portrayed in magazines, on the Internet, on television, or in movies. They require teachers who will provide facts when adoption or foster care concerns arise, but who maintain sensitivity to the unique and private nature of adoption and foster care for the individual student. Prying or placing children on the spot in front of their peers is never advisable.

## SUMMARY

The nature of adoption and foster care has changed in recent years. According to Smith and Riley (2006), when children enter school and become aware of differences, their self-esteem is impacted by the responses of those around them. If adoption is accepted as normal and positive, children feel safe and valued. When the mention of adoption or foster care is met with silence or with inappropriate comments, children feel shame or disapproval. Teachers must convey to students that children live in all kinds of families and that no type of family is better or worse than any other. Accurate information and acceptance in the classroom are crucial for children living in foster care and those who have been adopted.

# CHAPTER 2

## Respecting Adoption and Foster Care in the Classroom through Sensitive Language, Assignments, and Literature

Just as family members help children and youth understand and deal with issues related to foster care or adoption, teachers, too, have a tremendous impact on a child's sense of self. Like other Americans, however, teachers may be influenced by television, news reports, movies, books, or the Internet. They may have misperceptions about families formed through adoption or about children living in foster care families. If teachers do not have the knowledge or skills to choose lesson plans, language, reading materials, and activities that offer a sensitive and accurate picture of children living in alternative family structures, they may unknowingly perpetuate stereotypes or even provoke hurtful questions or teasing aimed at the child who has been adopted or placed in foster care (Smith & Riley, 2006).

Seemingly small actions on the part of the teacher may have unintended consequences for the child who lives with other than biological family. For example, sometimes schools or classrooms engage in "Adopt a . . ." type projects in which children collect money to support particular causes like pet shelters or caring for manatees. Or, conversely, an individual might "adopt" a classroom and provide resources for the children in the room. Young children who have been adopted might be confused by these projects, believing they are no different than animals that are adopted or worrying that the individual who is adopting their classroom may remove them from their home. In addition, elementary level teachers often assign children a project to create a timeline of their life. They may require that children include information and photographs from each year they have lived. Children who have been adopted beyond infancy, especially those adopted from other countries, may not have early information or photographs such as when they first began to walk or to talk. So, too, the child who has lived in a series of foster care families may be missing early information, or their photographs might contain a changing cast of family members. Moreover, children who have been adopted and those in foster care may not want to share the information they do have; therefore, this assignment can create frustration, anxiety, or fear for the child who must decide among undesirable alternatives: *Do I "make up" information about myself? Do I share information I would rather keep personal? Do I draw pictures for some years and look different from everyone else? Do I just skip over some years and perhaps get a bad grade?*

Similarly, teachers' casual questions and remarks can communicate acceptance or shame for families created in nontraditional ways. Imagine, for example, that before class begins students are discussing a movie or something they have heard on the news. One student might say, "The movie about the *Orphan* said 'Never adopt' and who would want an evil kid anyway!" So, too, the teacher might overhear one child say to another, "*I don't know how any mother could give her kid away, but I guess women like that just fool around without caring about what happens to the kid!*" Or, during the discussion of a story, such as *Pictures of Hollis Woods* (Giff, 2002), that children are reading in class, the teacher might hear one child ask another, "*You're in foster care. Did you ever run away like in the story?*" The teacher's response to comments like these can greatly impact the security of the child living in foster care or the child who has been adopted. Teachers who agree that mothers should "never give a child away" or that "kids who live in foster care have lots of problems" are perpetuating stereotypes and misinformation regarding adoption and foster care.

Given the diverse nature of families today, teachers can assume that their classes will indeed contain children living with other than biological relatives. Using positive language and providing accurate communication about adoption and foster care is critical. So, too, is providing alternatives for all children when giving potentially sensitive assignments. Finally, thinking carefully about how adoption or foster care are portrayed in the stories and books read in the classroom may prepare teachers to help their students view adoption and foster care as positive ways to build families. In this way, all children, regardless of the nature of their families, can feel safe at school.

## USING POSITIVE LANGUAGE

The old saying "*Sticks and stones may break my bones, but words can never hurt me*" is well-intended yet simply not true! Words can and do hurt children at school every day! Knowing how to phrase difficult concepts through positive language is a crucial skill for all teachers (Meese, 1999, 2002), particularly for those who have in their classrooms students who have been adopted or who are living in foster care.

Children who have been adopted are frequently asked questions of a sensitive and personal nature by other children and adults alike. Questions such as "*Where are your **real** parents?*" "*Do you know anything about your **natural** parents?*" "*Do you look like your **real** parents?*" or "*What would you do if your **real** parents showed up to take you back?*" are not uncommon for children of adoption. Although children who have been adopted may be perfectly capable of handling such questions on their own, when needed, teachers can assist children to answer by emphasizing that the child has parents just like everyone else in the classroom and that adoption is an acceptable and permanent way to form a family. For example, the teacher might say in response to a child who has just asked a sensitive question of a classmate, "*Jay, Cody has a real mother and father just like you. Remember, they were both here helping out our class on Field Day.*" Or, the teacher might respond, "*Jay, when parents adopt their children, the children are in their family forever. Nothing can change that! They are their parents' son or daughter just like you are your parents' son.*" Or, the teacher might offer, "*Jay, sometimes, children who have been adopted may not want to share their adoption stories. That's up to them and we have to respect their privacy. You wouldn't want everyone in the class to know all the things your family knows about you! So let's respect Cody's privacy, too.*" The task for the teacher is to convey accurate information about adoption in a positive and accepting manner, while also acknowledging that adoption stories involve personal and private information that a classmate may or may not wish to share.

Similarly, children living in foster care may be confronted with difficult questions such as "*I saw on the Internet where this girl got put in foster care because her mom was a drug addict. Is that what happened to you?*" Again, the teacher can intervene, if needed, by asserting that children are placed in foster care for many different reasons and that these reasons have nothing to do with the children themselves. The teacher can also convey to others that "*these reasons are personal and private and we need to respect the wishes of classmates as to what information they might choose to share.*"

Finally, teachers can reinforce the understanding that children in foster care do have families that take good care of them, even if only temporarily, and that it is difficult to live away from one's parents. For example, teachers might ask, *"Have you ever had to stay with someone else or stay at camp for a long time? How did it feel to be away from your parents for so long?"* Questions such as these might help students begin to think about their classmates in a different way and understand the universality of feelings associated with being away from one's family.

Depending on the age and maturity of students, teachers can also convey through well-chosen language that families are not just formed through biological connections, but are formed through legal connections as well. No one would assert that husbands and wives are not close relatives *because they are not "blood relatives!"* As a matter of fact, husbands and wives are usually listed as "next of kin" even though they are certainly not "related by blood!" We would not normally refer to our parents in casual conversation with others as our "blood-related parents" or our "genetic parents!" Yet, when discussing adoption or foster care, we seem to emphasize that people who are not genetically related cannot be *real "family."* We insist on making a distinction between "blood relatives" (e.g., the *real* parents) and "adoptive" or "foster" parents. In addition, people tend to suggest by the words they use that children can be "given away" or "put up for adoption" as though the decision not to parent a child is made casually instead of as a result of many and varied difficult circumstances.

**Table 2.1**
**Positive Language for Adoption and Foster Care**

| Words to Avoid | Say Instead |
|---|---|
| Adoptive Mother, Father, Brother, Sister, Parents | Mother, Father, Brother, Sister, Parents |
| Like a Mother, Father, Brother, Sister or Like Parents | Mother, Father, Brother, Sister, Parents |
| Have a child of their own | Their child—Children are legally and emotionally the parents' child regardless of biology or adoption! |
| Natural Mother, Father, Parents, Brother, Sister | Birth *or* Biological Mother, Father, Parents, Brother, Sister |
| Real Mother, Father, Parents, Brother, Sister | Birth *or* Biological Mother, Father, Parents, Brother, Sister |
| Real *or* Natural Mother, Father, Parents | First Mother, Father, or Parents |
| | Mother who has chosen adoption for her child. |
| Put up for adoption *or* Given away for adoption *or* Placed out for adoption | The birth mother made a plan for her child. |
| | The birth mother made a plan so her baby would have parents. |
| | The birth mother chose adoption as the best plan for her baby. |
| | The parental rights were terminated. |
| Illegitimate | Child born to unmarried parents. |
| Abandoned or deserted child | Child separated from birth parent(s). |
| | Birth parent(s) was(were) unable to parent. |
| Adoptable child | Child waiting for a family. |
| Put in foster care *or* Sent away to foster care | Temporarily placed in foster care. |
| | Waiting for a family. |
| | The parental rights were terminated. |
| (*Name of child*)'s mother could not take care of him/her. | The birth mother could not take care of any baby at that time, and so she made a plan for her baby to have parents who could take good care of him/her. |

Experts now suggest that teachers avoid historical phrases such as "real" or "natural" mother/father/ parents and "put up for" or "given away for " adoption (Shoettle, 2000, 2003; Wood & Ng, 2001). These phrases may instill confusion or even fear among children who have been adopted and their classmates. Instead, teachers can use more respectful language such as that suggested in Table 2.1. Knowing how to phrase information about adoption and foster care in an accepting and positive manner can make a difference in whether or not students feel secure and safe in their relationships with others in the classroom.

## ADAPTING SENSITIVE ASSIGNMENTS

Cassandra's teacher assigns a project for which she must write an autobiography giving details about key events during each year of her life. Her autobiography must include pictures and specific dates for each of the key events she describes. Nastia's teacher requires her life sciences students to trace genetic possibilities for both eye and hair color and illustrate this information on a family tree. Rushi's English teacher asks students to write an essay in which they must describe the family member they most resemble in appearance and personality. Benita and the other first graders in her classroom are making Mother's Day cards.

These are typical projects and assignments given in the elementary and middle school grades. Most children have no problem completing such tasks, and the teachers who assign them are not intending to create difficulty or provoke sensitive emotions for their students. Suppose, however, that Cassandra is a child who has lived in five foster care families during her 11 years of life. Nastia and her younger brother, Rushi, spent their first few years living in an orphanage in Russia before their adoption five years ago. Neither child has any information regarding their biological family. They have no photographs prior to their adoption and even their birth dates simply reflect the day on which they arrived at an orphanage. Benita's family has arranged an open adoption. Her birth mother periodically visits Benita, her parents, and her siblings at their home. Autobiographies, genetics, family trees, and Mother's Day cards are examples of assignments and projects with unintended "minefields" for children who have been adopted and for those living in foster care! Such projects may also trigger unexpected reactions from children who have lost parents through death or divorce!

Such assignments appear to magnify differences between children who do not live with biological relatives, particularly those who have been adopted or placed in foster care, and those who do. Projects such as these seem to emphasize missing pieces of information, differences in physical characteristics of children and their parents, and the risk of exposing personal and private information that children may or may not wish to share (Shoettle, 2003). In addition, tasks like these may result in a barrage of questions and comments from peers at a time when children may be thinking privately about the full meaning of adoption, grieving over the loss of a family, or integrating adoption into their identity. With forethought, however, teachers can easily adapt these assignments.

### Timelines

The objective for this assignment in the lower grades typically is for students to learn to sequence a series of five or six events. Rather than insisting that all students include a point on the timeline for each year of life beginning with birth and ending with the present year, teachers might provide the option of choosing the "best year" or "best month" or "best day," requiring children to sequence and illustrate at least six events from that year, month, or day. Similarly, rather than requiring that all students include photographs, teachers can provide alternatives from which to choose. Children might be given the choice to draw a picture, use stickers, or use photographs to illustrate various events. In this way, children who have no baby pictures might safely choose a pink or blue "newborn baby" sticker to illustrate their birth, draw a picture to illustrate their first steps, and include photographs as appropriate (Meese, 2002).

### Who's Who/Super Star/Student of the Week Bulletin Boards

Bulletin boards of this type are designed to build self-esteem, help classmates get acquainted, and promote classroom cohesion. For children who have been adopted or for those in foster care families, however, being the "Super Star" may point out differences that can be difficult to explain to peers (Schoettle, 2003). In this case, rather than requiring a baby picture or a family photograph, teachers might simply ask all students to bring in their *favorite* pictures of themselves or to bring in any picture of themselves from a "younger age." Similarly, children can be asked to share through photographs or pictures cut from magazines their favorite movies, foods, music, games, sports teams, and such as they get acquainted (Meese, 1999). The focus in this assignment should be on *current interests and getting acquainted* rather than on the past.

### Family Trees

Because of the complex nature of family structure today, some schools no longer require projects related to the "Family Tree" (Schoettle, 2003). When assigned, though, students who have been adopted or placed in foster care might wonder "which family" to include on the tree. Teachers can be flexible regarding how many or which relatives are to be included, how many branches the tree must contain, whether or not the tree must contain pictures, or how the tree is created. For example, the child who has been adopted might include only her family on her tree. Or, she might include both her family and her biological family on separate branches of the tree. Another child might create the tree by making biological family the "roots" and his foster family the tree branches. Yet another student might illustrate family connections by placing family in the branches and deceased or other biological relatives as leaves fallen to the base of the tree. The teacher might also emphasize that the family tree can illustrate the *important people* in a student's life including stepparents, baby-sitters, teachers, or those close friends whom family members call "Aunt" or "Uncle." Of course, teachers must take care when asking students to share the family trees they have created. Permitting students to volunteer to share, rather than requiring *all* to share, may be a safer option for students in foster care or those who have been adopted. Again, providing a range of choices for creating and sharing the tree will enable all children in the classroom to safely participate.

### Autobiographies

When teachers assign an autobiography, they want students to sequence events, organize information, and write in coherent, connected sentences and paragraphs. Sometimes, in lieu of an autobiography, students are assigned a poster on which they must illustrate their years of life. Insisting that all students include important events from all years of life from birth to the present precipitates the same difficulties as the timeline assignment. Instead, the teacher might ask all students to write about three or four favorite or most "memorable" years or events in their lives (Schoettle, 2003) or to include only those events in their lives that they wish to share as most important to them. Some students who have been adopted or placed in foster care may, of course, choose to write a complete autobiography. Requiring all students to share their autobiographies or "life posters" in front of classmates, however, certainly may not be advisable. Again, allowing students to volunteer to share provides a safe choice for children living in diverse family situations.

### Family History/Family Traditions/Interviewing Older Family Members

To promote interviewing and writing skills, social studies or English teachers may ask students to interview family members from a previous generation, such as grandparents, or to write about important family customs and traditions. Others might require students to trace their family history, finding the origin of the child's last name or the country of origin for some of the family's traditions. Many children will enjoy finding out about their German or Irish ancestry and heritage, yet others will think *"I was born in Guatemala. I love German food but how do I explain my German family heritage?"* or *"I'm with my red-haired foster family and I've never celebrated St. Patrick's Day until now!"* or *"I have no idea what my heritage is. I don't want to make myself sound like someone I'm not and I'm tired of people always thinking I'm interested in Ukraine anyway!"* Again, the teacher can create safe options from which all students can choose. Perhaps students can be told to interview *anyone* from a previous generation. This individual, then, could be a grandparent or simply an elderly friend who lives nearby who might share his or her family history and traditions. Similarly, students might research the ancestry of another person, such as an historical figure, or write about the customs and traditions of a chosen country. And, of course, they can conduct an interview or research information using their family, their birth family, or their foster family if they so choose! The key, again, is to structure a range of options so that all students in the classroom can feel safe with the information they choose to disclose.

### Genetics/Inherited Characteristics/Medical History

As students approach the upper grades, they are developing their sense of identity. They strive to understand where they belong and who they are. Part of this struggle for students living in foster care and for those who have been adopted may involve thinking about family characteristics they may have inherited. Children who have been adopted, especially those of intercountry adoptions, may have no information regarding the genetic or medical history of their birth families. The child may wonder about simple things such as where her curly hair or blue eyes came from, or about more complex matters such as genetics and medical conditions. Students may worry about unknown genetic tendencies, as for breast cancer or depression, passed on to them by birth parents, and children living in foster care may worry that the alcoholism or other difficulties experienced by their birth parents may be something they have inherited. Teachers sensitive to these issues can provide safe options by constructing case scenarios students can analyze for genetic possibilities or by pairing students and asking them to use their own physical characteristics to determine genetic possibilities for offspring.

Regardless of the type of assignment, teachers can think about the diversity in family living arrangements among children in the classroom and then provide a range of safe alternatives from which all students can choose. Careful attention to rubrics used for grading such assignments and projects is also essential. For example, if teachers give children options for completing autobiographies, timelines, or family trees, but then include on the grading rubric points for including particular items such as "identifies mother's parents and father's parents" or "states time of birth," they will quickly "undo" the safe choices they intended to provide (Meese, 2002). Finally, teachers may find that some of the most productive opportunities for promoting acceptance and providing accurate information regarding adoption and foster care will arise while guiding students to discuss books and stories they are reading in the classroom.

## ADOPTION AND FOSTER CARE IN CHILDREN'S LITERATURE

Issues regarding adoption and foster care can creep into classroom discussions in unexpected ways! For example, when students are discussing current events they have viewed on the Internet, read in a magazine, or heard on the nightly news or news magazines, unusual or uncomfortable questions and comments can quickly occur. Discussions surrounding immigration, economics, famine, or the adoption of children by celebrities might prompt difficult comments and questions, whether spoken or not, that teachers do not expect: "*I was adopted from Guatemala. I wonder if my friends think I'm an illegal immigrant?*" or "*Women who can't care for their babies shouldn't be allowed to have them.*" or "*People who take care of foster care kids are just doing that for the money because they can't get jobs.*" Or "*People who adopt children have a lot of money and just buy their babies.*" Informed teachers can take the opportunity during discussions of current events to use positive language and to give students accurate information and a deeper, more positive understanding of the many complex issues related to adoption and foster care. Probably no area of the curriculum, however, is as potentially laden with *possibilities* for misperceptions, inappropriate comments, or questions about adoption and foster care as that of children's literature used daily in the classroom.

Even simple, well-known fairy tales are fraught with images of children who have been abandoned and left to find their way in the world. Familiar stories from *Children's and Household Tales* by the Brothers Grimm, such as "Rapunzel" (1812) and "Snow White" (1823), conjure up images of children who have been left to the care of evil forces and who are waiting for rescue. Other classics, such as *Madeline* (Bemelman, 1939), an early Caldecott Honor Book, or *Madeline's Rescue* (Bemelman, 1953), the 1954 Caldecott Medal winner, depict the orphan as a child with an indomitable spirit. More contemporary tales contain characters such as J. K. Rowling's Harry Potter, an orphan who battles the evil "Valdemort" and emerges victorious in the final book with a family of his own, or the Baudelaire orphans, in the popular series of 13 books written by Daniel Handler and known as *Lemony Snicket's: A Series of Unfortunate Events*, which chronicles the difficulties experienced by three siblings after their parents die in a fire. Other current and well-known orphans are depicted as superheroes such as Superman, Spiderman, Batman, and Robin. Although fairy tales and fantasy novels are enjoyable forms of literature for children, they do not reflect the *reality* of most children who have been placed in foster care or those who have been adopted. Children who live in diverse family structures, just like all children, need to see their lives reflected in the books they read (Gilmore & Bell, 2006). Again, teachers must be prepared to provide accurate information that will portray adoption and foster care *as it exists today* and to interpret literature containing references to adoption and foster care through the lens of history whenever necessary.

### Historical Influences on Adoption and Foster Care Literature

As societal and cultural trends have impacted views of adoption and foster care (see Chapter 1), these viewpoints have inevitably been reflected in literature. Nelson (2006) suggests that children's literature clearly parallels these trends in the United States. For example, early literature focused on the "working orphan." In these early works, children were depicted as employees to be apprenticed or "placed out" with the needs of the adults taking precedence over the needs of the children. Thus, in tales such as *Oliver Twist*, a social novel designed to focus attention on child labor and "poorhouses" written by Charles Dickens in 1838, Oliver is portrayed as a child who is abandoned at birth, removed from a "baby farm" at age nine, and victimized by employers and acquaintances alike. Similarly, most children today are familiar with the story of *Little Orphan Annie*, based on the comic strip written by Harold Gray. Gray took his inspiration for this comic strip from the popular poem *Little Orphant Annie*, written by the "children's poet" James Whitcomb Riley in 1885. The poem clearly illustrates the plight of the "working orphan":

> Little Orphant Annie's come to our house to stay,
> An' wash the cups an' saucers up, an' brush the crumbs away,
> An' shoo the chickens off the porch, an' dust the hearth, an' sweep,
> An' make the fire, an' bake the bread, an' earn her board-an'-keep.

Early literature also emphasized the American dream, individual effort, and the spirit of adventure or survival. Literature in the 1800s, therefore, frequently described orphans, particularly orphan boys, as rugged survivors who made their own way and secured their own fortunes through hard work, quick wit, and good fortune. These stories can best be characterized as "orphan adventure tales" or "orphan survival tales." Remi, the protagonist in Hector Henri Mallot's *Nobody's Boy*, written in 1878, was one such character in a long tradition of orphan adventure stories. Today, Remi has even become a character in the popular Japanese animé series enjoyed by many children.

By the late 1800s, however, with escalating anxiety regarding the proliferation of orphanages, the rising number of orphans in the United States, and the increasing mechanization of the new industrial society, literature portraying children living in large institutions began to turn sentimental (Nelson, 2006). Orphanages were described as evil environments mass producing children and places devoid of love. During this time period, stories about orphans glorified those who were able to survive or escape the rigors of orphanage life. Anne Shirley, the strong-spirited main character in L. M. Montgomery's *Anne of Green Gables* (1908), epitomizes the orphan in literature of this time period. Anne demonstrates the need of children to be nurtured in families rather than constrained by the orphanage system. Although Anne was originally "placed out" and was to have been a boy to "help out" on the farm, she quickly won the hearts of stern Marilla Cuthbert, Marilla's brother Matthew, and the entire community. She ultimately became a valued and loved member of her family. Anne brought joy, spirit, and love to Marilla who also cared deeply for Anne.

### Contemporary Children's Literature on Adoption and Foster Care

During the latter half of the 1900s, orphans began to be characterized in literature as more than merely recipients of love from nurturing adults. Orphans began to be depicted as individuals who contributed to the emotional well-being of adults just as much as the adults contributed to the emotional well-being of the child (Nelson, 2006). *Tell Me Again about the Night I Was Born*, written by Jamie Lee Curtis in 1996, illustrates how precious the child now is to the family and how important knowing the adoption story is to the young child. Just as in the past, literature today reflects contemporary societal beliefs about adoption and foster care; therefore, children's authors now write books about adoption stories, the search for family, love, and identity, the need to belong, and the strength of multiethnic and multinational families.

Current children's literature for preschool through grade two, then, usually focuses on themes related to the nature of families, accepting differences, and understanding one's adoption story. Colorful picture books, animal character books, and narrative adoption stories with photographs and beautiful illustrations are readily accessible, such as the story of a child adopted from China, *I Love You Like Crazy Cakes*, written by Rose Lewis about the adoption of her own daughter and illustrated by Jane Dyer in 2000. For children in grades 3–8, works of nonfiction (e.g., *Orphan Train Rider: One Boy's True Story* by Andrea Warren, 1996) and novels that can be categorized as historical fiction (e.g., *Train to Somewhere* by Eve Bunting, 1996, or *Bud, Not Buddy* by C. P. Curtis, 1999) are available with adoption and foster care themes. Also particularly prevalent for children in grades 3–8 are other works of fiction. Some of these pieces are realistic fiction containing believable story elements, but many others may still be characterized as "orphan adventure tales" (e.g., *The Invention of Hugo Cabret: A Novel in Words and Pictures* written by Brian Selznick in 2007). In addition, some current literary works for children in this age group involve fantasy, tales of magic, and supernatural events, such as *The Moorchild* (McGraw, 1996). Today, children's literature written about adoption and foster care for youngsters in grades 3–8 focuses on themes related to loss, belonging, love, identity, and difference, as well as on expanding children's understanding or comprehension of the nature of family or of one's adoption story.

## Interpreting Literature on Adoption and Foster Care in the Classroom

Children's literature on adoption and foster care, then, mirrors the social and cultural trends of the time period. The three major trends used in the literature over the past 150 years include "worker," "survivor," and "precious" child (Nelson, 2006). Thus, when children are reading historical fiction in the classroom such as *Train to Somewhere* (Bunting, 1996), teachers must be prepared to interpret the piece within its historical context and the literary trend presented (i.e., orphan as "worker"). For example, before and during guided reading, teachers might provide accurate information such as:

*From the 1850s until about 1930, many children were living in orphanages in big cities like New York and Boston. There were so many children in orphanages because many families had come to the big cities to find work in factories. They came from farms or they immigrated to the United States from other countries. The factories did not pay workers very much. Even though parents worked very long hours, many families could not afford a place to live in the city. They lived in overcrowded and very poor apartments, often without heat or water, and some parents got very sick or were killed in the factories. Children were placed in the orphanages when their parents died or could no longer take care of them properly. A man named Charles Brace thought that the orphanages were not healthy places for children to live, so he decided to help these children find new homes out west. Many children traveled on the trains west. Most of the children were placed with loving families, but a few did have to work for their room and board. Today, children are no longer placed with families in this way.*

Similarly, when reading current novels involving fantasy or "orphan adventure tales" teachers must help children view the work from a realistic lens. For example, *The Invention of Hugo Cabret: A Novel in Words and Pictures*, an orphan adventure tale, can easily be interpreted by teachers. First, teachers can help children understand that the story is set in Paris in the early 1900s. Although street children do exist around the world today and this topic might be relevant for a social studies discussion with older readers, key points to emphasize within this story include that Hugo had a family who loved him and that he ended up in bad circumstances through no fault of his own. He did, however, use his talents to reinvent himself and ultimately he found a family. Accurate information and positive language conveying acceptance are critical skills for teachers when discussing historical or contemporary adoption and foster care themes depicted in children's literature.

## SUMMARY

Smith and Riley (2006) maintain that teachers still have much to learn about supporting children in their classrooms who have been placed for adoption or foster care. Whenever situations arise in the classroom that highlight perceived differences among children who are no longer living with their birth parents and those who are, teachers must be well-prepared! Providing safe choices for all children when planning assignments is one way in which teachers can assist students living in diverse family structures. Similarly, careful preparation prior to reading children's literature having adoption or foster care themes will enable teachers to correct misperceptions and respond to difficult questions or comments. Accurate information and positive language conveying acceptance, or providing individual assistance to children as needed, are critical teaching skills for supporting children who have been adopted or placed in foster care. So too is providing children's literature that depicts adoption and foster care as they really exist today!

# CHAPTER 3

## *Selecting Children's Literature on Adoption and Foster Care*

Many books and stories concerning adoption or foster care now exist for children in grades K–8, but how can teachers select *appropriate* literature for children in their classrooms to read? How can teachers ensure that young readers will see adoption and foster care portrayed accurately, sensitively, and realistically as these exist today? How can teachers help children select books that are free from stereotypes and misperceptions about children who have been adopted or placed in foster care? How can teachers help children select books containing characters with whom they can identify? One consideration for choosing reading material in the classroom, of course, is matching the readability level of the text to the child's actual reading level. Another important consideration when choosing materials on sensitive topics such as adoption and foster care is providing children with literature that has been recognized to be of high quality, such as books receiving prestigious awards like the Caldecott Medal and Honor winners, the Newbery Medal and Honor winners, and the American Library Association list of Notable Children's Literature. Finally, teachers may wish to consider the developmental tasks and issues across the grade levels important for children who have been adopted or placed in foster care in order to guide readers to choose stories or books focusing on appropriate developmental themes.

### FINDING BOOKS CHILDREN CAN READ

Numerous online resources are readily available today to help teachers match a child's reading level to the intended audience of a book. Most readability formulas analyze sentence length and story vocabulary to determine an *estimated* reading level, but teachers must remember that each of these formulas provides just that—an estimate. The type of text (e.g., a narrative versus expository text), the pictures and overall organization, and the degree of interest and information a child has on a topic all affect the actual readability level of a book for the individual child. Two widely used and easily accessible databases from which teachers can select books at the child's reading level are the Lexile Measure searchable book database (MetaMetrics, 2009) and the Accelerated Reader "book find" database (Renaissance Learning, 2009).

## Lexile Measures

The Lexile measure is based on semantic difficulty (i.e., word frequency) and syntactic complexity (i.e., sentence length). Books are "chunked" into 125 word segments that are analyzed for sentence length and compared to words in the 600 million word Lexile data bank. The words and sentence lengths for every segment are then placed into a formula to determine the Lexile level. Thus, teachers can match readers to materials estimated to be at their reading levels with the expectation that children will comprehend with at least 75 percent accuracy. In addition, Lexiles are given in a range since children may comprehend materials 50L to 100L above or below the actual Lexile level. Approximate grade level ranges for Lexile scores of typical readers are shown in Table 3.1.

Lexile codes are also included to give teachers specific information relevant for some books. These codes are the following: (1) AD (Adult Directed) for materials such as picture books that encompass a wide range of actual reading levels; (2) NC (Nonconforming) for books that have Lexile measures higher than the intended reading level of the book but that can be used to match high ability readers to materials at their developmental interest level; (3) HL (High Interest/ Low Reading Level) for books at lower reading levels that are of interest to struggling, more mature, readers; (4) IG (Illustrated Guide) for nonfiction books containing reference material but read like stories; (5) GN (Graphic Novel) for books that are mostly dialogue and written in a comic-book style; (6) BR (Beginning Reading) for books designated at Lexile level OL or below for the emergent reader and usually designed for the child to read aloud with an adult; and (7) NP (Non-Prose) for books having more than 50 percent of the content in nonstandard formats such as poems, songs, or recipes. Teachers can quickly determine the Lexile level for many different books by visiting the Lexile searchable database at www.lexile.com.

## Accelerated Reader

The Accelerated Reader (AR) program is widely used in schools across the United States. In this program, the student's reading level is first determined. Next, the child reads books designated at that level and then completes comprehension quizzes on the computer for each book he or she has read. Prizes are typically given as incentives to help children advance their reading levels. The AR program determines readability using the ATOS (Advantage-TASA Open Standard) formula. The formula analyzes the number of words per sentence, the number of characters per word, and the average grade

**Table 3.1**
**Range of Lexile Scores Across Grade Levels**

| Approximate Grade Level | Lower Range | Upper Range |
| --- | --- | --- |
| 1 | Up to 300L | 200L to 400L |
| 2 | 140L to 500L | 140L to 500L |
| 3 | 330L to 700L | 330L to 700L |
| 4 | 445L to 810L | 650L to 850L |
| 5 | 565L to 910L | 750L to 950L |
| 6 | 665L to 1000L | 850L to 1050L |
| 7 | 735L to 1065L | 950L to 1075L |
| 8 | 805L to 1100L | 1000L to 1100L |
| 9 | 855L to 1165L | 1050L to 1150L |
| 10 | 905L to 1195L | 1100L to 1200L |
| 11 and 12 | 940L to 1210L | 1100L to 1300L |

level of the words contained in the book. The calculation of reading level is based on the entire book and also includes information from over 30,000 children reading about one million books. Using the Accelerated Reader system, teachers can easily compare the grade-equivalent score from any reading test to the AR reading level of books using standard grade notation such as 2.5, 4.3, and so forth. The "book find" feature, found online at www.arbookfind.com, allows teachers to quickly determine the reading level of thousands of popular books.

## FINDING QUALITY CHILDREN'S LITERATURE

Locating books at the appropriate reading level is certainly an important first step, but ensuring that children read high-quality literature is equally crucial. For quality, many teachers rely on books winning awards from the Association for Library Service to Children, a division of the American Library Association (ALA). These books are often familiar to teachers, parents, and library media specialists and are readily available in most public and school libraries. The ALA award-winning books include the Caldecott Medal and Honor Books, the Newbery Medal and Honor Books, the Children's Notable List, and the Coretta Scott King Author Award for the best African American author and illustrator. Some of these award-winning books across the grade levels do have themes related to adoption and foster care, although the awards have been criticized recently. For example, Nisse (2008) maintains that the characters in the Newbery Medal winning books from 1922 until 2007 lack diversity across age, race, gender, family structure, and economic status. For lists of ALA award-winning books, detailed information about the criteria used for each of these awards, and information about the selection process, teachers can consult the American Library Association Web site at www.ala.org.

### The Caldecott Medal and Honor Books

Named in honor of an English illustrator, Randolph Caldecott, the Caldecott Medal has been awarded by an ALA committee annually since 1938. This award is presented to the most distinguished American picture book published in the United States for the preceding year. Books not winning the medal but deserving of special recognition are called the Caldecott Honor books. From 1938 through 2009, 72 books have won the Caldecott Medal and 224 have been designated Caldecott Honor books. Interestingly, although 296 books have merited attention through the Caldecott award program, only a handful actually relate to adoption, foster care, or orphans (e.g., *The Invention of Hugo Cabret: A Novel in Words and Pictures* by Brian Selznick won the Caldecott Medal in 2008).

### The Newbery Medal and Honor Books

The Newbery Medal was named to honor an eighteenth-century bookseller, John Newbery. Like the Caldecott, the award is determined by a committee representing the Association for Library Service to Children and is presented annually. Unlike the Caldecott, however, the Newbery is given to the most distinguished contribution to American children's literature published in the United States during the preceding year and is based on the author's interpretation of the theme or concept, presentation of information, development of a plot, delineation of characters and setting, and appropriateness of style. From 1922 until 2009, 88 books have received this prestigious award. Another 287 books worthy of special attention have been recognized as Newbery Honor books. Among the 375 Newbery Medal and Honor books written since 1922, fewer than 30 clearly contain themes relevant to orphans, adoption, or foster care. Among these are *The Higher Power of Lucky* written by Susan Patron and winning the Newbery Medal for 2007 as well as the popular *Bud, Not Buddy*, the 2000 Newbery Medal Winner written by Christopher Paul Curtis.

### The Children's Notable List

The American Library Association's Children's Notable List annually identifies the "best" books written for children ages birth through 14. Selected by committee, the Notable books are to be of commendable quality and creativity and published in the United States during the preceding year. They include books of fiction, information, poetry, and pictures that reflect and encourage children's interests in exemplary ways. The Children's Notable List automatically includes all of the Caldecott Medal and Honor Books and the Newbery Medal and Honor Books as well as books receiving other important ALA awards such as the Coretta Scott King Award for African American authors and illustrators, the Michael L. Printz Award for excellence in young adult literature, and the Schneider Family Book Award, which honors an author or illustrator of a book about the disability experience intended for child and adolescent audiences. Among the ALA Children's Notable books are a number of very popular literary works including some related to orphans in general (e.g., *Madeline's Rescue* by Ludwig Bemelmans, a 1953 ALA Notable book), to foster care (e.g., *Pictures of Hollis Woods* by Patricia Reilly Giff, an ALA Notable book for 2003, and *Locomotion* by Jacqueline Woodson, also a 2003 Notable book), and to adoption (e.g., *Emma's Yucky Brother* by Jean Little, a 2002 Notable book, and *Me, Mop and the Moondance Kid* by Walter Dean Myers, a 1988 Notable book).

## GUIDELINES FOR ANALYZING CHILDREN'S LITERATURE ON ADOPTION AND FOSTER CARE

Whether teachers plan to read a book aloud to children in the classroom, to guide children through the reading of a story, or to help children choose pieces to read independently, teachers should select or recommend works of literature that realistically present themes related to adoption and foster care. They must also ensure that the themes are appropriate for the developmental needs of the individual child or the age group. Rather than unknowingly using literature likely to perpetuate misperceptions or stereotypes regarding children in foster care or children who have been adopted, the teacher can make advance preparations. When misperceptions are likely, she or he can either choose a different story or prepare in advance to respond to incorrect information with accurate interpretations of the events portrayed. In addition, when stories contain stereotypical images of children and youth from diverse family situations, the teacher can respond with positive language and model acceptance for children in the classroom. Obviously teachers must reflect carefully on the type, or genre, of literature to be used and the developmental appropriateness of the themes and the overall presentation for children at the given grade level. Table 3.2 illustrates the common genres of literature, the historical trends suggested by Nelson (2006), and the typical themes related to adoption and foster care for children in grades PK–8.

Certainly when selecting children's literature teachers must consider the child's reading level and the readability level of the chosen book. Beyond these simple considerations, however, how are teachers to determine whether or not a book about adoption or foster care merits selection either for the group or for an individual child? The following guidelines are useful for teachers when analyzing children's literature about adoption or foster care:

- *Analyze the Reading Level:* Match the reading level of the child to the approximate readability level of the selected book. Locate reading levels for books online at the Accelerated Reader or Lexile Web sites. Keep in mind that reading level is approximate and denotes a wide range. The child familiar with a topic (e.g., a child adopted from

China and familiar with Chinese words or images) may read literature at a higher grade level than he or she might ordinarily read. In addition, considerable overlap in reading and interest level exists across books designed for middle and older readers in grades 3–8. Finally, the content, concepts, and themes of some books may not be suitable for children at earlier grade levels even though the actual readability of the work is appropriate.

- *Search for Evidence of Quality:* Books that have received an award such as the Caldecott Medal and Honor Books, the Newbery Medal and Honor Books, or the Children's Notable List have been determined by a committee of experts to be of high quality. For books that are not award winners, Prater and Dyches (2008) suggest other evidence teachers might use to determine quality. For example, teachers might examine the color, design, layout, and overall attractiveness of the illustrations. Will the illustrations appeal to children at a particular grade level? In addition, teachers might consider whether or not concepts or themes are engaging and integrated throughout the story and whether or not the plot is well-developed and believable. Children must be able to see adoption or foster care depicted realistically throughout the book before teachers can promote understanding and acceptance.

- *Look for Stereotypes:* Stereotypes involve gross generalizations about a particular group of people; therefore, teachers can examine literature for characters depicted in a derogatory manner. For example, are children who have been adopted or placed in foster care frequently described in a story as "troubled" or as "difficult" youngsters? Are orphans portrayed as manipulative, as dishonest thieves, or as inferior to others? Are they

**Table 3.2**
**PK–8 Literature about Adoption and Foster Care: Trends, Styles, and Themes**

| Group | Grades | Ages | Important Trends | Genre | Common Themes |
|---|---|---|---|---|---|
| Younger Readers | PK–2 | Up to 7 | Precious child | Picture books | Understanding adoption and foster care |
| | | | | Adoption story books | Understanding the nature of families |
| | | | | Animal character books | Accepting differences |
| | | | | Books about family | |
| Middle Readers | 3–5 | 8–10 | Worker | Nonfiction | Feeling different |
| | | | Adventurer/ Survivor | Historical fiction | Understanding that adoption and foster care mean loss |
| | | | Precious child | Realistic fiction | Coping with emotions of abandonment, guilt, and grief |
| | | | | Orphan adventure tale | Wanting to be accepted and to belong |
| | | | | | Longing to feel safe and loved |
| Older Readers | 6–8 | 11–14 | Worker | Nonfiction | Developing an identity |
| | | | Adventurer/ Survivor | Historical fiction | Search for family |
| | | | Precious child | Realistic fiction | Wanting to be accepted and to belong |
| | | | | Orphan adventure tale | Longing to feel safe and loved |
| | | | | Fantasy | Letting go of the past |

treated as people to be pitied? Conversely, are the children pictured as superheroes surviving against incredible odds or performing remarkable feats of magic? Similarly, teachers might want to examine the adults involved in the story. Are foster parents typically described as "abusive" or parents who adopt portrayed as "overinvolved?" Good children's literature should refrain from stereotypical images that perpetuate misperceptions and misunderstandings. Instead good literature should present all children and adults as unique individuals. Good literature should also emphasize the similarities among children who have been adopted or placed in foster care and those who have not rather than highlighting the differences.

- *Examine Character Development:* Are the main characters depicted in a realistic and credible manner? Sometimes in literature intended for young readers, animals are the main characters rather than children (e.g., *The Mulberry Bird: An Adoption Story*, written by Anne Braff Brodzinsky in 1996). Although using animal characters can be a safe way to present difficult concepts to young readers, children must be able to see their own lives reflected in the books they read. Teachers should look for books that portray children in a way that is consistent with current thought about adoption and foster care. The emphasis should be on acceptance and similarity to others; therefore, teachers will want to locate books that contain both male and female characters having realistic reactions and emotions. In this way, children can identify or empathize with the characters as they read.

- *Check the Plot:* Are the events believable and are solutions to conflicts realistic? Novels written as fantasy or orphan adventure tales may require careful interpretation by the teacher. Children who have been adopted or placed in foster care should not have to demonstrate extraordinary physical prowess, gifts, or abilities in order to solve their difficulties, find a home, or obtain love. Books implying that only the "typical" family of biologically related individuals can be "true" family will alienate the child and adversely impact his or her self-image. To gain acceptance or approval, children living in foster care and those who have been adopted should be portrayed as just that—*children* who have families and who handle situations in a realistic manner!

- *Check the Style and Purpose for Reading:* Certainly if children are reading about an actual event, historical fiction or nonfiction will be the teacher's likely choice. Teachers can then prepare in advance to interpret events related to adoption and foster care, such as the orphan trains, through an accurate historical lens. When the group is engaged in a novel study or when fiction is recommended as pleasure reading for an individual child, the teacher may wish to select more realistic fiction, stories with believable characters, plots, and settings, as opposed to orphan adventure tales or fantasy. In addition, numerous picture books and stories about adoptions and families, many containing beautiful illustrations even though they were not Caldecott Medal or Honor books, are available to select for younger readers today.

- *Match Book Themes to Developmental Issues:* Finally, the teacher must examine the overall themes in books about foster care and adoption. Themes should be appropriate to the general developmental needs of children at the particular grade level and to the specific developmental issues of children who have been adopted or placed in foster care. For example, young readers will need literary selections designed to foster an understanding of all types of families and of individual differences. For independent or adult-assisted reading, children in grades PK–2 may also enjoy reading personal adoption stories. In contrast, the middle or older reader will appreciate books focusing on deeper themes relevant for his or her developmental level. Themes such as longing to belong, coping with emotions like loss, guilt, or grief, handling comments made by peers or by adults, developing one's identity, integrating adoption or foster care into one's identity, or searching for family are important issues occupying the thought processes of many children at this level who have been adopted or placed into foster care. Teachers must also keep in mind that books at this level may include extremely sensitive topics such as teen pregnancy or child abuse, which may not yet be appropriate for many students in grades 5–8. When similarities among all children are emphasized through reading literature containing difficult themes, children living with biological family can learn more about their friends who live in diverse family situations, and children placed in foster care or placed for adoption can learn more about themselves and their situations.

## SAMPLING ADOPTION AND FOSTER CARE LITERATURE FOR K–8 CHILDREN

Locating books on adoption and foster care for children in grades K–8 is far easier than analyzing the quality and appropriateness of the books found! A quick search on the Internet using key words such as *orphan, adoption, foster care,* or *nontraditional families* quickly results in literally thousands of book titles alone! When popular fairy tales and children's series such as the Harry Potter books, the Lemony Snicket books, and the Madeline books are eliminated, and when all books containing plots such as children raised by animals, children living alone in places like deserted islands, children surviving the Holocaust or fleeing a war-torn country with a family member, children having a parent in prison, and children running away from abusive parents are eliminated, *many* book titles focusing specifically on adoption or foster care still remain.

Three excellent sources for readily locating children's literature on adoption and foster care for youngsters in grades K–8 include the aforementioned lists of award-winning books from the American Library Association (i.e., the Caldecott Medal and Honor Books, Newbery Medal and Honor Books, and Children's Notable List at www.ala.org), the Accelerated Reader Book Finder quick search (www.arbookfind.com), and the Tapestry Books list, an online catalog of books written specifically for children who have been adopted (www.tapestrybooks.com). More than 400 titles can be found using *only* these resources and also eliminating the categories listed previously when searching for children's literature on adoption or foster care for youngsters in grades K–8. For example, the Accelerated Reader site lists 299 titles relevant to adoption and foster care. Some of these, however, are geared toward the upper grade levels (e.g., books for students in grades 9–12 about teen pregnancies that resulted in adoption) or involve the "adoption" of animals. Several of the books listed on this site are also award-winning books. Moreover, from the Tapestry Book lists, 53 additional titles can be found that are not also on the Accelerated Reader or ALA Awards lists. Finally, the 400 titles do include many award-winning books as follows:

- Caldecott Medal and Honor Books—4 titles
- Newbery Medal and Honor Books—27 titles
- Children's Notable List Books—34 titles (not including those also on the Caldecott or Newbery Medal or Honor book lists)

From these search results, as well as from additional searches at specific public or school libraries, teachers can readily access a number of books related to adoption and foster care for younger, middle, and older readers. Choosing a book that is *appropriate,* however, may be trickier! Teachers are reminded that books estimated to be at a particular Lexile or AR reading or interest level may not necessarily contain content, concepts, and themes appropriate for children at that grade level. Teachers are always encouraged to analyze the appropriateness of each book for the specific intended readers using the guidelines presented earlier in this chapter.

For example, some books designated for young readers in grades K–2 may still be appropriate for less mature middle readers. A book such as Kathryn Miller's (1994) *Did My First Mother Love Me?* is estimated at the second grade reading level but contains difficult content that third or fourth graders may still be considering. In this book, the main character, Morgan, asks her parents this poignant question, "Did my first mother love me?" Her mother reads Morgan a letter from her birth mother describing her love for her child and reassuring Morgan that she is precious. Certainly children in third or fourth grade may need to hear this message as well! Similarly, *Emma's Yucky Brother,* by Jean Little (2001), is rated at the second grade reading level, but the plot involving sibling adjustment and a child adopted from foster care may still be appropriate for third or even fourth grade readers. Conversely, some books designated for middle readers may be applicable for better, more mature readers who are yet second graders. *Bringing Asha Home,* written by Uma Krishnaswami (2006), for example, presents the story of a young boy preparing for the adoption of a little sister from India, and *Karen's Little Sister* (Martin, 1989) tells the story of an older sibling in a blended family who must adjust to all the attention received by her baby sister adopted from Vietnam.

In addition, more mature middle readers in the fourth or fifth grade obviously may be able to under-stand content and themes in books for older readers, and some books intended for middle readers may still be appropriate for many older readers. For example, a number of books written at approximately the fourth and fifth grade reading levels contain extremely painful concepts. Books such as *Home and Other Big Fat Lies* (Wolfson, 2006), *I'll Sing You One-O* (Gregory, 2006), and *Pictures of Hollis Woods* (Giff, 2002) are written at the fourth grade reading level; however, all three deal with children who are coping with loss, the realities of foster care, and some very disturbing memories. Although the reading level is appropriate for mature middle readers, older readers may be better able to handle the themes of hurt, anger, abandonment, and longing presented in these novels. Likewise, other books written at the fourth or fifth grade reading levels, such as *Jake's Orphan* (Brooke, 2000), *The Story of Tracy Beaker* (Wilson, 1991), or *Dillon Dillon* (Banks, 2002) may provide comfort and understanding for older children in the sixth, seventh, or eighth grades who are searching for acceptance and a sense of belonging.

Relying solely on matching a child's reading level to the readability level of a book is not the best strategy, then, for choosing literature related to adoption and foster care for use in the classroom or in the independent reading program. Teachers must carefully consider the themes contained in each work and the *appropriateness* of those themes for their readers in the classroom. The remaining three chapters in this book, therefore, will present 116 specific works of children's literature on adoption and foster care intended for children in grades K–8. The titles presented are not meant to be an exhaus-tive list, but rather comprise a list of titles *representative* of children's literature on adoption and foster care that were available to the author and found by searching ALA award-winning titles, the Acceler-ated Book Finder Web site, and the Tapestry Book Lists. The books include one Caldecott Medal Winner, two Caldecott Honor Books, eight Newbery Medal Winners, nine Newbery Honor Books, thirteen ALA Notable Children's Books, and two Coretta Scott King Author Award Books.

Of critical importance is the apparent lack of diversity in the literature across the grade levels for both the authors and the main characters. As suggested by Nisse (2008), children's books with adop-tion and foster care themes found through this search also lack diversity in gender and race. For exam-ple, of the 111 authors whose works are reviewed (*Note:* Five authors have two books each included and, therefore, were counted only once), 85 are female and only 26 are male. Moreover, among the authors, 98 are Caucasian. Only three African American female authors, two African American male authors, and eight authors of other races were found when constructing this sample of representative children's literature. In addition, in the 116 works of children's literature reviewed, 59 (i.e., 50 percent) main characters are female and only 28 (24 percent) are male. Nineteen of the titles include both male and female main characters and another ten include male *animal* characters. Although these characters range in ethnicity from ten clearly African American or biracial children to eleven who are Chinese, eight who are Korean, three who are Vietnamese, and three who are Russian, the majority of the main characters are Caucasian. This lack of diversity in both authors and characters is surprising given that of the 510,000 children living in foster care homes in 2006, the year for which the most recent statis-tics are available, 52 percent were male and 48 percent were female, a ratio that has remained stable since 2000 (Child Welfare Information Gateway, 2009). Additionally, only 45 percent of the children in foster care in 2006 were White/non-Hispanic. If children are to identify with the characters in a novel, they should be able to see themselves in those characters, a task made more difficult with the limited diversity apparent in K–8 children's literature regarding adoption and foster care placement.

In the following chapters, the representative literature is organized not only by estimated reading levels but also, more importantly, by developmental themes appropriate for young, middle, and older readers. Thus, the teacher may find books with a reading or interest level designated for younger readers included in the list for middle readers, or books with reading levels appropriate for middle readers included with those for older readers. Again, teachers are cautioned to think about the *appropriateness* of the characters and themes contained in the books first, and then to choose books at the correct estimated reading level.

## SUMMARY

Books on adoption and foster care for children in grades K–8 are readily available, and the reading levels for many of these works can be found online through the Accelerated Reader or the Lexile Framework book search features. Many books on adoption or foster care are also winners of major literary awards determined by the American Library Association, including the Caldecott Medal and Honor books, the Newbery Medal and Honor books, and the Children's Notable List. Quality literature, then, is easy to find, but much of the literature lacks diversity in gender and ethnicity for both authors and main characters. Teachers must carefully analyze the available works for the themes related to adoption and foster care that are appropriate for children at the intended grade level. Beyond choosing quality literature and determining estimated reading levels, guidelines for analyzing and selecting literature also include looking for stereotypes, examining character development, checking the plot, checking the style and purpose for reading, and, most importantly, matching book themes to developmental issues related to adoption and foster care appropriate for the specific readers.

# CHAPTER 4

# *Adoption and Foster Care Literature for Young Readers*

Marquez runs into his kindergarten classroom excitedly telling his friends about how he was adopted from Guatemala. Before school, Sondra's best friend asks their teacher why Sondra does not look like her mother, father, and brother. Dasha, a new child in the classroom, is hesitant to talk about where she moved from. Scenes such as these are very real and occur daily in classrooms across the United States. Recall from Chapter 1 that children ages 5–7 may freely tell their adoption story without much true understanding of what that story actually means. Inevitably, these adoption stories precipitate questions, comments, or confusion on the parts of other children. Developmental issues appropriate for children in grades K–2, then, include understanding one's adoption story and learning about the meaning of family. Accepting differences is also a common issue for children in this age group.

Typical children's literature on adoption and foster care for young readers, therefore, should reflect these important developmental understandings. Most of the literature appropriate for children in this age group is in the form of picture books, animal character books, adoption story books, or books about families, with the most common literary trend across these stories being "precious child" (Nelson, 2006). Children in this age group must be reassured that they are precious to their families and that their birth mothers or other caregivers made a plan for them. In addition, children in grades K–2 need to hear that all types of families are "okay," that adoption and love are permanent, and that it is "alright" to be different.

The list of books provided in Table 4.1 will help teachers quickly determine possible literary selections that may be appropriate for their particular K–2 readers. The table organizes the story titles alphabetically and indicates estimated reading levels (e.g., Lexile and/or AR levels when known), genre, awards received, and developmental themes. Although 42 titles are included in this list, the list is certainly not exhaustive, but rather is intended to include *representative* literature on adoption and foster care that *may* be appropriate for children in grades K–2. Many books designed to be read by younger readers will, of course, require adult assistance, and *teachers are reminded that books estimated to be at K–2 Lexile or AR reading levels may not necessarily contain content, concepts, and themes appropriate for individual children at those grade levels.* Teachers are always encouraged to analyze the appropriateness of each book for the specific intended readers using the guidelines previously presented in Chapter 3.

**Table 4.1**
**Children's Literature on Adoption and Foster Care for Young Readers**

| Title, Author, Date of Pub. | AR Level and/ or Lexile | Genre | Awards | Adoption and Foster Care Themes |
|---|---|---|---|---|
| *"A" Is for Adopted*, Eileen Cosby, 2000 | None found | Picture Book | None | Precious/chosen child; Permanence of family; Loved forever |
| *Adoption Is for Always*, Linda Girard, 1986 | None found | Adoption Story | None | Precious child; Understanding that adoption means loss; Permanence of adoption |
| *A Koala for Katie: An Adoption Story*, Jonathan London, 1993 | AR Int. Level Lower Grades BL 2.3 | Adoption Story | None | Permanence of love; Birth mother made an adoption plan; *Real* mother is the one who is parenting |
| *Allison,* Allen Say, 1997 | AR Int. Level Lower Grades, BL 2.3 | Adoption Story | None | Discovering adoption rather than being told by parents; Understanding adoption as loss |
| *A Mother for Choco*, Keiko Kasza, 1992 | AR Int. Level Lower Grades, BL 2.2; Lexile level 390L | Animal Character Book | None | Looking different from family and accepting differences |
| *A New Barker in the House*, Tomie DePaola, 2002 | AR Int. Level Lower Grades BL 2.0; Lexile level 240L | Animal Character Book | None | Forming a family; Looking different from family members; Transracial or intercountry adoption; Sibling adjustments |
| *Beginnings: How Families Come to Be*, Virginia Knoll, 1994 | None found | Adoption Story and Book about Family | None | Families are formed in many ways; Understanding adoption stories; Understanding "forever" families; Transracial adoption |
| *Did My First Mother Love Me? A Story for an Adopted Child*, Kathryn Miller, 1994 | AR Int. Level Lower Grades BL 2.8 | Adoption Story | None | Understanding adoption story; Precious child; Understanding birth mother made an adoption plan |
| *Emma's Yucky Brother*, Jean Little, 2001 | AR Int. Level Lower Grades BL 2.2; Lexile level 200L | Adoption Story | Children's Notable List Book for 2002 | Adoption from foster care; Fear and loss; Permanence of family and love; Sibling adjustments |
| *Families Are Different*, Nina Pellegrini, 1991 | Lexile level 540L | Book about Family | None | Learning to accept differences; Meaning of family; Transracial or intercountry adoptions |

| Title, Author, Date of Pub. | AR Level and/ or Lexile | Genre | Awards | Adoption and Foster Care Themes |
|---|---|---|---|---|
| *Finding Joy*, Marion Coste, 2006 | AR Int. Level Lower Grades BL 3.0 | Adoption Story | None | Understanding adoption story; Transracial or intercountry adoptions |
| *Guji Guji*, Chih-Yuan Chen, 2004 | AR Int. Level Lower Grades BL 3.0; Lexile level AD650L | Animal Character Book | None | Learning to accept differences; Meaning of family |
| *Horace*, Holly Keller, 1991 | AR Int. Level Lower Grades BL 3.2 | Animal Character Book | None | Meaning of family; Learning to accept differences; Loved forever |
| *How I Was Adopted: Samantha's Story*, Joanne Cole, 1995 | Lexile level 520L | Adoption Story | None | Understanding adoption story; Meaning of family |
| *I Love You Like Crazy Cakes*, Rose Lewis, 2000 | AR Int. Level Lower Grades; BL 3.8; Lexile level AD550 | Adoption Story | None | Understanding adoption story; Remembering the birth mother; Permanence of family; Love of parent for child |
| *Is That Your Sister? A True Story of Adoption*, Catherine Bunin & Sherry Bunin, 1992 | None found | Adoption Story | None | Transracial adoption; Accepting differences; Meaning of family |
| *Jin Woo*, Eve Bunting, 2001 | AR Int. Level Lower Grades; BL 2.7; Lexile level 390L | Adoption Story | None | Sibling adjustments; Permanence of love; Intercountry adoption |
| *Just Add One Chinese Sister*, Patricia McMahon & Conor McCarthy, 2005 | AR Int. Level Lower Grades; BL 2.8 | Adoption Story | None | Understanding adoption story; Meaning of family; Transracial and intercountry adoption; Sibling adjustments |
| *Let's Talk About It: Adoption*, Fred Rogers, 1994 | None found | Book about Family | None | Meaning of family; How families are formed; Accepting differences |
| *Mommy Far, Mommy Near: An Adoption Story*, Carol Peacock, 2000 | AR Int. Level Lower Grades; BL 2.7; Lexile level 360L | Adoption Story | None | Understanding adoption story; Transracial and intercountry adoption; Love of family |
| *My Mei Mei*, Ed Young, 2006 | AR Int. Level Lower Grades; BL 2.5; Lexile level 590L | Adoption Story | None | Sibling adjustments; Intercountry adoption |
| *Never Never Never Will She Stop Loving You: The Adoption Love Story of Angel Annie*, Jolene Durrant, 1999 | None found | Adoption Story | None | Understanding adoption story; Remembering birth mother; Permanence of love from both family and birth family; Precious child |

**Table 4.1 (continued)**

| Title, Author, Date of Pub. | AR Level and/ or Lexile | Genre | Awards | Adoption and Foster Care Themes |
|---|---|---|---|---|
| *Nikolai, The Only Bear*, Barbara Joose, 2005 | AR Int. Level Lower Grades; BL 2.6 | Animal Character Book | None | Understanding adoption story; Intercountry adoption; Understanding differences |
| *Nothing At All*, Wanda Ga'g, 1941 | None found | Animal Character Book | Caldecott Honor Book, 1943 | Finding a family; Finding a place to belong |
| *Our Baby from China: An Adoption Story*, Nancy D'Antonio, 1997 | Lexile level 580L | Adoption Story | None | Understanding adoption story; Permanence of family; Transracial and intercountry adoption |
| *Our Twitchy*, Kes Gray, 2003 | AR Int. Level Lower Grades; BL 2.9 | Animal Character Book | None | Accepting differences; Meaning of family |
| *Sisters*, Judith Caseley, 2004 | AR Int. Level Lower Grades; BL 2.3 | Adoption Story | None | Sibling adjustments; Intercountry and transracial adoption |
| *Stellaluna*, Janell Cannon, 1993 | AR Int. Level Lower Grades; BL 3.5; Lexile level 550L | Animal Character Book | American Booksellers Book of the Year, 1994 | Accepting differences; Foster family |
| *Tell Me Again About the Night I Was Born*, Jamie Lee Curtis, 1996 | AR Int. Level Lower Grades: BL 2.8; Lexile level 108OL | Adoption Story | None | Understanding adoption story; Safety and security with family; Birth mother and birth father on family tree |
| *The Best Single Mom in the World*, Mary Zisk, 2001 | None found | Adoption Story | None | Understanding adoption story; Intercountry and transracial adoption; Meaning of family; Single parent adoption |
| *The Coffee Can Kid*, Jan Czech, 2002 | AR Int. Level Lower Grades; BL 3.1; Lexile level 470L | Adoption Story | None | Understanding adoption story; Intercountry and transracial adoption; Remembering the birth mother |
| *The Family Book*, Todd Parr, 2003 | None found | Book about Family | None | Meaning of family; Accepting differences |
| *The Mulberry Bird: An Adoption Story (Revised)*, Anne Brodzinsky, 1996 | None found | Animal Character Book | None | Permanence of love; Birth mother made an adoption plan; Meaning of family |
| *The Red Blanket*, Eliza Thomas, 2004 | AR Int. Level Lower Grades; BL 3.3 | Adoption Story | None | Understanding adoption story; Intercountry and transracial adoption; Single parent adoption |

| Title, Author, Date of Pub. | AR Level and/ or Lexile | Genre | Awards | Adoption and Foster Care Themes |
|---|---|---|---|---|
| *The White Swan Express: A Story About Adoption*, Jean Okimoto & Elaine Aoki, 2002 | AR Int. Level Lower Grades; BL 4.3 | Adoption Story | None | Understanding adoption story; Intercountry and transracial adoption; Single parent and gay/ lesbian adoption |
| *Through Moon and Stars and Night Skies*, Ann Turner, 1990 | AR Int. Level Lower Grades; BL 2.1; Lexile level 250L | Adoption Story | None | Understanding adoption story; Intercountry and transracial adoption; Safety and security of loving family |
| *Waiting for May*, Janet Stoeke, 2005 | AR Int. Level Lower Grades; BL 3.4 | Adoption Story | None | Understanding adoption story; Intercountry and transracial adoption; Sibling adjustments |
| *We Wanted You*, Liz Rosenberg, 2002 | AR Int. Level Lower Grades: BL 2.0 | Adoption Story | None | Understanding adoption story; Intercountry and transracial adoption; Permanence of love and family |
| *When Joel Comes Home*, Susi Fowler, 1993 | AR Int. Level Lower Grades; BL 3.3 | Adoption Story | None | Understanding adoption from point of view of family friends |
| *When You Were Born in China: A Memory Book for Children Adopted from China*, Sara Dorow, 1997 | None found | Adoption Story | None | Understanding adoption story; Intercountry and transracial adoption |
| *When You Were Born in Korea: A Memory Book for Children Adopted from Korea*, Brian Boyd, 2000 | None found | Adoption Story | None | Understanding adoption story; Intercountry and transracial adoption |
| *You're Not My Real Mother*, Molly Friedrich, 2004 | AR Int. Level Lower Grades; BL 2.5 | Adoption Story | None | Understanding adoption story; Intercountry and transracial adoption; *Real* mother is the one who is parenting |

## USING LITERATURE ON ADOPTION AND FOSTER CARE IN THE K–2 CLASSROOM

As noted earlier in this chapter, children in grades K–2 need reassurance that their families love them and that they are precious to their families. They also need to learn that many types of families exist and that although families may be quite different from each other it is quite acceptable to be different. Understanding adoption and foster care stories, understanding that the birth mother made a plan for her child to have a loving family, and learning that adoption and love are permanent are all crucial ideas for young readers to attain. Furthermore, children who have not been adopted or placed in foster care need to learn that their friends have caring families and that their personal stories are private and are to be respected.

When children in grades K–2 are reading literature on adoption and foster care, the teacher might plan follow-up activities involving safe choices for *all* children (see Chapter 2) and create discussion questions to reinforce the key concepts and themes important for children at this developmental level. Remember that the teacher's job will be to provide accurate information about adoption and foster care in a manner that children can comprehend, to assist individual children in handling curious peers, and to promote acceptance of diverse families. In addition, when teachers know that children in their classes are living in foster care or have been adopted, they might want to check with the child's parents first before engaging in activities or discussions of a sensitive nature. Finally, the teacher will want to take care to protect the privacy of individual children, never forcing children to share information they do not wish to share and never plying the child with questions regarding his/her personal adoption or foster care story. Teachers will want to strictly enforce the notion that personal stories for *all* children in the classroom are exactly that: *personal and private*. The teacher might choose the following types of activities to accompany the reading of children's literature on adoption and foster care at this level:

- Include pictures of multiethnic families throughout the classroom environment and check reading materials for evidence of multiethnic families.

- Read books such as those contained in Table 4.1 about different types of families and talk about how the families in the books are the same and how they are different. As children read the stories ask them: What kinds of families did you see in the story? Who was in the family? Are all of the families the same? What makes a family? Remind students that families are made up of lots of different people and that each type of family is great!

- Ask children to suggest ways they are different from a friend. Include specific questions such as:

  Who in the class has the same eye color as you? Who has a different eye color?

  Who in the class has the same hair color as you? Who has a different hair color?

  Who is the tallest boy/girl? Who is the shortest boy/girl?

  Who has brothers or sisters? How many brothers and sisters? Are they older or younger than you?

  What is your favorite food? What is your least favorite food?

  How are we all the same? How are we all different?

  As children make these suggestions, write their responses on chart paper or a poster. Review afterward the many ways that children are alike and different. Remind children that we are all unique and that our families are also all unique.

- Share a picture or a drawing of your family. Have children draw a picture of their home or their family. This can be a drawing of their house or a drawing of any people the child loves. The drawing could also be of any people who love the child, as shown in Figure 4.1.

- Share with children your favorite family activity. Have children talk about the favorite things they do with their families (e.g., eat out, go to the movies, play sports, etc.). Make a poster or list of all the favorite activities and emphasize how favorite activities are the same and how they are different. Be sure to provide safe alternatives for all children and refrain from forcing all children to share their favorite family activity.

- Share with children your favorite family holiday or tradition. Talk about what makes a tradition special. Let children share their favorite family holiday or tradition if they choose to do so. Develop a classroom "tradition" that children can share across the course of the school year. Reinforce the idea that traditions help bring people together since this is something special that they share time and time again.

- Create a timeline of your favorite year. Include at least six events from that year. (See Chapter 2 for safe choices regarding timelines.)

- Spotlight children on the "Who's Who" or "Superstar" bulletin board. Have each child share a favorite picture of him/her or have children bring in pictures of things that are important to them. (See Chapter 2 for safe choices regarding this type of bulletin board.)

**Figure 4.1**
**Drawing the People We Love**

- Teach children to respond to difficult questions that other children or adults may ask by using the W.I.S.E. up strategy suggested by Schoettle (2000). Children can learn to **W**alk away, to say **I**t is private and "I do not want to talk about it" or say "No" and change the subject, to **S**hare some information that they do not mind sharing, or to **E**ducate others by telling them correct information and helping them understand it. Note that this strategy can work for children in foster care, for those who have been adopted, or for any child who faces a difficult situation (e.g., parents divorcing) that he or she may not wish to talk about.

- Use the titles from Table 4.1, summarized in the annotated bibliography below, for recommended children's literature for young readers to prompt discussion about adoption or foster care.

## AN ANNOTATED BIBLIOGRAPHY OF SELECTED LITERATURE ON ADOPTION AND FOSTER CARE FOR GRADES K–2

The stories for young readers previously listed in Table 4.1 are arranged in the same alphabetical order by title in the following annotated bibliography. A summary is provided for each story as well as comments containing additional information or cautions relevant for the teacher's use of the story. In addition, themes to be emphasized in discussion or follow-up activities for each story are listed. Interestingly, only one book about adoption or foster care for young readers, other than the *Madeline* books mentioned in Chapter 3, received a Caldecott Honor Award and this was for the book *Nothing At All* written by Wanda Ga'g in 1941! Only one other book, *Emma's Yucky Brother* (Jean Little, 2002), was named to the Children's Notable List in 2002. Despite the lack of books at the K–2 grade levels that have received American Library Association awards, the illustrations and stories are quite charming for a number of the titles listed below.

## ANNOTATED BIBLIOGRAPHY

**Title:** *"A" Is for Adopted*
**Author(s):** Eileen Tucker
**Illustrator:** Norma S. Strange
**Publisher:** Swak-Pak Books, Tempe, AZ
**Date of Publication:** 2000
**Awards:** None
**Reading Levels:** No Lexile or AR levels found

**Summary:**
This is an ABC picture book telling the story of adoption in poetic form. For example, F stands for "family," N stands for "name," which is chosen carefully for a child who is loved. The author presents information about adoption accurately and lovingly.

**Comments and Specific Suggestions:**
The pictures are colorful and appealing. Some pages contain religious references; therefore, the book may not be appropriate for public school settings.

**Themes:**
Precious, "chosen," and loved child
Birth mother made a plan for her child
Permanence of family and love

**Title:** *Adoption Is for Always*
**Author(s):** Linda Walvoord Girard
**Illustrator:** Judith Friedman
**Publisher:** Albert Whitman and Company, Morton Grove, IL
**Date of Publication:** 1986
**Awards:** None
**Reading Levels:** No Lexile or AR Levels found

**Summary:**
Celia, a girl of about six or seven, has always known she was adopted, but now she is questioning her parents about the realities of her adoption. She wants to know whether or not she could not stay with her birth mother because she was "bad," and she worries that her birth mother might take her away someday. Celia's parents and her teacher reassure her that her birth mother did love her and that she will always be with her parents. Her parents reaffirm that they will always love her. Celia and her parents decide to celebrate her adoption day each year as well as her actual birthday.

**Comments and Specific Suggestions:**
Many young children who are adopted celebrate their adoption day or their "Gotcha Day" in addition to their birthday. This provides a link to a discussion of special family traditions and celebrations. In addition, the teacher will want to reinforce the notion that Celia was not "bad" and that her adoption had nothing to do with anything she might have done. The permanence of Celia's adoption and her family should also be emphasized.

**Themes:**
Understanding adoption story and that adoption means loss
Understanding permanence of adoption and of love
Feelings of confusion or sadness—"Was I adopted because I was bad?"

**Title:** *A Koala for Katie: An Adoption Story*
**Author(s):** Jonathan London

**Illustrator:** Cynthia Jabar
**Publisher:** Albert Whitman and Company, Morton Grove, IL
**Date of Publication:** 1993
**Awards:** None
**Reading Levels:** AR Int. Level Lower Grades, BL 2.3

## Summary:

Katie asks about her adoption story, something she has done many times. She asks if she grew in her "real mommy's" tummy. Katie's mother answers that of course Katie grew in her mommy's tummy, but that she is Katie's mother too. Katie then asks why her first mommy did not want her. Her mother reminds her that her birth mother loved her, but that she was too young to take care of a baby and wanted Katie to have a better life than she could provide for her. Later, Katie goes to the zoo with her parents and sees a baby koala clinging to its mother. This prompts Katie to ask who would take care of the baby if its mother could not anymore. Katie's parents clarify that this would be very sad, but a new mom would take good care of the baby and love the baby just as Katie's parents love her. Katie's father buys her a stuffed koala bear at the zoo gift shop and Katie pretends she is its mother protecting it and loving it. Katie says she will always protect her "baby." Katie's father replies that Katie will always be their little girl.

## Comments and Specific Suggestions:

The story contains colorful, "cartoon-type" illustrations. The situations, questions, and actions of the characters are realistic. In addition to clarifying that Katie's birth mother made a loving plan for her adoption, teachers might have children talk about pets or stuffed animals they have cared for. The story also lends itself to a discussion of what parents do for their children.

## Themes:

Permanence of love
Birth mothers love their children and make plans for their children to be in loving families
Concept of "real mother"

**Title:** *Allison*
**Author(s):** Allen Say
**Illustrator:** Allen Say
**Publisher:** Houghton Mifflin Company, Boston, MA
**Date of Publication:** 1997
**Awards:** None, although Allen Say is a Caldecott Medal winning illustrator for other books
**Reading Levels:** AR Int. Level Lower Grades, BL 2.3; Lexile Level 430L

## Summary:

This is the adoption story of a child, Allison, adopted from "far, far away from another country" such as Korea, Vietnam, or China. The child had only her doll, Mei Mei, when found. Allison received a kimono from her grandmother and while trying it on noticed that she looked different from her parents. She asked her parents why she did not look like them and then heard her adoption story for the first time. Allison was angry, and she destroyed her mother's precious Raggedy Andy doll and her father's baseball mitt and ball he received from his father. When a cat visited Allison's house and then returned again, she decided to make him a member of the family and began her reconciliation with her parents. This book illustrates the confusion, distrust, and anger of children when they are unaware of their adoption from their earliest possible memories.

## Comments and Specific Suggestions:

The book contains beautiful and realistic illustrations but should be used cautiously. Although the dialogue may represent true situations for children adopted from countries such as China, some of the words may create confusion or anxiety for young readers. For example, when Allison first discovers she is adopted, she asks, "Where's my Mommy? Where's my Daddy? They didn't want me?" to which her mother responds, "We're sure they wanted you, but we never met them," and her father states, "They were not able to keep you but they wanted you to have a mother and father" (pp. 9 and 10). For young children, these statements need clarification so that youngsters do not come away from the story with the understanding that parents may "give away" their children if they cannot "keep" them or jump to the faulty conclusion that the baby was "bad" so the parents could not keep her. Teachers will need to clarify that the birth mother and father were not able to take care of *any* baby at that time and so they made a plan to be sure the baby had a family that could love and care for her forever. In addition, when the cat returns, Allison "adopts" it and states that he can be part of their family. The story then ends with the statement, "The stray cat wasn't a stray anymore" (p. 30). The parallel between a child's adoption and a stray cat was probably not intended, but could possibly send the wrong message to other children—that children who are adopted are similar to "strays." This point will need further clarification by the teacher.

**Themes:**
Importance of adoption story
Parent-child trust

**Title:** *A Mother for Choco*
**Author(s):** Keiko Kazya
**Illustrator:** Same
**Publisher:** G. P. Putnam's Sons, a Division of the Putnam & Grosset Book Group, New York
**Date of Publication:** 1992
**Awards:** None
**Reading Levels:** AR Int. Level Lower Grades, BL 2.2; Lexile Level 390L

**Summary:**
Choco is a little bird who is alone and wishes he had a mother. He sets off to search for her. He looks for animals having features like his, but no one looks like him. Mrs. Bear does not look like him at all, but he tells her, "I need a mommy." Mrs. Bear asks him what a mommy would do, and he says that a mommy would hold him, kiss him, and sing and dance with him. Mrs. Bear does these things with him and suggests that maybe she could be his mother since she already has three children, Hippy, Ally, and Piggy. Choco learns that even though he does not look like his mother, he is happy and loved. He is happy that his new mother looks just as she does.

**Comments and Specific Suggestions:**
This book was originally published in Japan in 1982. It is an animal character book. Teachers might help children engage in a discussion about what mothers do for their children. The key idea to develop here, of course, is that mothers love and care for their children in many ways. The focus should be on the similarities among children regardless of their family structure.

**Theme:**
Difference (Looking different from family is not as important as being loved and happy with a family)

**Title:** *A New Barker in the House*
**Author(s):** Tomie DePaola
**Illustrator:** Same
**Publishe:r** G. P. Putnam's Sons, New York
**Date of Publication:** 2002
**Awards:** None
**Reading Levels:** AR Int. Level Lower Grades, BL 2.0; Lexile Level AD240L

**Summary:**
The twins, Morgie and Moffie, get a new little brother adopted from a country where Spanish is spoken. Marcos, also called Markie, does not speak English. Morgie and Moffie dream about what they will do when Markie arrives, and after his arrival they scare and confuse him with their play and their food. Slowly the twins adjust to Markie and they begin learning some Spanish. Markie begins to adjust and learn some English.

**Comments and Specific Suggestions:**
The book contains cartoon-type illustrations in vivid bright acrylics. This is part of a series of books about the Barker family and the twins Morgie and Moffie. An animal character book, the story depicts realistic situations about the adjustment of siblings when intercountry adoption presents a language barrier and when children in the family look different from one another. Teachers can certainly lead children in a discussion about siblings. For example, the teacher might ask children such questions as the following: Do they look the same as or different from their brothers and sisters? Are they older, younger, or middle children? Have they ever been jealous of a brother or a sister and when? The point to be emphasized is the commonality in feelings about siblings across the families of children in the classroom.

**Themes:**
Forming a family
Adjusting to a new language and new culture after intercountry adoption
Sibling adjustment to an intercountry adoption
Transracial or intercountry adoption

**Title:** *Beginnings: How Families Come to Be*
**Author(s):** Virginia Kroll
**Illustrator:** Stacey Schuett
**Publisher:** Albert Whitman and Company, Morton Grove, IL
**Date of Publication:** 1994
**Awards:** None
**Reading Levels:** None found

**Summary:**
This book tells the story of children who were adopted at different ages and from different circumstances. Each story is told through a "question and answer" conversation between the child and his or her mother or father. Each child obviously knows his or her adoption story and actively engages in its retelling. Ruben, who appears to be Latino, was the birth child of a large family. Katherine Grace was adopted as an infant from Korea and her family is awaiting the adoption of her brother from a country in South America. Mark was adopted by his Uncle Joe, a single father, after his mother died, and Olivia was adopted by a single mother as well. Olivia, however, has an open adoption. Her birth mother and father, both teens, invited Olivia's mother to her birth and gave her the name "Olivia." Habib was adopted as an infant. His African American family decided to adopt him on the fifth night of Kwanzaa, Nia or Purpose, and they named him Habib, meaning "Beloved." Finally, Nicole, a child with a disability who appears to be African American or Latino, was adopted by a Caucasian family after she had already been in several foster families. Nicole's "forever family" located her by searching the "Blue Book" where waiting children are listed by Social Services.

**Comments and Specific Suggestions:**
The book contains very colorful illustrations of elementary level children and realistic portrayals of different types of families having adopted children today. Following this story, when appropriate and with parent approval, children who have been adopted might be permitted the opportunity to share their own adoption story with the group.

**Themes:**
Understanding adoption stories
Families are formed in many ways
Forever families are people who love and care for each other always
Transracial and intercountry adoption
Adopting a child with a disability

**Title:** *Did My First Mother Love Me? A Story for an Adopted Child*
**Author(s):** Kathryn Ann Miller

**Illustrator:** Jami Moffett
**Publisher:** Morning Glory Press, Buena Park, CA
**Date of Publication:** 1994
**Awards:** None
**Reading Levels:** AR Int. Level Lower Grades, BL 2.8

## Summary:

Morgan feels loved by her mother and father, but she asks her mother the question, "Did my first mother love me?" Her mom reads her the letter written by her first mother. This is a letter filled with love and describing everything Morgan's birth mother wants for her. Morgan's birth mother reassures her that she desired to take good care of Morgan's future by planning it as best as she could. Finding the best possible family was, to her, the most important thing she could do for Morgan. The letter contains the statement that Morgan's birth mother wished to be the one to give her child wonderful things, but she knew her wish would not come true. Instead, Morgan's birth mother states that she gave Morgan's parents the precious gift of her dearest child.

## Comments and Specific Suggestions:

The black and white illustrations are quite moving and the book contains a special section at the end describing for parents how to talk with their child who has been adopted. This is an accurate and caring portrayal of the love of parents and of the birth mother. The language of adoption at the end of the book is helpful and appropriate for teachers as well as for parents.

## Themes:

Understanding adoption story
Precious child
Finding the best possible family
Love of the birth mother, who made a plan for her child, and love of the parents

**Title:** *Emma's Yucky Brother*
**Author(s):** Jean Little
**Illustrator:** Jennifer Plecas
**Publisher:** HarperCollins Publishers, New York
**Date of Publication:** 2001
**Awards:** ALA Children's Notable List, 2002
**Reading Levels:** AR Int. Level Lower Grades, BL 2.2; Lexile Level 200L

## Summary:

Emma's family adopts four-year-old Max who has been in a foster care placement. Max visits a few times and then spends the night. He misses his foster parent, Jane, but agrees to be adopted by Emma's family. Max breaks Emma's doll and runs away. Emma finds Max and tells him she fixed the doll. She also says, "Next time ask me for help. That's what sisters are for" (p. 63). Max returns home, and Emma and Max learn about becoming loving brothers and sisters.

## Comments and Specific Suggestions:

This is a short chapter book with realistic situations and reactions from the characters. The illustrations are colorful. Teachers might use this book to talk about sibling relationships much like the suggestions with *A New Barker in the House*.

## Themes:

Adoption from foster care
Sibling adjustment
Dealing with fear and loss
Loving and realizing love is permanent

**Title:** *Families Are Different*
**Author(s):** Nina Pellegrini
**Illustrator:** Same
**Publisher:** Holiday House, New York
**Date of Publication:** 1991
**Awards:** None
**Reading Levels:** Lexile Level 540L

**Summary:**
Six-year-old Nico, a kindergartner, and her older sister, Angel, were adopted from Korea as babies, but four years apart. Nico sometimes feels angry or sad that she looks different from her parents, especially when her friends, Molly and Anna, look so much like theirs. Sometimes when she hears strangers say things like, "Oh your baby looks just like you," she feels different, too (p. 14). Nico talks with her mother about her feelings and her mom tells Nico, "There are different kinds of families . . . they are all glued together with a special kind of glue called LOVE" (p. 15). Nico then starts to notice lots of different families among those she knows. She sees a child who looks like his African American father but not like his Caucasian mother, a boy and girl who live with their grandparents, a girl who lives with her father, stepmother, and half sister, and many others. Nico decides, "Now I don't think I'm strange at all. I'm just like everyone else . . . I'm different" (p. 25).

**Comments and Specific Suggestions:**
The illustrations are quite colorful and realistic. The book would be a good way to open a discussion about what makes a family and the many types of families that are wonderfully different.

**Themes:**
Feeling different and learning to accept differences
Meaning of family
Transracial and Intercountry adoption

**Title:** *Finding Joy*
**Author(s):** Marion Coste
**Illustrator:** Yong Chen
**Publisher:** Boyds Mill Press, Honesdale, PA
**Date of Publication:** 2006
**Awards:** None
**Reading Levels:** AR Int. Level Lower Grades, BL 3.0

**Summary:**
Shu-Li (i.e., Shao Xui Li meaning "elegantly beautiful") is a child who was placed under a bridge by her biological parents. On the red blanket in which she was placed was pinned a note, "This is our Shu-Li. Please take care of her. No room for girls" (p. 1). Shu-Li was found and taken to an orphanage. Meanwhile, across the ocean were a mother and father who were getting older. They had two older boys and an older girl who were all grown up, and they decided to adopt a little girl. The mother flew across the ocean wondering whether or not her family could love a baby born to strangers. When Shu-Li is adopted, she is given the new name "Joy," and her family all accepts and loves her easily. Her parents keep the red blanket and the note in a chest in the attic and plan to take it out and tell Joy her story when the time seems right.

**Comments and Specific Suggestions:**
Joy is obviously very much loved by both of her families, and this love is clearly communicated through the words and the beautiful illustrations. Like the story *Allison*, however, one wonders why the parents do not plan to talk with Shu-Li from the very beginning about her adoption. An adoption story can be integrated into bedtime stories and casual conversation from the earliest memories onward. Children might also wonder why there was "no room for girls." This discussion, carefully crafted, involves an excellent lesson in Chinese history, culture,

and politics—in an agricultural and patriarchal society, boys perform labor and take care of parents as they age. In some areas of China, one of the most populated countries on Earth, a one-child policy has been implemented, which has forced parents to place firstborn girls in market places or on doorsteps and "try again." For background information and an interesting discussion of this phenomenon, as well as the subsequent adoption of thousands of girls from China by citizens of the United States, read *The Lost Daughters of China* (Evans, 2000). Teachers might also visit the Web site of Families with Children from China at www.fwcc.org.

**Themes:**
Love of both families
Intercountry and transracial adoption
Understanding the adoption story

**Title:** *Guji Guji*
**Author(s):** Chih-Yuan Chen
**Illustrator:** Same
**Publisher:** Kane/Miller Book Publishers, La Jolla, CA
**Date of Publication:** 2004
**Awards:** None
**Reading Levels:** AR Int. Level Lower Grades, BL 3.0; Lexile Level AD650L

**Summary:**
A crocodile egg rolls down a hill and lands in a duck's nest. The mother duck hatches all of the eggs, names all of the babies, and loves all of her ducklings just the same. Guji Guji is given his name because that is what he said when he was hatched. One day Guji Guji meets three crocodiles who try to convince him that he is a crocodile too and that he should lead the ducks to a bridge and have them jump into the water so the crocodiles can eat them. Guji Guji takes his family to the bridge, but they all throw big stones into the water instead of jumping. The crocodiles snap at the stones and break their teeth, and Guji Guji continues to live happily ever after with his family as a "crocoduck."

**Comments and Specific Suggestions:**
This is a delightfully funny little tale that was originally published in Taiwan in 2003. The story was inspired by a friend of the author, an American adopted from Korea as a baby. The author's friend always felt isolated and different from his family. Although this is an animal character book, the book is useful for developing the concept of different types of families, as well as the notion of love and loyalty among family regardless of how different family members may look.

**Themes:**
Family and accepting differences
Loving family and loyalty to family

**Title:** *Horace*
**Author(s):** Holly Keller
**Illustrator:** Same
**Publisher:** A Mulberry Paperback Book, an Imprint of William Morrow & Co., New York
**Date of Publication:** 1991
**Awards:** None
**Reading Levels:** AR Int. Level Lower Grades, BL 3.2

**Summary:**
Horace is a leopard covered with spots, but his mother and father are tigers covered with stripes. His mother tells Horace his adoption story every night at bedtime, but Horace always falls asleep before it is finished. Horace gets annoyed with his parents when they tell him to do things like finish eating his oatmeal or brush his teeth or wear

his boots, and sometimes he wishes he had different parents. At his birthday party, Horace realizes he looks differ-ent from his cousins and family, and so he sets off to find others who look like him. He visits a carnival and a park and finally returns home to his family where he hears his whole adoption story before falling asleep. Horace real-izes that his family chose him and that he chose them too. Horace knows that he is happy with his family.

## Comments and Specific Suggestions:
This is an animal character book containing nice illustrations that should delight young readers. The thoughts and reactions of Horace are also realistic for children. The book is useful for learning about what makes a family regardless of how different family members appear.

## Themes:
Understanding adoption story
Loving family
Accepting differences

**Title:** *How I Was adopted: Samantha's Story*
**Author(s):** Joanna Cole
**Illustrator:** Maxie Chambliss
**Publisher:** William Morrow & Company, New York
**Date of Publication:** 1995
**Awards:** None
**Reading Levels:** Lexile Level 520L

## Summary:
Samantha, known as Sam, tells the story of her adoption and ends her story by asking, "Were you adopted too?" (p. 7). Sam's was an infant adoption and she says, "Many children stay with the woman who gave birth to them. Some children do not. Some children need to be adopted the way Mommy and Daddy adopted me" (p. 14). The message conveyed by Samantha is that her parents wanted a child and love her very much. Samantha also talks about the many types of adoptions and families.

## Comments and Specific Suggestions:
The book begins with guidance to parents and teachers regarding how children ask questions about their adoption and history and that these questions change as children age. Children require answers they can understand, and they incorporate new information as they grow and mature. Although Samantha tells the story of her adoption from the level she can understand, some children may conclude from her story that the child who has been adopted could not stay with the "woman who gave birth to them" because they were "bad." The teacher will need to take care to clarify this point. The final question (i.e., were you adopted too?) can be a springboard to additional discussion as well. The teacher can take the opportunity to provide accurate information about what adoption means.

## Themes:
Understanding adoption story
Families are formed in many ways
Love of family and meaning of family

**Title:** *I Love You Like Crazy Cakes*
**Author(s):** Rose Lewis
**Illustrator:** Jane Dyer
**Publisher:** Little, Brown, and Company, Boston, MA
**Date of Publication:** 2000
**Awards:** None
**Reading Levels:** AR Int. Level Lower Grades, BL 3.8; Lexile Level AD550L

**Summary:**
A baby was well taken care of by nannies in China, but all of the girls had something missing, a mother. Far away, a woman wanted a baby. When she received a picture of her baby she flew to China. The mother knew right away, when the nannies brought her baby to her, that she was falling in love. Back at home, the baby cried when other family members held her and stopped crying when her mom held her again. As the mother rocks her daughter to sleep the first night at home, she cries for the baby's Chinese birth mother who could not watch her baby grow and she hopes that somehow her baby's birth mother will know that her child is happy, safe, and loved.

**Comments and Specific Suggestions:**
The story is based on the author's own trip to adopt her daughter from China. The watercolor illustrations are beautiful and warm. The story is also available in Spanish. Rose Lewis is a single mother who also wrote a sequel to *I Love you Like Crazy Cakes* entitled *Every Year on Your Birthday* (Lewis, 2007), a book chronicling key events in the first five years of her child's life. This book might lead to a carefully constructed timeline project. (See Chapter 2.)

**Themes:**
Understanding adoption story
Intercountry or transracial adoption
Love of parent and birth mother for child
Permanence, safety, and security for child

**Title:** *Is That Your Sister? A True Story of Adoption*
**Author(s):** Catherine Bunin and Sherry Bunin
**Illustrator:** Sheila Kelly Welch
**Publisher:** Our Child Press, Wayne, PA
**Date of Publication:** 1992
**Awards:** None
**Reading Levels:** None found

**Summary:**
A six-year-old girl, Catherine, tells the story of how she feels about being adopted and about having a younger sister who is also adopted. The children do not look alike or look like their mother, and sometimes Catherine wishes she were like her friend Melissa, who was also adopted but who looks like her mother. Melissa does not have to explain all the time! Catherine wonders why her birth mother "allowed" her to be adopted. She does not remember her foster family, although her sister, Carla, remembers a little bit about her foster family. Catherine tells the story of how the social worker brought Carla to visit and helped them go to court to adopt Carla. Catherine also says, "... kids still don't get it. I know because someone will always say, 'Yeah, but don't you know who your real mom and dad are?' I know, but they don't get it. I tell them that my real mom and dad are the mom and dad who take care of me and love me ... But no matter how I try, I can't seem to explain that very well ... you know, sometimes I hate talking about adoption with a lot of dumb kids and with grownups, too" (pp. 14–15).

**Comments and Specific Suggestions:**
This book is quite realistic and deals with the difficult questions young readers may experience from their peers. The main character, Catherine, makes the point that people ask too many questions and this makes her feel different. Teachers might use this statement as a springboard for a discussion about times when children have felt different. For example, children might have felt bad or different when relatives such as grandparents, aunts, or uncles have asked them lots of questions or have said embarrassing things to them.

**Themes:**
Dealing with difference
Transracial adoption and adoption from foster care
Understanding the meaning of family

**Title:** *Jin Woo*
**Author(s):** Eve Bunting
**Illustrator:** Chris Soentpiet
**Publisher:** Clarion Books, an Imprint of Houghton Mifflin, New York
**Date of Publication:** 2001
**Awards:** None
**Reading Levels:** AR Int. Level Lower Grades, BL 2.7; Lexile Level 390L

**Summary:**
Jin, whose name means "Happy Jewel," was adopted from Korea. His older brother, David, also adopted, wonders if his parents were that excited about him. David worries that his parents will not love him now that Jin Woo is coming. The parents demonstrate that they have lots of love for both boys by including David in the preparations and giving him responsibility for Jin Woo's special 100-day ring. David makes Jin Woo laugh for the first time on their way home, and upon arriving home the neighbors and family members all say that David's parents had a big celebration for him too. David begins to be Jin Woo's big brother when he gets his dad to take down his duck mobile that has always calmed him in his room and put it up over Jin Woo's crib.

**Comments and Specific Suggestions:**
This is a good book for siblings who are expecting a new arrival home, whether or not that sibling is expected through adoption or through birth. The book accurately portrays the emotions of fear and jealousy from the older sibling. The characters and reactions are realistic and the illustrations are colorful. The illustrator, coincidentally, was adopted.

**Themes:**
Permanence of love
Sibling adjustment
Intercountry and transracial adoption

**Title:** *Just Add One Chinese Sister: An Adoption Story*
**Author(s):** Patricia McMahon and Conor Clarke McCarthy
**Illustrator:** Karen A. Jerome
**Publisher:** Boyds Mills Press, Honesdale, PA
**Date of Publication:** 2005
**Awards:** None
**Reading Levels:** AR Int. level Lower Grades, BL 2.8

**Summary:**
This is the true adoption story of the author and how she, her son, Conor, and her husband traveled to China to adopt their daughter. The story is told by the author as if she is answering questions from Claire as they work together on a scrapbook about Claire's adoption. Letters and comments written by Conor during the wait and the adoption process are included along with artifacts that tell part of the story, such as a sock from the first day Claire laughed, tickets from the airplane trip, and a picture of the White Swan Hotel in Guangzhou.

**Comments and Specific Suggestions:**
This is a delightful story with an accurate portrayal of adoption from China. The colorful pictures are realistic and many are made to look like photographs to be included in a scrapbook. Children might be encouraged to produce their own life book or scrapbook. Of course, children must be given safe options to include the information they wish to share in a manner they choose.

**Themes:**
Understanding adoption story
Transracial and intercountry adoption

Sibling adjustment and involvement in the adoption
Forming a family
Fear/frustration for child of intercountry adoption with new language, people, smells, and food

**Title:** *Let's Talk About It: Adoption*
**Author(s):** Fred Rogers
**Illustrator:** Jim Judkis
**Publisher:** The Putnam and Grosset Group, New York
**Date of Publication:** 1994
**Awards:** None
**Reading Levels:** None found

**Summary:**
The book is designed to help parents and teachers get children talking about what families are and how families are formed. In simple language, Mr. Rogers communicates that families are people who care about each other and that being in a family means belonging as well as giving and receiving love. The message is clear: We can belong in our family through birth or adoption, and we belong and love even when we get angry at our parents or siblings or our parents get angry at us.

**Comments and Specific Suggestions:**
Mr. Rogers had a sister adopted into his family when he was only 11 years old. This is a great Mr. Rogers book, a little dated, but with a very positive message that all children need to hear.

**Themes:**
Meaning of family—belonging and love
Understanding how families are formed
Dealing with differences

**Title:** *Mommy Far, Mommy Near: An Adoption Story*
**Author(s):** Carol Antoinette Peacock
**Illustrator:** Sharon Costello Brownell
**Publisher:** Albert Whitman and Company, Morton Grove, IL
**Date of Publication:** 2000
**Awards:** None
**Reading Levels:** AR Int. Level Lower Grades, BL 2.7; Lexile Level 360L

**Summary:**
Elizabeth and her younger sister, Katherine, were both adopted from China. When Elizabeth plays the game "Look" with her mother, she notices that they look very different. She later asks her mother, "When did your mommy get you from China?" Elizabeth's mother explains about her birth and her other mommy in China. Over time, Elizabeth comes to understand her adoption by explaining to Katherine, by pretending to talk to her other mommy, and by asking questions that her mother answers carefully and lovingly (e.g., telling Elizabeth about the one child rule in China). Elizabeth also asks to have her adoption story retold repeatedly. In the summer, Elizabeth sees a child and mother together who are both Chinese. Her mother notices how sad Elizabeth looks and carries her home. Elizabeth and her mother engage in a conversation letting Elizabeth know how very much she is loved: "My mommy is lost," I said. "That mommy loved you very much," my mother said. "She didn't keep me." "No but she wanted to. Very badly . . ." my mother said, "That mommy loved you, Elizabeth. And I love you. And Daddy loves you . . ." (p. 24).

**Comments and Specific Suggestions:**
The feelings and emotions portrayed by Elizabeth are quite real and accurate for children adopted from China. Teachers might lead children in a discussion of feelings they might have had when they lost something important

to them. The story enables young children to understand these feelings of sadness and loss at their developmental level.

**Themes:**
Understanding adoption story
Intercountry and transracial adoption
Meaning of family

**Title:** *My Mei Mei*
**Author(s):** Ed Young
**Illustrator:** Same
**Publisher:** Philomel Books, a Division of Penguin Group, New York
**Date of Publication:** 2006
**Awards:** None, but Ed Young has won a Caldecott Medal for other works
**Reading Levels:** AR Int. Level Lower Grades, BL 2.5; Lexile Level 590L

**Summary:**
The author tells the story of his own daughter as she learns what it means to be a sister. Antonia, adopted from China, pretends she has a little sister, "Mei Mei," and that she is the big sister, "Jieh Jieh." When the family flies to China to adopt another girl, Amanda, three-year-old Antonia feels left out. Back home, though, she discovers over time how to be a big sister and she does not have to pretend anymore. She shows her little sister how to do things, and by the end of the story both girls are waiting for another Mei Mei.

**Comments and Specific Suggestions:**
The illustrations are beautiful, and this is an accurate portrayal of an older sibling adjusting to the adoption of a younger one. Big sisters or big brothers might be encouraged to talk about the things they do for their younger siblings, or, conversely, younger siblings might discuss the things their older siblings do for them.

**Themes:**
Sibling relationships and adjustment
Intercountry adoption

**Title:** *Never Never Never Will She Stop Loving You: The Adoption Love Story of Angel Annie*
**Author(s):** Jolene Durrant
**Illustrator:** Illustrations by children who have been adopted; Photography by Steve Allred
**Publisher:** JoBiz! Books, St. George, UT
**Date of Publication:** 1999
**Awards:** None
**Reading Levels:** None found

**Summary:**
Written by a parent who has adopted a child, the message throughout the book is that the family and birth family, mother and birth mother, will *always* love the child. The story begins by explaining that the child has one mother who makes sandwiches, reminds the child to eat his vegetables or do his homework, kisses him goodnight, and loves him always. Then, all the ways in which the birth mother cared for her child, such as eating properly and making an adoption plan, are conveyed so that young children can easily understand. The illustrations, drawn by children who have been adopted, add to the book's appeal.

**Comments and Specific Suggestions:**
Notes to birth mothers and fathers and to parents are included in the beginning of the book. In addition, the author makes some suggestions regarding how the public can support the adoption process. The focus throughout the book is clearly on the birth mother and her difficult decision as well as ongoing love for her child.

For young children, the permanence of a birth mother's love may be very comforting. For somewhat older children, particularly those who came from less than ideal first family situations, the message may create confusion, sadness, or self-doubt as children wonder why their birth mother did not love them the same way as "Angel Annie."

**Themes:**
Understanding adoption story
Remembering birth mother
Permanence of love from both family and birth family
Precious child

**Title:** *Nikolai, The Only Bear*
**Author(s):** Barbara Joose
**Illustrator:** Renata Liwska
**Publisher:** Philomel Books, a Division of Penguin Young Readers Groups, New York
**Date of Publication:** 2005
**Awards:** None
**Reading Levels:** AR Int. Level Lower Grades, BL 2.6

**Summary:**
Nikolai is in an orphanage in Novosibirsk, Russia, with 99 "keepers" and 100 orphans. He is the only bear and he does not talk or play or sing like the other orphans. Nikolai sees other orphans come and go, but he still does not get adopted. One day Dr. Larissa writes a letter to America. A man with a fuzzy head and a furry face visits Nikolai at the orphanage, and when Nikolai growls, the man growls back. When Nikolai claws the air, the smooth-faced woman with the man claws the air, too, instead of telling Nikolai to "play nice." She gives Nikolai hugs and makes him feel "soft bearish" as he climbs on her lap. The three go home as a family to America.

**Comments and Specific Suggestions:**
This is an animal character book. The story is a bit unusual, and teachers may need to clarify that orphans are not like animals with a keeper in an orphanage. For children who have waited for a family for a long time, or for those who have felt different from others, however, this may be an appropriate story choice.

**Themes:**
Understanding adoption story
Understanding differences (e.g., cross-cultural differences since Nikolai is the "only bear")
Meaning of family

**Title:** *Nothing At All*
**Author(s):** Wanda Ga'g
**Illustrator:** Same
**Publisher:** Coward-McCann, Inc., New York
**Date of Publication:** 1941
**Awards:** A Caldecott Honor Book in 1943
**Reading Levels**: None found

**Summary:**
Nothing At All is one of three orphan dogs living in forgotten kennels. His two siblings, one with pointy ears and one with curly ears, are found by children and taken home to be loved. Nothing at All is invisible and alone as he follows behind the others. A bird shares a magic trick with the puppy so that he can slowly become visible. He turns into Something-After-All and is spotted by his two siblings who then take him home to their new family where he lives "happily ever after."

**Comments and Specific Suggestions:**
The author-illustrator is best known for her 1929 Newbery Honor book, *Millions of Cats* (1928). The illustrations are engaging, although the unusual typesetting in the original version may be hard for some children to read. Children who are waiting for families may certainly feel invisible, but the animal characters in this book solve the problem through magic rather than through finding a realistic solution to the problem. In addition, Nothing At All must work hard to get a family instead of learning that all children deserve a loving family regardless of their actions. Although the book was named a Caldecott Honor Book, teachers should consider other more contemporary choices first.

**Themes:**
Feeling unloved and "invisible" without a family
Finding a place to belong

**Title:** *Our Baby from China: An Adoption Story*
**Author(s):** Nancy D'Antonio
**Illustrator:** Photographs by Nancy D'Antonio
**Publisher:** Albert Whitman and Company, Morton Grove, IL
**Date of Publication:** 1997
**Awards:** None
**Reading Levels:** Lexile Level 580L

**Summary:**
This little book tells the true story of the adoption from China of Ariela Xiangwei D'Antonio, the author's daughter. The story is told in the style of a captioned photo album using both words and photographs of the actual trip. Included are photographs of sightseeing excursions in China, the first pictures of Ariela, photos of the caregivers and other adopting families, and photographs of the plane ride home and of the welcome from Ariela's "forever family."

**Comments and Specific Suggestions:**
*Our Baby from China* presents an accurate and realistic account of an intercountry adoption from China. One caution is in order, however. The New York City skyline is presented in one of the photographs with the twin World Trade Center towers still standing, a picture that might produce reactions from older children or from some parents.

**Themes:**
Understanding adoption story
Intercountry and transracial adoption
Meaning of family

**Title:** *Our Twitchy*
**Author(s):** Kes Gray
**Illustrator:** Mary McQuillan
**Publisher:** Henry Holt and Company, New York
**Date of Publication:** 2003
**Awards:** None
**Reading Levels:** AR Int. Level Lower Grades, BL 2.9

**Summary:**
Twitchy is a bunny that begins to wonder why his parents do not hop like him. His parents, Sedge and Milfoil (a horse and a cow), tell Twitchy they are not his Bunnymom and Bunnypop. They say, "Twitchy, your Bunnymom and Bunnypop brought you to us when you were very little. They couldn't look after you because they already had sixteen children to feed. They wanted someone to love and care for you properly, so we said we would, and we did, and we have ever since" (p. 6). Sedge and Milfoil then have Twitchy look in the river and tell them what he sees. He says that he sees big eyes that twinkle when they look at him and big smiles that make him

happy, but he still runs away. Later, Twitchy returns to the burrow (i.e., a train tunnel chosen by Sedge and Milfoil since it would be like a burrow for their son). He cries, ". . . I can change. I can be a cow or a horse, but please be my real mom and pop" (p. 20). Twitchy's parents respond, "We ARE your real mom and pop . . . We've always been your real mom and pop. And you'll always be our Twitchy . . . We might not be bunnies, but we've always loved and cared for you just the same," said Sedge. "We don't want you to change" (p. 21).

**Comments and Specific Suggestions:**
Adoption is never mentioned in this animal character book, but it is certainly implied. The description of Twitchy's adoption story is, however, a little disturbing and may need clarification for young readers who may draw the conclusion that parents having many children may simply choose a child to "give away." In addition, Twitchy is not told his adoption story from his earliest memories and, thus, must discover the truth at a later age. Teachers will want to provide accurate information about adoption in a manner that children in their classroom can understand. The illustrations are bright and colorful "cartoon-type" pictures.

**Themes:**
Understanding the meaning of family (i.e., *real mom* and *real dad*)
Accepting differences

**Title:** *Sisters*
**Author(s):** Judith Caseley
**Illustrator:** Same
**Publisher:** Greenwillow Books, an Imprint of HarperCollins, New York
**Date of Publication:** 2004
**Awards:** None
**Reading Levels:** AR Int. Level Lower Grades, BL 2.3

**Summary:**
Kika is newly adopted and adjusting to having a home, parents, pets, and a sister. Kika does not know when she was born, but does remember that she was in a big room with lots of children. Melissa, Kika's sister, anxiously awaited Kika's adoption and arrival, but Kika is not immediately the sister Melissa hoped for. She is not a playmate and a companion. Both sisters ultimately adjust to each other and learn how to love and be sisters. Melissa signs "love" on Kika's birthday card and Kika thinks, "I know what it means. We are sisters" (p. 27).

**Comments and Specific Suggestions:**
Sibling adjustment is portrayed realistically in this story, particularly for siblings through an intercountry adoption.

**Themes:**
Sibling adjustment
Intercountry and transracial adoption

**Title:** *Stellaluna*
**Author(s):** Janell Cannon
**Illustrator:** Same
**Publisher:** Harcourt Brace and Company, New York
**Date of Publication:** 1993
**Awards:** None—Was an American Booksellers Book of the Year Winner for 1994
**Reading Levels:** AR Int. Level Lower Grades, BL 3.5; Lexile Level 550L

**Summary:**
A mother bat loves, cares for, and comforts her baby, but when attacked by a barn owl, the baby is accidentally dropped by his mother. He eventually falls into a bird's nest with three chicks, Flap, Flitter, and Pip. This family cares for him and he tries to be like them, flying during the day, sleeping upright, and eating bugs. One day the little

bat flies too far away from the others and is found by other bats hanging the "wrong way" by his "thumbs." His mother, who had escaped the barn owl, finds the bats and she teaches him that he can hang upside down, fly well at night, and eat fruit rather than bugs. The bat takes his mother to meet Flap, Flitter, and Pip, who try to fly at night. They realize they are good friends and even though they are different that still "feels so much alike" (p. 41).

**Comments and Specific Suggestions:**
Like *Little Lost Bat* (2006) (see Chapter 5), the story gives interesting facts about bats (i.e., fruit bats), encouraging easy connections to science or social studies lessons. The illustrations are beautifully rendered for both the bats and birds. Although this is an animal character book that is not specifically about adoption, orphans, or foster care, it could be used with young children to begin a discussion about difficult topics such as foster care. The bird family, for example, is a loving and supportive "foster family" for the little bat. In addition, the notion of accepting differences among friends is clearly evident throughout the story.

**Themes:**
Dealing with differences among friends
Foster care family

**Title:** *Tell Me Again About the Night I Was Born*
**Author(s):** Jamie Lee Curtis
**Illustrator:** Laura Cornell
**Publisher:** Joanna Cotler Books, an Imprint of HarperCollins Publishers, New York
**Date of Publication:** 1996
**Awards:** None
**Reading Levels:** AR Int. Level Lower Grades, BL 2.8; Lexile Level 108OL

**Summary:**
A little girl asks to be told about the night she was born, but she knows her birth and adoption stories from memory. The child knows how much her parents love her, and she helps to "retell" her story. She includes facts such as her birth mother gave birth to her and her parents flew to adopt her as soon as they received a phone call late one night. The love the child knows is evident as she says, "Tell me how you couldn't believe something so small could make you smile so big."

**Comments and Specific Suggestions:**
A beautiful family tree, including the birth mother and birth father, are shown in the engaging and colorful illustrations. If appropriate, using the suggestions given in Chapter 2, teachers might engage children in a follow-up activity in which they create their own family trees. The book is also available in Spanish.

**Themes:**
Understanding adoption story
Meaning of family—Security and confidence in family

**Title:** *The Best Single Mom in the World*
**Author(s):** Mary Zisk
**Illustrator:** Same
**Publisher:** Albert Whitman and Company, Morton Grove, IL
**Date of Publication:** 2001
**Awards:** None
**Reading Levels:** None Found

**Summary:**
Mary Zisk wrote this book for her daughter, whom she adopted. The story is a young girl's retelling of her adoption story in a conversation with her mother. The story emphasizes how they became a family. The child

sometimes wishes she had a father, too, but she has her grandfather. "Sometimes I wish we had a dad in our family. But Grandpa takes me to special places. And we can talk about anything" (p. 24). The mother tells her daughter her adoption story at bedtime and tells her, "You'll be my little snuggle bunny forever and always" (p. 27).

### Comments and Specific Suggestions:
The story involves a single parent adoption and, therefore, a nontraditional family structure. Other children in the classroom may have a single parent even if they have not been adopted. The child and mother both appear Asian in the illustrations, but a Matryoshka, or nesting dolls, in one picture also hints at a Russian origin. Both instances would make the story equally appropriate for children of intercountry adoption.

### Themes:
Understanding adoption story
Intercountry adoption
Meaning of family
Single parent adoption

**Title:** *The Coffee Can Kid*
**Author(s):** Jan M. Czech
**Illustrator:** Maurie J. Manning
**Publisher:** Child and Family Press, an Imprint of Child Welfare League of America, Arlington, VA
**Date of Publication:** 2002
**Awards:** None
**Reading Levels:** AR Int. Level Lower Grades, BL 3.1; Lexile Level AD470L

### Summary:
This is an adoption story of a child from Korea. Annie's father tells her adoption story once again, with Annie's help, after she climbs up to get a coffee can from the top shelf of a closet. The can holds a picture of Annie as a baby and a letter from her birth mother. Annie's father tells her the letter says that her birth mother loves her and that "not a day will go by that she doesn't think of you" (p. 17). Annie wants to know that she can look at the letter and picture whenever she wants to and her father tells her she can as long as she is careful. Annie thinks the can should be on a lower shelf!

### Comments and Specific Suggestions:
In this adoption story, the birth mother is clearly described as someone who loved her baby and made a plan for a better life for her child. The birth mother is described as too young to care for any child, and the birth grandmother as too old to take care of a baby. In addition, the family did not have enough food to eat. The story is positive, realistic, and focused on the love of parents for their children. Teachers can easily engage children in a discussion about "artifacts" their families might have such as old family photos, medals, and such, or they might have children talk about things they keep in special places like Annie's coffee can!

### Themes:
Understanding adoption story
Intercountry and transracial adoption
Love of birth mother

**Title:** *The Family Book*
**Author(s):** Todd Parr
**Illustrator:** Same
**Publisher:** Megan Tingley Books, a Division of Little, Brown and Company, New York
**Date of Publication:** 2003
**Awards:** None
**Reading Levels:** None Found

**Summary:**
All sorts of families are portrayed through colorful illustrations in this easy reader. Examples of diverse families include: families with members of the same and different race/ethnicity, stepfamilies, families with adopted children, families with two moms or two dads, single parent families, quiet and noisy families, and neat and messy families. The message is clear: Families are different, but all families are made up of people who love each other and help each other be strong.

**Comments and Specific Suggestions:**
The pictures are colorful and bold. The book is quite useful for teaching the concept of diverse family structures. Most children will see their family reflected in some way in this book.

**Themes:**
Meaning of family
Accepting differences

**Title:** *The Mulberry Bird: An Adoption Story (Revised)*
**Author(s):** Anne Braff Brodzinsky
**Illustrator:** Diana L. Stanley
**Publisher:** Perspectives Press, Indianapolis, IN
**Date of Publication:** 1996
**Awards:** None
**Reading Levels:** None found

**Summary:**
The story chronicles a baby bird that is well cared for by its mother. One day a storm breaks the nest and the baby bird falls to the ground. An owl carries the baby to a new family of shorebirds. The new parents love and care for the baby. When the mother bird finds her child and sees that it is safe and loved, she is very sad, but she flies away forever. The baby bird's parents tell the baby that his birth mother loved and cared for him. Finally, the baby bird decides that being adopted "... was having two families—one far away but not forgotten, and one that greeted him each morning" (p. 47).

**Comments and Specific Suggestions:**
First published in 1986, the book was revised in 1996 to reflect changes in adoption. Anne Brodzinsky and her husband, David Brodzinsky, have published extensively on the psychology of adoption and children's adjustment to adoption. Feelings of anger, sadness, and confusion are included in this animal character story. The owl is the "agent" who helps place the baby in a "good" family.

**Themes:**
Love of birth mother/single parent
Meaning of family

**Title:** *The Red Blanket*
**Author(s):** Eliza Thomas
**Illustrator:** Joe Cepeda
**Publisher:** Scholastic Press, New York
**Date of Publication:** 2004
**Awards:** None
**Reading Levels:** AR Int. Level Lower Grades, BL 3.3

**Summary:**
Ms. Thomas is a 46-year-old, single woman who in 1994 traveled to China to adopt five-month-old PanPan. Ms. Thomas describes how she prepared for her adoption and her trip by buying a red blanket she had seen months

ago in a children's store. She took the blanket with her as she traveled to China and arrived at the orphanage where she adopted PanPan. Back at the hotel, PanPan cried and could not be comforted since there were no familiar caretakers, or babies, or sounds, or songs. In desperation, Ms. Thomas remembered the red blanket and tucked it around her daughter. PanPan stopped crying and held on to her mother's fingers. After arriving home, PanPan grew up still keeping her red blanket close to her and sleeping under it at night. Ms. Thomas says, "You carry it with you everywhere. 'It's special,' you explain if anyone asks. The blanket is worn and faded by now, and some people think it's just a raggedy piece of cloth. But we know better, you and I . . . It will always be beautiful" (p. 28).

**Comments and Specific Suggestions:**
This is part of the adoption story the author told her daughter, PanPan, from the time she was about three years old and able to understand her story. The need for comfort and security derived from familiar sounds, sights, and smells is quite realistic for children of intercountry adoption. Most children, regardless of adoption or foster care, will have a similar story of a favorite blanket or stuffed animal to share in class.

**Themes:**
Understanding adoption story
Intercountry and transracial adoption
Single parent adoption
Comfort, safety, and security from family

**Title:** *The White Swan Express: A Story About Adoption*
**Author(s):** Jean Davies Okimoto and Elaine M. Aoki
**Illustrator:** Meilo So
**Publisher:** Clarion Books, New York
**Date of Publication:** 2002
**Awards:** None
**Reading Levels:** AR Int. Level Lower Grades, BL 4.3

**Summary:**
The stories of four families from across North America are cleverly woven together as the prospective parents travel to Guangzhou in the province of Guangdong, China, to adopt their babies. Once in China, the couples form a group to travel by bus to Guangzhou and then by another bus to their hotel, The White Swan. They dub their bus the "White Swan Express." The adoptions take place in a large government building where the babies are brought to their new parents. The new families shop, tour the city, buy souvenirs, and return home where they plan to keep in touch with each other.

**Comments and Specific Suggestions:**
The story is based on the adoption experience of one of the authors, Elaine M. Aoki. The afterword gives information regarding the adoption process in China. The book provides an accurate portrayal of adoption from China. Four families are depicted, including the Maynards from Miami, Florida; Andrea Lee and Charlotte Appleford from Seattle, Washington; Rebecca Mandel from Minnesota; and the Suzukis, a couple from Toronto, Canada. The family diversity is obvious, a single parent, lesbian/gay parents, and older parents.

**Themes:**
Understanding adoption story
Intercountry and transracial adoption
Accepting differences and diversity

**Title:** *Through Moon and Stars and Night Skies*
**Author(s):** Ann Turner
**Illustrator:** James Graham Hale
**Publisher:** A Charlotte Zolotow Book, An Imprint of HarperCollins, New York
**Date of Publication:** 1990

**Awards:** None
**Reading Levels:** AR Int. Level Lower Grades, BL 2.1; Lexile Level 250L

**Summary:**
A little boy tells his mother the well-known story of his adoption. He tells how he was given pictures of his "momma" and "poppa," his white house with a big green tree, a red dog, and his bed with a teddy bear quilt. He tells his mother how he flew a very long way and was afraid, but he recognized his mother and father, his new house, the big tree, the red dog, and his bed with the quilt from the pictures he had been given. The boy gets to know his mother's smile and her song, just like the leaves in the tree. He becomes acquainted with his father's warm eyes and with his warm teddy bear quilt. The boy knows that he is safe and arms will always be there to hold him.

**Comments and Specific Suggestions:**
The illustrations are colorful. The book is an excellent portrayal of an intercountry adoption of a child beyond infancy. The focus is clearly on safety, security, and love of family.

**Themes:**
Understanding adoption story
Intercountry and transracial adoption
Love and permanence of family

**Title:** *Waiting for May*
**Author(s):** Janet Morgan Stoeke
**Illustrator:** Same
**Publisher:** Dutton Children's Books, A Division of Penguin Young Readers Group, New York
**Date of Publication:** 2005
**Awards:** None
**Reading Levels:** AR Int. Level Lower Grades, BL 3.4

**Summary:**
The story is based on the author's own adoption of her daughter, Chang Hai Fan, from China. The author also describes how her three sons, combined into just one son for the purpose of the story, reacted to the adoption of their sister. The boys looked forward to the adoption and loved their new sister immediately. The story is told from the point of view of the "boy" getting a younger sister, a Mei Mei in Chinese. In addition, because the boy's grandmother was "Grandma May" and because the family waited so long that they finally adopted in the month of May, they chose to call their new family member "May." At first, May cried because she was frightened of the new sounds and smells, but when she saw the turtle button on the boy's shirt, she climbed on his lap and began to smile for the first time.

**Comments and Specific Suggestions:**
This is an accurate story of a Chinese adoption. The story is warm and supportive and is told from the point of view of a child becoming a sibling. During and following the reading of this story, children might be engaged in a discussion of how they got their names or nicknames. In addition, as suggested with some of the previously listed books, children might talk about their feelings or reactions when a new brother or sister arrived home.

**Themes:**
Understanding adoption story
Sibling adjustment
Intercountry and transracial adoption

**Title:** *We Wanted You*
**Author(s):** Liz Rosenberg
**Illustrator:** Peter Catalanotto

**Publisher:** Roaring Brook Press, a Division of the Millbrook Press, Brookfield, CT
**Date of Publication:** 2002
**Awards:** None
**Reading Levels:** AR Int. Level Lower Grades, BL 2.0

**Summary:**
This adoption story clearly communicates that the parents always wanted their child and that they waited and searched for their child. The parents engage in activities such as painting the boy's room, fixing an old rocking chair, and making a quilt as they prepare for their son's arrival. They also went immediately when they received the telephone call that a child had been located for them. The parents also communicate that they did not give birth to their son, Enrique, but they will always take care of him and love him, and they have always wanted him.

**Comments and Specific Suggestions:**
A rather unique method is used for telling this story. The story is placed alongside pictures showing not just a baby, but also a growing boy and then a young man interacting with his family. The juxtaposition of these elements conveys the permanence of the family and its love for the child.

**Themes:**
Understanding adoption story
Intercountry and transracial adoption
Permanence of family and love

**Title:** *When Joel Comes Home*
**Author(s):** Susi Gregg Fowler
**Illustrator:** Jim Fowler
**Publisher:** Greenwillow Books, a Division of William Morrow & Company, New York
**Date of Publication:** 1993
**Awards:** None
**Reading Levels:** AR Int. Level Lower Grades, BL 3.3

**Summary:**
A little girl anxiously awaits the adoption of Joel by her parents' best friends, Jean and George. The girl talks about all of the things she will do with Joel when he comes home. "When Joel comes home," I said, "I'll pick the most beautiful flowers from our garden. When Jean walks off the plane, I will give them to her and say, 'These are for you, because now you're a mom just like my mom' " (p. 4). Nothing goes as planned on the day the girl goes to the airport to meet Jean and George as they arrive back home with Joel. George, however, promised to let the little girl be the first person at home to hold baby Joel, and this promise comes true. The girl says, "Hey Joel . . . I've been waiting for you!" and George responds, "We were all waiting for each other" (p. 20).

**Comments and Specific Suggestions:**
The author and illustrator are a husband and wife team who also adopted one of their own children. The interesting feature of this story is that it is from the point of view of a family friend, the little girl, awaiting the adoption. Children might be encouraged to talk about their feelings when something special, such as a birthday party, does not happen the way they thought it would.

**Themes:**
Meaning of family
Friends and family celebrating adoption
Understanding adoption story as family friends

**Title:** *When You Were Born in China: A Memory Book for Children Adopted from China*
**Author(s):** Sara Dorow

**Illustrator:** Photographs by Stephen Wunrow
**Publisher:** Young and Young Book Company, St. Paul, MN
**Date of Publication:** 1997
**Awards:** None
**Reading Levels:** None found

**Summary:**
The book presents an account of the adoption process in China. Black and white pictures present information about the country, about why children are placed in orphanages, and about the love and care of the nurses for the children in the orphanages. The story depicts the role of the adoption agency and the excitement of the new parents as they arrive to adopt their children.

**Comments and Specific Suggestions:**
Like *When You Were Born in Korea*, the message conveyed is one of an ancient country in which many people care and try to do the best thing for babies. The birth mother, the orphanage caregivers, the adoption agency, and the love and excitement of the new family are clearly described. The appreciation of the new parents for those who first cared for their baby is also obvious. The book gives a wealth of information about China and the one-child-per-family policy. This information is offered in a respectful manner, as is the description of the babies in the orphanage. This sensitive information (i.e., sharing cribs with bottles propped up and children propped on potty chairs in "split bottom" pants) and the depiction of older children serving as caregivers for small children could be disconcerting to young readers.

**Themes:**
Intercountry adoption and transracial adoption
Meaning of family—Care and love of many to help child have a "forever family"
Understanding adoption story

**Title:** *When You Were Born in Korea: A Memory Book for Children Adopted from Korea*
**Author(s):** Brian Boyd
**Illustrator:** Photographs by Stephen Wunrow
**Publisher:** Young and Young Book Company, St. Paul, MN
**Date of Publication:** Originally published in 1993; 6th printing in 2000
**Awards:** None
**Reading Levels:** None found

**Summary:**
Like *When You Were Born in China*, this book describes the process and people involved in an adoption from Korea. Black and white photographs from real adoptions in Korea enhance understanding of the adoption story. The book describes the many reasons why birth parents would decide to place their child for adoption and the different ways in which they might do that. The emphasis is on the decision: It was made before the child was born and had nothing to do with the child's behavior or actions. The quality of care received by the child from nurses, social workers, and foster families in Korea is also emphasized. Finally, a careful description is made of the escorts who travel with the babies to present them to their new parents in the United States. The welcome and happiness of the new family is clearly evident in the photographs.

**Comments and Specific Suggestions:**
Information is included about the country and culture of Korea. This information is conveyed in a respectful manner and the predominant message is one of many caregivers planning for a loving home for the child.

**Themes:**
Intercountry adoption and transracial adoption
Meaning of family—Care and love of many to help child have a "forever family"
Understanding adoption story

**Title:** *You're Not My Real Mother*
**Author(s):** Molly Friedrich
**Illustrator:** Christy Hale
**Publisher:** Little, Brown and Company, New York
**Date of Publication:** 2004
**Awards:** None
**Reading Levels:** AR Int. Level Lower Grades, BL 2.5

**Summary:**
The author faced this accusation (i.e., you are not my real mother) from her daughter, P-Quy, whom she adopted from Vietnam. Ms. Friedrich's response to this accusation is both humorous and accurate. She talks about all those things that she does that mothers do: placing 20 bandages on a knee that needs only one, driving to get Polar Bear when he is left behind at a friend's house, helping cook stew, teaching manners, counting by tens and saying the alphabet, giving hugs and kisses, jumping on the trampoline, doing cannonballs in the pool, staying up late to catch fireflies, and falling asleep before finishing the bedtime song she is singing. P-Quy decides that she does have a real mother because of all these things her mother does for her. Ms. Friedrich also concludes that she is thankful to P-Quy's birth mother everyday for giving her daughter life.

**Comments and Specific Suggestions:**
This is a warm and engaging portrayal of what it means to have a mother. The story could easily be followed with a discussion of the many little things that mothers and fathers or other family members do for their children that demonstrate love and affection everyday.

**Themes:**
Meaning of family and of "real mom"
Understanding adoption story
Intercountry and transracial adoption
Love of family

## SUMMARY

Understanding diverse family structures, accepting differences, and deriving safety and security from the permanent love of family members are certainly developmental issues for *all* children in grades K–2. For children who have been adopted or placed in foster care, such issues are also crucial, but these children have additional developmental tasks as well. They will need to understand their adoption or foster placement story, and they will need to understand the visible differences that come when their families have been formed through intercountry or transracial adoption. Sibling adjustments and responding to the questions or comments of peers are very real concerns as well. Teachers can provide children's literature suggested in this chapter to help all children understand the nature of diverse families and to foster understanding and respect for children living in families formed through adoption or foster care. The important trend across the literature for young readers is that of *precious child*.

# CHAPTER 5

# *Adoption and Foster Care Literature for Middle Readers*

Whereas children in grades K–2 may talk freely about their adoption story and openly discuss differences among themselves, their friends, and their families, by grades 3–5 children become more reserved. Youngsters in this age group have an increasing cognitive ability and social awareness. They also have a greater capacity to evaluate themselves as compared with their peers, a characteristic that often manifests itself in a competitiveness demonstrated by children ages eight to ten. To these children, being different may be unacceptable; thus, the child who has been adopted or who lives in foster care may feel quite different from his or her peers and be hesitant to engage in discussions or activities that may seem to highlight those differences.

In order to prompt discussion and reflection, social workers and adoption professionals often assist children in grades 3 and up to develop "lifebooks." Resembling a scrapbook, a lifebook provides questions or a structured framework to help children who have been adopted consider any information they may have about their life, such as their date and place of birth, information about their adoption day, and any facts they might have about their birth family. Similarly, lifebooks help children placed in foster care chronicle the people who have been in their life. The lifebook can also help the child in foster care deal with grief and gain an understanding of the events that have affected his or her life (O'Malley, 2000, 2006a, 2006b).

For all students ages 8–10, important developmental issues include mastering skills, dealing with and accepting differences, and wanting to be accepted and to belong. These critical tasks for all children are magnified for those adjusting to families through adoption or those waiting in foster care for a permanent family. In addition, the increasing cognitive ability and more logical thought of children in grades 3–5 enables them to understand that families can be formed through caring as well as through both legal and biological connections. They also begin to understand that adoption and foster care both mean loss (Brodzinsky, Schechter, & Henig, 1992). Thus, youngsters at these grade levels may be dealing with strong emotions. Feelings of sadness, grief, abandonment, shame, anger, fear, and guilt may occupy the thoughts of children who have been adopted or placed in foster care, even though these emotions may not be evident to teachers or parents through visible behavior.

In addition, all children long to be accepted and to belong somewhere, but this longing may be particularly acute for children waiting for a family in a foster care placement. Unfortunately, some children in foster care may have experienced multiple family placements and may have come to believe over time that they are not worthy of love. These children might push others away through angry words or hostile reactions rather than risk another loss, again magnifying their perceived differences from peers in the classroom. For those who have been adopted, thoughts about their birth mother, birth father, or country or culture of birth may preoccupy their minds (Brodzinsky, Schechter, & Henig, 1992). Although children who have been adopted most likely feel safe, secure, and loved by their families, they may still wonder why their birth families chose not to raise them. They may also wonder whether or not their birth parents ever think about them, and when those adopted from other countries hear about war, famine, or economic difficulties abroad, they may feel guilty that they have so many benefits that their birth family members do not. Such difficult thoughts and emotions must eventually be integrated into the budding identity of the child who has been adopted or placed in foster care.

As their teachers know, the increasing level of skill and thought among children in grades 3–5 requires that middle readers engage in wide reading. These learners will need to read independently for pleasure as well as in guided groups to learn vocabulary, content, and additional skills from both narrative and expository types of text; therefore, children in these grades will be expected to read works of both fiction and nonfiction. Common works of nonfiction and historical fiction about adoption and foster care for this age group often contain stories about the "orphan trains" such as *Train to Somewhere* (Bunting, 1996). Books about the orphan train riders and pieces of fiction such as *Jake's Orphan* (Brooke, 2000) represent the major literary trend of "orphan as worker" (Nelson, 2006). Fictional works at this level may also portray orphans as adventurers or survivors, such as the first book in the popular series *The Box Car Children* (Warner, 1989) or the 1987 Newbery Medal Winner, *The Whipping Boy* (Fleischman, 1986). Many other titles are realistic fiction designed to help children explore strong emotions or see themselves as the "precious child." Books such as *Dillon Dillon* (Banks, 2002) or *The Story of Tracy Beaker* (Wilson, 1991) help children understand feelings of loss, grief, abandonment, and longing.

Children's literature about adoption and foster care for middle readers, then, encompasses all three major literary trends (i.e., precious child, orphan as worker, and orphan as adventurer/survivor) (Nelson, 2006) and genres ranging from nonfiction and historical fiction to realistic fiction and orphan adventure tales. In addition, the themes in adoption and foster care literature appropriate for children at this level continue to include comprehending the adoption or foster care story at an increasing level of complexity as well as themes dealing with feelings of difference, coping with strong emotions related to the birth family, understanding the need to belong and be accepted, and wanting to feel safe and loved. Table 5.1 lists 30 books for middle readers regarding foster care and adoption to help the teacher quickly select those most appropriate for the children in his or her classroom. As in Chapter 4, the table organizes the story titles alphabetically and gives estimated reading levels (e.g., Lexile and/ or AR levels when known), genre, awards received, and developmental themes. The list is certainly not exhaustive, but rather provides *representative* literature related to adoption and foster care that may be appropriate for children in grades 3–5.

## USING LITERATURE ON ADOPTION AND FOSTER CARE IN GRADES 3–5

Although children in grades 3–5 are developing greater cognitive capacity and social awareness, they may still find issues associated with adoption and foster care disconcerting. Remember that children in this age group are just beginning to consider very complex and difficult issues; therefore, the content, concepts, and themes of some books may not be appropriate for some middle readers even though the actual readability of the work is suitable. Similarly, the teacher might notice that several titles included in Table 5.1 have Accelerated Reader interest or reading levels lower than grades

**Table 5.1**
**Children's Literature on Adoption and Foster Care for Middle Readers**

| Title, Author, Date of Pub. | AR Level and/or Lexile | Genre | Awards | Adoption and Foster Care Themes |
|---|---|---|---|---|
| *Adoption Is Okay,* Sylvia Rhodes, 1999 | None found | Nonfiction | None | Comprehending adoption story; Coping with strong emotions; Intercountry adoption of older child |
| *And Tango Makes Three*, Justin Richardson and Peter Parnell, 2005 | AR Int. Level Lower Grades, BL 3.5; Lexile Level AD720L | Nonfiction | None | Dealing with feeling different; The nature of families |
| *Because of Winn-Dixie*, Kate DiCamillo, 2000 | AR Int. Level Middle Grades, BL 3.9; Lexile Level 610L | Realistic fiction | Newbery Honor Book for 2001 | Coping with strong emotions—abandonment and loss; Learning to trust and be a friend |
| *Ben and the Sudden Too-Big Family*, Colby Rodowsky, 2007 | AR Int. Level Middle Grades, BL 5.4; Lexile Level 1010L | Realistic fiction | None | Coping with strong emotions—sibling adjustment; Intercountry and transracial adoption |
| *Bonesy and Isabel*, Michael Rosen, 1995 | AR Int. Level Lower Grades, BL 4.9 | Realistic fiction | None | Coping with strong emotions—loss; Intercountry and transracial adoption |
| *Bringing Asha Home*, Uma Krishnaswami, 2006 | AR Int. Level Lower Grades, BL 3.0; Lexile Level 560L | Realistic fiction | None | Intercountry adoption; Comprehending adoption story; Sibling adjustment |
| *Bud, Not Buddy*, Paul Curtis, 1999 | AR Int. Level Middle Grades, BL 5.0; Lexile Level 950L | Historical fiction | Newbery Medal Winner for 2000; Coretta Scott King Author Award for 2000 | Coping with strong emotions of loss; Need to be loved and belong; Foster care and racism during the Depression years |
| *Coming on Home Soon*, Jacqueline Woodson, 2004 | AR Int. Level Lower Grades, BL 2.9; Lexile Level 550L | Realistic fiction | Caldecott Honor Book for 2005 | Coping with strong emotions of loss; Need to feel safe and loved |
| *Dillon Dillon*, Kate Banks, 2002 | AR Int. Level Middle Grades, BL 4.1; Lexile Level 520L | Realistic fiction | None | Coping with strong emotions of loss; Comprehending adoption story; Dealing with feeling different; Wanting to feel safe and loved |
| *Finding the Right Spot*, Janice Levy, 2004 | None found | Realistic fiction | None | Coping with strong emotions of loss, loneliness, grief, and loyalty; Comprehending foster care story |

**Table 5.1 (continued)**

| Title, Author, Date of Pub. | AR Level and/or Lexile | Genre | Awards | Adoption and Foster Care Themes |
|---|---|---|---|---|
| *Jake's Orphan*, Peggy Brooke, 2000 | AR Int. Level Middle Grades, BL 5.4; Lexile Level 790L | Historical fiction | None | Need to be loved and belong; Orphan as worker; Developing an identity/ having a name |
| *Karen's Little Sister*, Ann Martin, 1989 | AR Int. Level Middle Grades, BL 3.0; Lexile Level 480L | Realistic fiction | None | Coping with strong emotions —sibling adjustment; Intercountry and transracial adoption |
| *Little Lost Bat*, Sandra Markle, 2006 | AR Int. Level Lower Grades, BL 4.2; Lexile Level AD880L | Fiction (Animal character book with "bat facts" included) | None | Need to feel safe and loved; Comprehending adoption story |
| *Lucy's Family Tree*, Karen Schreck, 2001 | AR Int. Level Middle Grades, BL 4.2 | Realistic fiction | None | Dealing with feelings of difference; Intercountry and transracial adoption |
| *Lucy's Wish*, Joan Nixon, 1998 | AR Int. Level Middle Grades, BL 3.8; Lexile Level 600L | Historical fiction | None | Need to feel safe and loved in a family; Coping with emotions of loss; Orphan train rider stories |
| *Megan's Birthday Tree: A Story About Open Adoption*, Laurie Lears, 2005 | AR Int. Level Lower Grades, BL 3.4 | Realistic fiction | None | Comprehending adoption story; Understanding open adoption |
| *Me, Mop, and the Moondance Kid*, Walter Myers, 1988 | AR Int. Level Lower Grades, BL 3.9; Lexile Level 640L | Realistic fiction | An ALA Notable Children's Book for 1988 | Need to be loved by family and to belong; Coping with strong emotions— disappointment and anger |
| *Parents Wanted*, George Harrar, 2001 | AR Int. Level Middle Grades, BL 4.3 | Realistic fiction | None | Need to belong, be accepted and have a family and home; Comprehending foster care story |
| *Rebecca's Journey Home*, Brynn Sugarman, 2006 | AR Int. Level Lower Grades, BL 4.1 | Realistic fiction | None | Comprehending adoption story; Intercountry and transracial Adoption; Sibling adjustment; Family diversity |
| *There's a Hamster in My Lunch Box*, Susan Clymer, 1994 | None found | Realistic fiction | None | Comprehending adoption story; Intercountry and transracial adoption |
| *The Box Car Children, Book #1*, Gertrude Warner, 1989 | AR Int. Level Middle Grades, BL 2.7 | Fiction— orphan adventure tale | None | Need to belong and have a family; Survival of siblings |
| *The Finding*, Nina Bawden, 1987 | AR Int. Level Middle Grades, BL 4.5 | Realistic fiction | None | Comprehending adoption story; Developing one's identity |

| Title, Author, Date of Pub. | AR Level and/or Lexile | Genre | Awards | Adoption and Foster Care Themes |
|---|---|---|---|---|
| *The Handle and the Key*, John Neufield, 2002 | AR Int. Level Middle Grades, BL 4.1 | Realistic fiction | None | Coping with strong emotions —abandonment; Need to belong and have permanence of family; Sibling adjustment |
| *The Pinballs*, Betsy Byars, 1977 | AR Int. Level Middle Grades, BL 3.8; Lexile Level 600L | Realistic fiction | An ALA Notable Children's Book for 1977 | Coping with strong emotions —loss of control, anger, feeling responsible for past; Comprehending foster care story |
| *The Story of Tracy Beaker*, Jacqueline Wilson, 1991 | AR Int. Level Middle Grades, BL 4.4; Lexile Level 790L | Realistic fiction | None | Coping with strong emotions —anger; Need to belong and feel loved; Comprehending foster care story |
| *The Whipping Boy*, Sid Fleischman, 1986 | AR Int. Level Middle Grades, BL 3.9; Lexile Level 570L | Fiction— orphan adventure tale | Newbery Medal Winner for 1987 | Survival; Learning to trust and be a friend |
| *Three Names of Me*, Mary Cummings, 2006 | AR Int. Level, Lower Grades, BL 3.1 | Realistic fiction | None | Comprehending adoption story; Dealing with differences; Intercountry and transracial adoption |
| *Three's a Crowd*, Jamie Suzanne, 1987 | AR Int. Level Middle Grades, BL 3.6 | Realistic fiction | None | Comprehending foster care story; Coping with strong emotions; Longing for return of parents |
| *Touchdown for Tommy*, Matt Christopher, 1985 | AR Int. Level Middle Grades, BL 3.3; Lexile Level 570L | Realistic fiction | None | Comprehending foster care story; Need to be loved and to belong |
| *Train to Somewhere*, Eve Bunting, 1996 | AR Int. Level Lower Grades, BL 2.8; Lexile Level 440L | Historical fiction | An ALA Notable Children's Book for 1997 | Coping with strong emotions —abandonment and loss; Need to belong; Orphan train story |

3–5. The themes and concepts in books such as *And Tango Makes Three* (Richardson & Parnell, 2005), *Megan's Birthday Tree: A Story About Open Adoption* (Lears, 2005), and *Train to Somewhere* (Bunting, 1996) may fit some young readers, but they are included in this chapter as having content or themes more appropriate for students at the third to fifth grade levels. In addition, teachers may still wish to consider for their middle readers some of the books about accepting differences and diverse families that are intended for younger readers (see Chapter 4), and conversely, for children who are more mature, particularly those in the fourth or fifth grades, several books listed in Chapter 6 for older readers may also be quite appropriate. Given the complexity of issues, as well as the range of developmental, interest, and reading levels among children in grades 3–5, teachers obviously must use caution when selecting or recommending stories about adoption or foster care for students in this age group.

In addition to using some of the suggested literature for small group or independent reading, teachers may wish to consider some of the titles in Table 5.1 to read aloud to children in the classroom.

Novels such as *Because of Winn-Dixie* (DiCamillo, 2000), *Bud, Not Buddy* (Curtis, 1999), and *Dillon Dillon* (Banks, 2002) are beautifully written, poignant tales of loss and grief that lend themselves to guided discussion about how the main characters cope with their emotions and change over time. In *Bud, Not Buddy*, for example, the main character, Bud, states, "... This was the third foster home I was going to and I'm used to packing up and leaving, but it still surprises me that there are always a few seconds, right after they tell you you've got to go, where my nose gets all runny and my throat gets all choky ... but it seems like my eyes don't cry no more" (p. 3). Early in this story, then, Bud's emotions are evident. Teachers might help children explore these strong feelings and set the purpose for continued reading through questions such as "Why do you think Bud would feel like crying when he finds out he is being moved to a new foster home?" "How would you have felt if you were Bud?" and "What do you think Bud means by 'my eyes don't cry no more'?" Other questions that can be used with many of the books at this level include: Why do you think (*the character*) acts that way? Has (*the character's*) behavior changed by the end of the story? If so, how? What do you think led to (*the character's*) change in attitude or behavior? Beyond discussion questions such as these, teachers can easily use the following types of activities with the books listed in Table 5.1 to extend and enrich children's understanding of adoption and foster care:

- Following *Lucy's Wish* (Nixon, 1998) or *Train to Somewhere* (Bunting, 1996) students can read additional books on the orphan trains. Joan Nixon, the author of *Lucy's Wish*, has written a series of eight "orphan train" books, many of which are appropriate for middle grade readers. Throughout any discussion of the orphan trains, of course, teachers should emphasize that orphan trains no longer exist, that most children placed through the orphan trains found loving homes, and that children are no longer adopted in this way.

- Enrichment links to social studies or science can easily be made for books at this level. Children may study the railroads and organization of railroad workers such as the porters during the Great Depression or they can be challenged to research evidence of racism (*Bud, Not Buddy*). In addition, children can investigate traditions or holidays from other countries (e.g., El Salvador, India, China, or Russia) or find the names of real people who rode the orphan trains.

- Use the Web to research authors such as Walter Myers, Joan Nixon, or Betsy Byars. What inspired these authors to write their stories? For example, children might be surprised to find that Walter Dean Myers, author of *Me, Mop and the Moondance Kid*, was born in West Virginia and that his mother died when he was only two. He was placed in a foster home in Harlem where he subsequently remained.

- Use a grade-level appropriate story map to organize the elements of the selected book including the setting, characters, plot, conflict, and theme or use a Venn Diagram to compare and contrast the main characters from two books such as *Because of Winn-Dixie* (DiCamillo, 2000) and *Finding the Right Spot* (Levy, 2004) as illustrated in Figure 5.1.

- Create a picture of the main character or a favorite character from the selected book. As an alternative, students might depict their favorite event in the story by drawing a picture or constructing a diorama. For example, children might draw a picture of Dillon Dillon watching the new mother loon take care of the baby chicks or construct a replica of the boxcar home of the *Box Car Children* (Warner, 1989).

- Challenge children to create a scrapbook or "lifebook" from the point of view of the main character in the story. Students might draw pictures, cut pictures or words from magazines, or use self-photos if they prefer. Encourage children to create captions for each page of their scrapbooks.

- Create a list of the "survival tools" used by characters in the book. For example, for the *Box Car Children* students might list the tree stump used as a step and the sand used as scouring powder to keep things clean. More advanced students might examine the characters' emotional "survival tools" such as the vivid imagination, humor, and drawings used by Tracy to navigate her placement in a children's home in *The Story of Tracy Beaker* (Wilson, 1991). Similarly, children may enjoy examining Bud's "Rules and Things to Have a Funner Life and Make a Better Liar Out of Yourself" from *Bud, Not Buddy* (Curtis, 1999) and then constructing a list of their own "best rules" for survival.

**Figure 5.1**
**Venn Diagram for** *Finding the Right Spot* **and** *Because of Winn-Dixie*

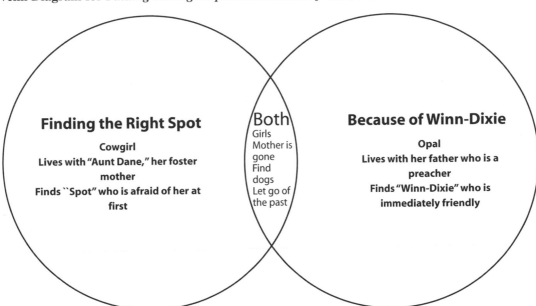

## AN ANNOTATED BIBLIOGRAPHY OF SELECTED LITERATURE ON ADOPTION AND FOSTER CARE FOR GRADES 3–5

The 30 books for middle readers listed in Table 5.1 are arranged in the same alphabetical order by title in the following annotated bibliography. In addition, a summary is provided for each book as well as comments containing more information, suggestions, or cautions that may be helpful as the teacher plans to use the story. The themes to be emphasized in discussion or follow-up activities for each title are listed. Fewer books are described for middle readers than for younger and older readers due to the developmental level of children in grades 3–5 as compared with the increasing complexity of the issues emerging in children's literature about adoption and foster care at those grade levels; therefore, the teacher is encouraged to consult both Chapters 4 and 6 for additional literature that may be appropriate for some children in the classroom.

Although fewer books are listed here than for other K–8 readers, the quality of many of the titles listed is high. For example, 7 of the 30 books received recognition from the American Library Association. Two books, *The Whipping Boy* (Fleischman, 1986) and *Bud, Not Buddy* (Curtis, 1999), won the Newbery Medal for 1987 and 2000, respectively. In addition, *Coming on Home Soon* (Woodson, 2004) was a Caldecott Honor Book for 2005 and *Because of Winn-Dixie* (DiCamillo, 2000) was a Newbery Honor Book for 2001. Finally, three books were on the Children's Notable Book List for 1977, 1988, and 1997. These were, respectively, *The Pinballs* (Byars, 1977), *Me, Mop, and the Moondance Kid* (Myers, 1988), and *Train to Somewhere* (Bunting, 1996).

## ANNOTATED BIBLIOGRAPHY

**Title:** *Adoption Is Okay*
**Author(s):** Sylvia Rhodes
**Illustrator:** Natalie Rahberg

**Translation:** Russian translation by Natasha Nechiporenko
**Publisher:** Key to the Heart Publications, Garland, TX
**Date of Publication:** 1999
**Awards:** None
**Reading Levels:** None found

## Summary:

This book is intended for Russian orphanage workers as well as U.S./Russian adoption professionals. Its purpose is to explain to children their impending adoption. The book describes in very simple and clear language what will happen and how the child might feel about each of these events. For example, the child is told that he/she will have a new momma and papa, and that feeling angry, sad, or confused is normal. Children are also told that they may miss the people and the familiar sounds and smells of Russia, but that they should talk with their new parents about these things. Having new rules and becoming frustrated with the inability to speak the same language as parents are two additional concerns addressed in the book. Finally, the book concludes with the message that the child will have a "forever family" and that he or she is a special part of two different families.

## Comments and Specific Suggestions:

The illustrations are very bold and dark, and they are drawn in a vivid Russian style. The faces depicted in the drawings, however, may appear very stern to children in the United States. Each page contains the Russian translation, in Cyrillic, of the English words. The focus on emotions and communicating with parents is quite appropriate for children who have been adopted at an older age from Russia. Following the story, students might enjoy researching Russia or learning letters from the Cyrillic alphabet.

## Themes:

Comprehending adoption story
Coping with strong emotions
Intercountry adoption
Older child adoption

**Title:** *And Tango Makes Three*
**Author(s):** Justin Richardson and Peter Parnell
**Illustrator:** Henry Cole
**Publisher:** Simon & Schuster Books for Young Readers, New York
**Date of Publication:** 2005
**Awards:** None
**Reading Levels:** AR Int. Level Lower Grades, BL 3.5; Lexile Level AD720L

## Summary:

A true story of two male penguins in the Central Park Zoo in New York City, Roy and Silo become a couple. They do everything together, including building a nest of stones. Roy and Silo bring a rock that looks like an egg to the nest and try to hatch it. The penguin keeper notices and swaps the rock for an egg that needed care. Roy and Silo took turns hatching the egg, and Tango became the baby of both penguins when he emerged from the egg. The adult penguins proceed to parent Tango and teach him skills such as how to swim.

## Comments and Specific Suggestions:

The story is written as if it is fiction; yet this is an unusual, but true, story of an animal "adoption." Although the interest level is given as "lower grades," the story is included here due to the complex issue involved: its obvious parallel with adoption by persons who are gay or lesbian. Teachers should be aware that this is an extremely sensitive issue! The emphasis by the teacher should be on the loving care of the penguins for their child. If the story is used in the classroom, teachers might have children find out additional information about the Central Park Zoo ( www.centralpark.com), penguins, or Tango as extension activities after reading the book.

**Themes:**
The nature of families
Coping with feeling different

**Title:** *Because of Winn-Dixie*
**Author(s):** Kate DiCamillo
**Illustrator:** None
**Publisher:** Candlewick Press, Somerville, MA
**Date of Publication:** 2000
**Awards:** Newbery Honor Book for 2001
**Reading Levels:** AR Int. Level Middle Grades, BL 3.9; Lexile Level 610L

**Summary:**
Ten-year-old Opal has just moved to Naomi, Florida, with her father. As the story begins, she enters a Winn-Dixie store only to encounter a big dog in the produce section. While petting the dog, Opal is challenged by the store manager, and she quickly tells him that the dog is hers and that his name is "Winn-Dixie." She decides to take Winn-Dixie home. Opal and her father, a preacher, live in the Friendly Corners Trailer Park. She has no friends and she is sad because her mother has been gone since she was the age of three. Opal asks her father to tell her ten things about her mother, one for each year of her life. As she learns these stories about her mother, easygoing Winn-Dixie helps her make friends with people in the town, including characters such as the feisty librarian, Franny Block, elderly Gloria Dump, and eccentric Otis. Like her mother, Opal loves stories so she decides to collect stories about her new friends hopefully to tell her mother someday. This is a wonderful story of letting go.

**Comments and Specific Suggestions:**
Although this book is not technically about adoption or foster care (i.e., Opal lives with her biological father), it is nevertheless a story about loss and letting go of the past. Children in grades 3–5 who are in foster care and those who have been adopted are often learning to deal with loss and grief. This beautifully written story may help all children cope with loss and open an important discussion. The book is also available in a movie version released in 2005 by Twentieth Century Fox. Following the reading of the story, students might collect interesting or humorous stories from older family members or friends to be compiled into a classroom collection.

**Themes:**
Coping with strong emotions—abandonment and loss
Letting go of the past
Learning to trust and be a friend

**Title:** *Ben and the Sudden Too-Big Family*
**Author(s):** Colby Rodowsky
**Illustrator:** None
**Publisher:** Farrar, Straus and Giroux, New York
**Date of Publication:** 2007
**Awards:** None
**Reading Levels:** AR Int. Level Middle Grades, BL 5.4; Lexile Level 1010L

**Summary:**
Ten-year-old Ben does not remember his mother because she died in an automobile accident when he was only about one. Ben has lived with his father, Mitch, who has always been there for him. When Mitch meets and then marries Casey, Ben thinks that is "cool"; however, when Mitch and Carrie decide to adopt a baby girl, Mingmei (Maudie Mingmei), from China, Ben has his doubts! After traveling with his family to China to adopt Mingmei, the family takes a vacation in Duck, North Carolina. Ben is overwhelmed by all of the people in his new extended family who gather for the 50th wedding anniversary of Casey's parents, Nanny and Fred. Twenty-three relatives arrive at the celebration, including Nanny's odd twin sister, "Poornora." Following his initial discomfort at not knowing the family's jokes and traditions, Ben realizes that he is now part of this large family and of his own new family of four, and he decides that having all of this family is "cool."

**Comments and Specific Suggestions:**
The characters in this story are delightful and the book has a real "family flavor." As Mitch tells Ben about the one-child policy in China and the reason so many baby girls are adopted from that country, he does use outdated expressions such as "... mothers would resort to hiding their daughters or *giving them up* ..." and "... occasionally a boy is *put up for adoption* ..." (p. 25). The teacher can easily remedy this by using the correct language during discussion (i.e., the birth mother made a plan for her baby to have a loving home). The themes in this book are evident in Ben's words and thoughts: "It suddenly seemed as if I had a whole new identity. I wasn't just Ben anymore ... I was the big brother" (pp. 36–37) and "I wondered if in all those years since my mother died, my father had actually been lonely ... I thought about how, through the years, Mitch had never told me much about my mother, maybe on account of it made him too sad. And how—and this is where it gets a little bizarre—now that we have Casey, maybe someday he'll be able to tell me more" (pp. 80–81). The teacher will want to ask questions to probe why Mitch never spoke to Ben about his mother and why Mitch may finally open up now that he has married Casey and adopted Maudie Mingmei.

**Themes:**
Coping with strong emotions—sadness and loss
Letting go of the past
Understanding what it means to be part of a family
Sibling adjustment
Intercountry and transracial adoption
Developing a new identity (as a sibling and as a part of a family)

**Title:** *Bonesy and Isabel*
**Author(s):** Michael Rosen
**Illustrator:** James Ransome
**Publisher:** Harcourt Children's Books, New York
**Date of Publication:** 1995
**Awards:** None
**Reading Levels:** AR Int. Level Lower Grades, BL 4.9

**Summary:**
Ivan and Vera have adopted Isabel from El Salvador. Isabel understands that her parents care for her and she loves the farm on Sunbury Road as well as the farm animals. She also loves Bonesy, the old retriever farm dog who she secretly feeds under the table. When Bonesy dies, Isabel is able to share the sorrow with Vera and Ivan. She begins to bond with her new family, to learn English, and to accept new ways.

**Comments and Specific Suggestions:**
This is a simple story about becoming a new family through an intercountry adoption. The oil paintings throughout the book are beautiful. Children may enjoy researching El Salvador to find facts about the country and its culture following the reading of this story.

**Themes:**
Coping with strong emotions—love and loss
Comprehending adoption
Intercountry and transracial adoption
Older child adoption—understanding new culture and language

**Title:** *Bringing Asha Home*
**Author(s):** Uma Krishnaswami
**Illustrator:** Jamel Akib
**Publisher:** Lee and Low Books, New York
**Date of Publication:** 2006
**Awards:** None
**Reading Levels:** AR Int. Level Lower Grades, BL 3.0; Lexile Level 560L

**Summary:**

Eight-year-old Arun is a young boy who tells his best friend how he wishes he had a sister to celebrate with on the special Hindu holiday, Rakhi, a special day for brothers and sisters. He is very excited when his parents tell him they are adopting a baby girl, Asha, from India, but Arun is dismayed over how long the process takes. As the year progresses, Arun plans ways to love his sister before she arrives. He gets a baby swing for Asha to put on his swing set, and he makes a mobile out of paper airplanes for his sister's crib.

**Comments and Specific Suggestions:**

Relatively few books are available regarding adoption from India. This story is a warm portrayal of love for an adopted sibling. In addition, following the book, students can research holidays, such as Rakhi, or other customs of the Hindu religion or of India.

**Themes:**

Comprehending adoption story
Sibling adjustment
Intercountry adoption

**Title:** *Bud, Not Buddy*
**Author(s):** Christopher Paul Curtis
**Illustrator:** None
**Publisher:** Delacorte Press, a Division of Random House, New York
**Date of Publication:** 1999
**Awards:** Newbery Medal Winner for 2000; Coretta Scott King Author Award for 2000
**Reading Levels:** AR Int. Level Middle Grades, BL 5.0; Lexile Level 950L

**Summary:**

Set during the Great Depression when many children found themselves as orphans placed in "Homes" or riding the rails, the main character, ten-year-old Bud Caldwell, finds his Momma dead when he is just six. Bud is placed into a series of foster homes for four years where he is mistreated and even beaten. After he runs away from his most recent foster home with the Amoses, he goes in search of someone he believes to be his father, Herman E. Calloway. He believes his mother has left him "clues" that Calloway, a member of a jazz band, must be his father because she has among her personal possessions flyers about the band as well as rocks with names of places and dates on them. While his mother was alive, he never knew what the rocks meant; however, he knew they were important because his mother had kept them. Across the course of the story, Bud makes his way to Grand Rapids, Michigan, where he finds the band and Herman Calloway, who is at first a grumpy and mean-spirited man. Bud finally learns his story. Herman Calloway is his grandfather. Herman and Bud's mother, Angela Janet, had picked up rocks from each place the band had played until Herman had pushed Angela so hard that she ran away. Herman never knew what had happened to his daughter; however, he had continued to pick up rocks from each town the band visited during the 11 years since Angela had been gone. Over time, Bud not only learns his life story, but he also realizes he has a home and a family with his grandfather's band.

**Comments and Specific Suggestions:**

Very few books have won both the Newbery Medal and the Coretta Scott King Award for the same year! Bud's humor, superstitious nature, and list of "Rules and Things to Have a Funner Life and Make a Better Liar Out of Yourself" are captivating! As historical fiction, the book can clearly be linked to an enriching study of the Great Depression, jazz, railroads, and racism during the 1930s. Bud's love for his mother and how he copes with her loss are strong themes throughout the work. As Bud moves from anger, "I started getting madder and madder. I was mad at the Amoses, but most of all I was mad at me . . . for getting trapped like this where there wasn't anybody who cared what happened to me" (p. 29) to remembering his mother's love, "She would tell me every night before I went to sleep that no matter what happened I could sleep knowing that there had never been a little boy, anywhere, anytime, who was loved more than she loved me. She told me that as long as I remembered that I'd be okay" (p. 73) to an understanding of how he carries his mother's love with him forever and that he needs to belong somewhere, "I was thinking. Deeza's momma was right, someone who doesn't know who their family is, is like dust blowing around in a storm, they don't really belong any one place" (p. 78). This final quote will, of course, require discussion as it is crucial to the book's theme. Students may also enjoy, with teacher guidance, writing their own list of "Rules and Things for Having a Funner Life!"

**Themes:**
Coping with strong emotions—grief and loss
Need to be loved and to belong
Foster care and racism during the Great Depression

**Title:** *Coming on Home Soon*
**Author(s):** Jacqueline Woodson
**Illustrator:** E. B. Lewis
**Publisher:** G. P. Putnam's Sons, a Division of Penguin Group, New York
**Date of Publication:** 2004
**Awards:** Caldecott Honor Book for 2005
**Reading Levels:** AR Int. Level Lower Grades, BL 2.9; Lexile Level 550L

**Summary:**
This is a beautifully written story about an African American family during World War II. "Mama" leaves to find work with the railroad in Chicago while all of the men are away at war. Ada Ruth, a young girl, stays home with Grandma, both of them eagerly waiting for a letter from Mama. After much waiting and worrying, the letter finally comes at the end of the story. During the wait, Ada Ruth and Grandma find a kitten and take care of it.

**Comments and Specific Suggestions:**
Although this is not technically a book about adoption or foster care, it is a story about missing family and about the stability of love. The need to feel safe and secure in the love of family is evident in Ada Ruth's conversation with her mother before Mama departs: "Ada Ruth, do you know I love you more than anything in the world?" "Yes, ma'am," I whispered. "More than rain. More than snow." Mama whispered back (p. 3). Children might discuss the many ways that people in their own lives, members of their family as well as others such as a special teacher or minister, help them to feel safe and loved. The teacher can list the contributions made by children on chart paper or on a poster board. Following this discussion, the teacher might ask children what they believe Mama wrote in her letter to Ada Ruth and Grandma. Children, then, might be asked to write Mama's letter or to write a return letter from Ada Ruth to Mama. On an additional note, Jacquelyn Woodson is also the author of *Locomotion*, published in 2003. (See Chapter 6.)

**Themes:**
Coping with strong emotions—Worry and loss
Need to feel safe and loved among family

**Title:** *Dillon Dillon*
**Author(s):** Kate Banks
**Illustrator:** None
**Publisher:** Farrar, Straus and Giroux, New York
**Date of Publication:** 2002
**Awards:** None
**Reading Levels:** AR Int. Level Middle Grades, BL 4.1; Lexile Level 520L

**Summary:**
When Dillon was ten, he asked his parents why he had been given the odd name "Dillon Dillon," a name that had caused him to be teased throughout his life. His parents told him that they had always meant to share that story with him, but the time had never been right. Dillon had been adopted as a baby. His birth parents, his father's sister, Maggie, and her husband, Jon, had been killed in a plane crash when Dillon was just 18 months old. His name at birth had been Dillon McDermott, and his parents had not wanted to take away his name, Dillon, even though their own last name just happened to be Dillon as well! Dillon, who has always felt "out of place" with his

family members, is angered, confused, and hurt by this revelation, particularly as he considers that his older brother, Didier, who was four when Dillon arrived, and his younger sister, Daisy, are his cousins. When Dillon's family stays at a cottage on a lake, he befriends two loons and watches their chick hatch. When the two loons are killed accidentally, Dillon knows he cannot care for the baby chick properly. He watches as another loon takes over and becomes the loving mother to the chick. As the story unfolds, Dillon realizes that his brother and sister *are* his siblings and that his mother and father *are* his parents. At the end of the book, Dillon is given a picture of Maggie and Jon and is told that his birth mother was a scientist who loved the loons and who studied them. She had an ability to "communicate" with the loons just like Dillon.

**Comments and Specific Suggestions:**
This is a lovely story about loss, family, and acceptance. Woven throughout the book are interesting legends about loons. Dillon's reaction to the news about his adoption is quite realistic, and the parallel between Dillon's situation (i.e., the loss of his birth parents and his subsequent adoption) and that of the baby loon is obvious. Dillon's conflicting emotions and final resolution of his feelings are apparent in lines such as: "These two people in front of him were only fill-ins" (p. 47); "He didn't want to be reminded that they were not even related by blood. That they had not shared that lifeline which he'd learned about in science class . . . All at once it dawned on Dillon. For his entire life he had felt something was missing. Something was wrong. Now he knew what that was. And as it began to sink deeper into his being, it hurt" (p. 51); "Could parents who adopt a child love him as much as two who are their own?" (p. 56); and "When he looked at his parents, . . . he saw two people who loved him" (p. 109). By the end of the story, Dillon realizes, "How like his own life was that of the chick" (p. 137). Following the reading of the book, as an extension activity, children might enjoy researching the loon or finding Native American legends about loons. Students can be encouraged to illustrate interesting legends or to create their own "legends." For additional information about loons, teachers can consult the book, *The Common Loon, Spirit of Northern Lakes*, by Judith McIntyre (1989), or Web sites such as http://michiganbackroads.com/Attractions/loons.htm, a site that contains loon legends and facts as well as audio of the unusual sounds of the loon, or http://nationalzoo.si.edu.

**Themes:**
Coping with strong emotions—loss, grief, confusion, distrust, and anger
Comprehending adoption story
Dealing with feelings of difference
Understanding the meaning of family and love

**Title:** *Finding the Right Spot*
**Author(s):** Janice Levy
**Illustrator:** Whitney Martin
**Publisher:** Magination Press, an Imprint of the American Psychological Association, Washington, DC
**Date of Publication:** 2004
**Awards:** None
**Reading Levels:** None found

**Summary:**
A young girl whose mother always called her "Cowgirl" because they wanted to live on a ranch someday is removed from her home because her mother drinks and is no longer able to keep a job. Cowgirl now lives with "Aunt Dane," her foster mother, who over time helps her to learn she is loved and to realize that it is "okay" to feel pain and to cry. When Cowgirl's mother misses a much-anticipated scheduled visit, Aunt Dane tells her that yesterday is gone and she should make the best of today. Cowgirl loves Aunt Dane but she is also torn by feelings of guilt and loyalty toward her mother. The title of the book has a double meaning. Cowgirl tries to befriend and pet a puppy. Initially the little dog will not let her touch it. Over time, Cowgirl finds the "right spot" for touching the puppy and sharing love with it, and she also finds the "right spot" for herself to flourish and be loved.

**Comments and Specific Suggestions:**
The book is available through the American Psychological Association and is specifically intended to help young people cope with the loss of a parent and placement in foster care. This book makes an interesting comparison

with *Because of Winn-Dixie*. Students might discuss how animals are used today to help people both physically and emotionally.

**Themes:**
Coping with strong emotions—loss, loneliness, uncertainty, disappointment, grief, and feelings of torn loyalty
Comprehending foster care story
Hope for the future and stability of love despite removal from biological family

**Title:** *Jake's Orphan*
**Author(s):** Peggy Brooke
**Illustrator:** None
**Publisher:** D.K. Publishing, New York
**Date of Publication:** 2000
**Awards:** None
**Reading Levels:** AR Int. Level Middle Grades, BL 5.4; Lexile Level 790L

**Summary:**
Set in 1926, Tree, a 12-year-old orphan, is "placed out" to work for a farmer in North Dakota. Tree is happy to be out of the orphanage in the city of St. Paul, but he is worried about having to leave his troublesome brother, Acorn, behind. Mr. Gunderson is hard to please, and Tree knows that at the end of the year he is likely to be sent back to the orphanage. When Acorn runs away from the orphanage and turns up at the farm, Mr. Gunderson refuses to take him in, insisting that he has room for only one, but the warmhearted Mrs. Gunderson will not allow him to send Acorn away even though he considers both boys "useless hay burners" just like the horses (p. 156). Mr. Gunderson's brother, Jake, however, understands Tree and Acorn. He protects Tree from his brother's wrath when Tree is involved in a fight with a bully at school. Later when Acorn kills some of the Gunderson's chickens after feeling betrayed by Mr. Gunderson selling the calf that had been promised to him, Jake tells Gunderson that foxes were in the hen house. At the end of the story, Jake adopts both Tree and Acorn and gives them both a home and a name: Theodore Jacob Gunderson (Tree) and Alexander Jacob Gunderson (Acorn). Tree finds what he has been longing for: "My eyes were misting over with tears, but I held his gaze. 'Like father and son,' he'd said . . . I found myself running clumsily across the kitchen floor to throw my arms around his strong, hard shoulders. He wrapped his arms around me, too . . . We had a place—me and Acorn" (p. 257). "Smith was the only name in our files at the orphanage. But Acorn and I both preferred Gunderson—Jacob Gunderson. A name, I always thought, should link a person to his beginnings" (p. 261).

**Comments and Specific Suggestions:**
Teachers will want to help students explore the final quote: What does Tree mean by "a name should link a person to his beginnings"? How do our names link us to others? Teachers can sensitively help children share first, middle, or family names and why these are important to the family. In addition, the author includes interesting notes at the end of the book. Although this is historical fiction, the author, Peggy Brooke, states that her story is set in the town where she and her husband live, at the site of her grandfather's old homestead. Facts about homesteading, the prairie in North Dakota, and the orphan trains are also included in these notes. Students can use the notes and online resources to research the North Dakota prairie, homesteading, or the orphan trains. Creating a diorama of the Gunderson farm or an illustration of their "family name" might make good follow-up activities for enrichment.

**Themes:**
Finding a home and a place to belong
Gaining a name and a sense of identity
Keeping family (siblings) together
Orphan as worker—orphan train story

**Title:** *Karen's Little Sister*
**Author(s):** Ann M. Martin

**Illustrator:** Susan Tang
**Publisher:** Scholastic, Inc., New York
**Date of Publication:** 1989
**Awards:** None
**Reading Levels:** AR Int. Level Middle Grades, BL 3.0; Lexile Level 480L

**Summary:**
Elizabeth is a second grader in a blended family where she and her brother, Andrew, live with their mom and also stay for extended periods of time with their father, their stepmother, her children from a previous marriage, and the children of their father and stepmother. When Elizabeth's father and stepmother decide to adopt a child from Vietnam, the new two-year-old, Emily, becomes the youngest girl in the family. Emily requires a lot of attention for an earache, and she must go to the hospital to have tubes put in her ears. Elizabeth is initially very jealous of all the attention Emily is receiving from her father and from her 13-year-old stepsister, Kristy. She says, "I used to be the youngest girl. Now Emily is the baby. She has ruined everything" (p. 10). During the course of the story, Elizabeth also takes care of an abandoned baby bird and finally gets her own pet, a rat! The bird helps Elizabeth realize that Emily must be very frightened and in pain, and she begins to accept and love Emily. "Emily and the bird were sort of alike. They needed big people to help them with some things" (p. 42). Kristy tells Elizabeth how special she is to be the "middle sister" and makes T-shirts for the three girls that say: "I'm the Big Sister/Middle Sister/Little Sister."

**Comments and Specific Suggestions:**
This short chapter book is book number six in the popular "Baby Sitters Little Sisters" series. Since Emily does not understand English and is not hearing well because of her ear infections, the reaction of fear upon her adoption and hospitalization are realistic. Also quite realistic are the feelings of jealousy experienced by Elizabeth. The large and complex blended family also makes this book useful for children from many diverse family structures. Teachers might engage children in a discussion about sibling order in their own families and how children feel about being the youngest, middle, or oldest child.

**Themes:**
Coping with strong emotions related to family
Sibling adjustment
Intercountry and transracial adoption
Blended family

**Title:** *Little Lost Bat*
**Author(s):** Sandra Markle
**Illustrator:** Alan Marks
**Publisher:** Charlesbridge, Watertown, MA
**Date of Publication:** 2006
**Awards:** None
**Reading Levels:** AR Int. Level Lower Grades, BL 4.2; Lexile Level AD880L

**Summary:**
A little bat is born and nursed by its mother who works hard to feed herself and her baby. The mother returns every day to nurse and comfort the baby bat. They communicate through scent and by sounds they make only to each other. One night the mother bat is caught by a barn owl and fails to return. The baby waits for its mother, cries, and crawls toward the cave entrance where it is overcome by hunger and exhaustion. Finally, another female bat that has lost her own baby to the cave floor below "... covers him with her furry warmth, holds him snug, and lets him nurse" (p. 27). The new female bat marks her baby with her own scent and calls softly in a sound just for him.

**Comments and Specific Suggestions:**
This is a tale of loss and sorrow with beautiful illustrations. Although this is an animal character book, the parallel between the birth mother and child and the parent and child are obvious. Also included at the end of the book

are many interesting facts about Mexican free-tailed bats and their nursery cave, Bracken Cave, in Texas. As an extension or enrichment activity following the reading of this story, children can be challenged to research various types of bats and to prepare a poster presentation of the information found. (See also *Stellaluna* in Chapter 4.)

**Themes:**
Comprehending adoption story—Birth mother loved and cared for her child but could not continue to take care of him; Mother loves, cares for, and comforts her child.
Need to feel safe, secure, and loved

**Title:** *Lucy's Family Tree*
**Author(s):** Karen Halvorsen Schreck
**Illustrator:** Stephen Gassler III
**Publisher:** Tilbury House, Gardiner, ME
**Date of Publication:** 2001
**Awards:** None
**Reading Levels:** AR Int. Level Middle Grades, BL 4.2

**Summary:**
Lucy was adopted from Mexico. She is worried about her family being "different" when she is given a "family tree" assignment as a class project. She asks her parents to write a note so she can be "excused" from the assignment because she does not want to be seen as too different from her classmates; however, her parents refuse to write the note. They ask her to think about the project and find three families that are like hers. Lucy, thinking about her "normal" friends, soon realizes that the twins next door look like their parents but feel different since they are the only Jewish children in the neighborhood. Robert, another friend, has two "moms." Lucy begins to see there are many different types of families. She creates her family tree by blending her Mexican heritage with her much-loved family.

**Comments and Specific Suggestions:**
The book includes suggestions for teachers to help children who have been adopted construct family trees. If appropriate, children can be encouraged, as a follow-up activity, to create their own family trees. (See Chapter 2 for specific suggestions for safe choices when assigning a family tree project.)

**Themes:**
Dealing with feelings of difference
Intercountry and transracial adoption

**Title:** *Lucy's Wish*
**Author(s):** Joan Lowery Nixon
**Illustrator:** None
**Publisher:** Delacorte Press, a Division of Random House, New York
**Date of Publication:** 1998
**Awards:** None
**Reading Levels:** AR Int. Level Middle Grades, BL 3.8; Lexile Level 600L

**Summary:**
Set in 1866, Lucy is ten years old when she loses her mother to a cholera epidemic. After living on the streets of New York City for a few weeks, she desperately wants a family and a sister. She finds out about the Children's Aid Society and their train west, and she is sent on the orphan train to a farm in Missouri. Her new mother, Mrs. Snapes, is kind; however, Mr. Snapes is always angry. Lucy finds out that her new sister, Emma, is teased by the other children who call her "simple." Nevertheless, she becomes attached to her new special sister and to her new family.

**Comments and Specific Suggestions:**
The story is Book Number One in the Orphan Train Adventures series written by Joan Lowery Nixon. Teachers might follow up this story by having children read and share other books in the series or by researching the orphan trains. (See also Andrea Warren's *We Rode the Orphan Trains* in Chapter 6 or Eve Bunting's *Train to Somewhere* later in this chapter.)

**Themes:**
Orphan Train and "placing out"
Understanding the need to belong
Coping with strong emotions related to family—sisters

**Title:** *Megan's Birthday Tree: A Story About Open Adoption*
**Author(s):** Laurie Lears
**Illustrator:** Bill Farnsworth
**Publisher:** Albert Whitman and Company, Morton Grove, IL
**Date of Publication:** 2005
**Awards:** None
**Reading Levels:** AR Int. Level Lower Grades, BL 3.4

**Summary:**
Megan was adopted by her parents as an infant immediately after her birth to Kendra, a young single woman. Megan's parents keep in touch with Kendra, and Megan writes to Kendra and sees her occasionally. After Megan's birth, Kendra planted a tree in her yard and every year she sends a picture of the tree to Megan on her birthday. When Kendra writes to tell Megan she is getting married and moving, Megan worries that if Kendra no longer has the tree she will forget about her. About her birth, Megan's mother says, "Kendra counted every one of your fingers and toes . . . then she kissed the top of your head and began to cry. Kendra loved you so much! Yet she knew she wasn't ready to take care of a baby, so she'd chosen Dad and me to be your parents" (p. 8). Megan replies, "I'm glad you and Dad adopted me . . . but I hope Kendra always remembers me" (p. 8). Megan tries hard to raise money to buy a new tree. As Megan is digging up a small tree, Kendra arrives and reassures Megan that she does not need a tree to remember her. She even has the real tree in her truck to go with her on her move! Kendra tells Megan, "Oh Megan, I don't need a tree or anything else to remember you! Even though we don't live together, you will always be a part of me" (p. 24).

**Comments and Specific Suggestions:**
Megan is clearly portrayed in the illustrations as resembling her birth mother. The subject of open adoption may be difficult for younger children to understand, but the message is clear in the story: Megan's mother will always love her and her birth mother will always remember her. This is a message that young children need to hear. Children can be encouraged to discuss people who do not live in their homes, but who they remember and who remember them. Teachers might ask: How do we know these people remember us even when we do not live together?

**Themes:**
Comprehending adoption story
Open adoption

**Title:** *Me, Mop, and the Moondance Kid*
**Author(s):** Walter Dean Myers
**Illustrator:** Rodney Pate
**Publisher:** Dell Publishing, a Division of Bantam Doubleday Dell Publishers, New York
**Date of Publication:** 1988
**Awards:** An American Library Association Notable Children's Book for 1988
**Reading Levels:** AR Int. Level Lower Grades, BL 3.9; Lexile Level 640L

**Summary:**

Eleven-year-old T. J., the narrator of the story, and his younger brother, Moondance, have been adopted by the Williams family. Their friend, Miss Olivia Parrish (Mop), has not been adopted and still lives at the "Dominican Academy" with Sister Marianne, Sister Carmelita, and others, although the "Academy" is soon to be closed and the children moved to a new location. The Kennedys, Jim and Marla, are coaching a little league baseball team on which T. J., Moondance, and Mop play. Mop thinks that Jim and Marla are "checking her out" to see whether or not she can play ball before they adopt her. She wants so badly to be adopted and stay near T. J. and Moondance that she has trouble even talking around Marla! The little league team does not play very well, but over time, Moondance becomes an excellent pitcher with the help of Sister Carmelita, who was a trophy-winning little league pitcher as a child, and a homeless man named Peaches. Mop also becomes an excellent catcher with their help, and the Elks win the little league championship over their rivals the Eagles. T. J. thinks, "I didn't really want Peaches to help me, but I kind of felt sorry for him. I couldn't tell how old he was really, but I knew he was old. And I knew he looked kind of thrown away too. I had felt like that before" (p. 51). At the end of the story, Mop is adopted by the Kennedys, but not just because she can play baseball.

**Comments and Specific Suggestions:**

Walter Dean Myers is a Newbery Award winning author. His mother died when he was only two, and he was placed in foster care in Harlem. Children might enjoy researching Mr. Myers and learning more about Harlem as an extension of this story.

**Themes:**

Coping with strong emotions related to birth family
Wanting to feel safe and loved in a family
Understanding the need to belong—being "tough" while longing to belong

**Title:** *Parents Wanted*
**Author(s):** George Harrar
**Illustrator:** None
**Publisher:** Milkweed Editions, Minneapolis, MN
**Date of Publication:** 2001
**Awards:** None
**Reading Levels:** AR Int. Level Middle Grades, BL 4.3

**Summary:**

Andy Fleck is a spirited 12-year-old boy who has been in a number of foster care families. Andy's biological father is in jail and his biological mother is an alcoholic, so he was removed from their care and is now distrustful with adults. Andy has Attention Deficit Hyperactivity Disorder (ADHD) and wants to be adopted by his new foster parents, the Sizeracy family, Jeff and Laurie. Unfortunately, Andy seems to "sabotage" any possibility for his adoption. He steals, makes accusations of child abuse, and vandalizes. Finally, Andy realizes that the Sizeracys are going to adopt him, and he learns not to lie and to trust others.

**Comments and Specific Suggestions:**

The story contains accusations about child molestation; therefore, teachers may wish to consider carefully the maturity level of students before using this book. The main character and his reactions are realistic, however, for a child with ADHD who has lived in numerous foster care placements. In addition, the story revolves around the important issue of trust. Students might, under careful teacher direction, talk about times when people have lied about something (e.g., celebrities or political figures from the news). How does a lie impact our ability to trust others or to be trusted ourselves?

**Themes:**

Coping with strong emotions—loss and trust
Understanding the need to belong—Being "tough" while longing to belong
Understanding the nature of family

**Title:** *Rebecca's Journey Home*
**Author(s):** Brynn Glenberg Sugarman
**Illustrator:** Michelle Shapiro
**Publisher:** Kar-Ben Publishing, Minneapolis, MN
**Date of Publication:** 2006
**Awards:** None
**Reading Levels:** AR Int. Level Lower Grades, BL 4.1

**Summary:**
The Stein family decides to adopt a baby girl from Vietnam, and they decide to name her Rebecca. The Hebrew version of the name is Rivka and the Vietnamese version is Le Tai Hong. The two older boys in the family, Jacob and Gabriel, are interested as their parents complete all of the paperwork and adopt Rebecca. They lovingly watch their new sister taken to the Mikvah, the ritual bath, to be immersed three times and formally converted to Judaism with her new name, Rivka. The boys are excited that Rebecca will be Vietnamese, American, and Jewish!

**Comments and Specific Suggestions:**
The author of this story adopted a child from Vietnam. Teachers can extend the story by encouraging children to research Vietnam (e.g., location, climate, customs, foods) or to research Jewish customs such as the Mikvah.

**Themes:**
Intercountry and transracial adoption
Siblings through adoption
Diversity in family and culture

**Title:** *There's a Hamster in My Lunch Box*
**Author(s):** Susan Clymer
**Illustrator:** Paul Casale
**Publisher:** Scholastic, Inc., New York
**Date of Publication:** 1994
**Awards:** None
**Reading Levels:** None found

**Summary:**
Elizabeth is a third grader who was adopted as an infant from Honduras. Elizabeth's teacher and classroom receive a surprise, a hamster named "Squeaks," from an anonymous donor. Hillary, Elizabeth's younger sister, was just adopted from Honduras and, therefore, Elizabeth wants her class to "adopt" Squeaks. "Anybody would be scared who had to go to a new home. Her little sister had sure been scared when she'd arrived on the plane from Honduras" (p. 8). When Squeaks disappears and is eventually found, Elizabeth gets to keep one of Squeak's babies as her own. The anonymous donor turns out to be Nora, the oldest child in the Honduran adoptees group made up of eight families in their city who had adopted children from Honduras. Nora tells Elizabeth, "When Amore [Nora's name for Squeaks] had babies, Mom said I couldn't keep any of them . . . I tried to think of what was best for the babies" (p. 105). During the course of the story, Elizabeth wants to hear her own adoption story again and to look at the pictures of her adoption. Her mother says, "When you adopt someone you care very much. Just like us, honey. You're my daughter for your whole life . . . Your birth mother couldn't give you a home like she wanted you to have . . . She couldn't even feed you enough to keep you healthy" (p. 76). Elizabeth's mother promises that Elizabeth can visit Honduras when she is 16, something Elizabeth has wanted to do but has been afraid to ask of her mother for fear of hurting her feelings.

**Comments and Specific Suggestions:**
The story is realistic and should be appropriate for most third graders. The parallel is obvious between Nora's comment that she did what was best for Squeak's babies and a birth mother making an adoption plan. The curiosity about visiting one's birth country and the worry that this desire will hurt the parents' feelings is also quite realistic. A few stereotypical remarks are made in the story. For example, Elizabeth thinks she is small for

her age. "Elizabeth gritted her teeth. She didn't like it when people teased her about being small. Mom said that most people born in Honduras were just littler than most people in the United States, so she'd probably be short all her life" (p. 22). "A two-color family . . . that was them" (p. 31). Teachers should be able to handle these stereotypical comments with a little forethought and discussion about understanding and dealing with differences.

**Themes:**
Comprehending the adoption story
Dealing with feelings of difference

**Title:** *The Box Car Children, Book #1*
**Author(s):** Gertrude Chandler Warner
**Illustrator:** L. Kate Deal
**Date of Publication:** 1989 (originally published in 1924 and again in 1942)
**Awards:** None
**Reading Levels:** AR Int. Level Middle Grades, BL 2.7

**Summary:**
Four siblings run away after their parents die. Henry, the oldest, is 14, and his younger brothers and sisters are 12-year-old Jessie, 10-year-old Violet, and Benny who is 6. Accompanied by their dog, Watch, they run away because they are afraid of their guardian, their grandfather James Alden, whom they have never met. The children find an abandoned box car to use as their home. Henry works for Dr. Moore to earn money for food and the children supply their box car home with items from the local dump. Dr. Moore suspects the children are James Alden's when Mr. Alden posts a reward for finding the children. Violet becomes ill and Henry takes her to Dr. Moore. Dr. Moore contacts Mr. Alden, who pretends to be "Mr. Henry" until the children get acquainted with him and find out that he is actually very nice. The children go to live with their grandfather and Mr. Alden moves the box car to their backyard as a playhouse.

**Comments and Specific Suggestions:**
This is a well-known short chapter book and is the first story in the popular "Box Car Children" series. During discussion, teachers might ask students why they believe Mr. Alden did not tell the children right away that he was their grandfather. Lead the children to understand how the children felt (e.g., fear, afraid they might be "broken up") and why they might have felt that way, and help students discuss the notion of trust. Then, help the children understand how we all need family to take care of one another. How did the children, as a family, take care of each other? Following the reading of this book, children might illustrate the box car, create a diorama of the box car, make a list of other survival equipment they could find or make for the box car, or read additional books from the series.

**Themes:**
Orphan adventure/Survival story
Understanding the need to have a family

**Title:** *The Finding*
**Author(s):** Nina Bawden
**Illustrator:** None
**Publisher:** Puffin Books, an Imprint of Penguin Books, New York
**Date of Publication:** 1987
**Awards:** None
**Reading Levels:** AR Int. Level Middle Grades, BL 4.5

**Summary:**
Alex was found as a baby along the banks of the Thames River in London near what was called "Cleopatra's Needle." He was featured on television and in newspapers when he was found and adopted by his family. When

elderly Mrs. Angel, whom Alex often visited with his grandmother, dies, she leaves her entire fortune to Alex. Alex is once again "famous" and begins to question his past and his identity. He runs away believing that his family would be better off without him. His older sister, Laura, and his family find him once again at the site of his original "finding" and Alex finally decides that he will celebrate the day he was found instead of his birthday.

**Comments and Specific Suggestions:**
The book contains an important theme for children who have been adopted: searching for one's past and one's identity. The title, "The Finding," suggests that Alex eventually "finds" himself and his identity as a member of his family. Finding out about Cleopatra's Needle may be an interesting follow-up activity. Additional information can be found online at http://www.historic-uk.com. (Click on History UK England and scroll down to find Cleopatra's Needle.)

**Themes:**
Comprehending adoption story
Coping with strong emotions related to family—loss, curiosity
Searching for identity

**Title:** *The Handle and the Key*
**Author(s):** John Newfield
**Illustrator:** None
**Publisher:** Dial Publishing, New York
**Date of Publication:** 2002
**Awards:** None
**Reading Levels:** AR Int. Level Middle Grades, BL 4.1

**Summary:**
Dan is an upper elementary level boy who was adopted by the Knox family after having lived in several foster homes. His parents are kind, but his older sister, Mary Kate, is quite insensitive. She tells Dan to leave. Dan is angry, hostile, and rebellious throughout the story, but eventually he and Mary Kate form a "truce" and he begins to adapt to his family.

**Comments and Specific Suggestions:**
The book is a little stereotypical in that Dan's parents are overly kind, Dan is overly rebellious, and Mary Kate is openly hostile to her new sibling. Mother sums up the theme, and the stereotypes, when she tells Mary Kate that she is uncertain whether or not Dan even knows where the "handle or the key" are to unlock his heart.

**Themes:**
Coping with strong emotions—abandonment, anger
Understanding the need to belong
Wanting to feel safe, secure and loved in a permanent home
Sibling adjustment

**Title:** *The Pinballs*
**Author(s):** Betsy Byars
**Illustrator:** None
**Publisher:** Harper and Row Junior Books, Harper Trophy Edition, New York
**Date of Publication:** 1987, Original edition published in 1977
**Awards:** An American Library Association Notable Children's Book for 1977
**Reading Levels:** AR Int. Level Middle Grades, BL 3.8; Lexile Level 600L

**Summary:**
Three children, Harvey, Carlie, and Thomas J. (T. J.), are all in the same foster care home with Mr. and Mrs. Mason. Carlie, the oldest, was placed in foster care after her third stepfather left her. She is now rebellious

and cynical because her mother left and has not returned for her since she was in the fourth grade. She considers herself a "stray" (p. 46). Harvey, the second oldest at 13, had both legs run over by an alcoholic father after his mother also left their family. Harvey copes with his circumstances by making lists. Thomas J. was found and kept as a toddler by two 80+-year-old twins, Thomas and Jefferson, hence his name, until they became too frail to care for him. T. J. knows nothing about his past, and he says his "favorite story had been about Baby Moses being sent out in a basket by his real mother to a better home. When he heard that story he always imagined his own mother waiting by the road, hiding in the poplar trees, waiting to see the twins take him in" (p. 62). At the Masons' home, Carlie learns to care for others and she helps Harvey accept that he will be okay after he loses the will to live. Carlie and T. J. get Harvey a puppy, something he has always wanted. After the death of the twins, Carlie also helps T. J. realize that he can speak up for himself and be a boy. She acknowledges that life has not been good to them, "You know, Thomas J. . . . wouldn't it be nice if we could get to our brains with an eraser?" (p. 134), but she learns to communicate to Harvey and to T. J. that they can make choices and have control over their own lives even given the bad things that have happened to them in the past. They decide they are not just like "pinballs" to be bounced around at random.

## Comments and Specific Suggestions:
Many issues experienced by children in foster care are contained in this story. The need to understand one's past and the need to feel some control over one's life are both important issues for children in foster care. In addition, children may feel responsible for the bad things that have happened to them. This emotion is evident when Carlie thinks, "For some reason insults didn't hurt her . . . But let somebody say something polite or nice to her—it made her feel terrible" (p. 28). The hurt is also apparent when "Harvey didn't glance up. He was really enjoying the list. It didn't bring back any unpleasant memories, not like the list called 'Promises My Mother Broke.' That list almost made him cry. Almost, but not quite. It wasn't as easy to cry as people thought" (p. 41). Before beginning the story, teachers will need to be sure today's children understand what a "pinball" is. Teachers will need to help children carefully consider why the children see themselves as *pinballs*, why nice comments make Carlie feel terrible, and why Harvey finds it hard to cry. How do the characters change over the course of the story, and what created that change in the children?

## Themes:
Comprehending foster care story
Coping with strong emotions—anger, hurt, abandonment, feeling in control versus no control
Feeling responsible for bad things in one's past

**Title:** *The Story of Tracy Beaker*
**Author(s):** Jacqueline Wilson
**Illustrator:** Nick Sharratt
**Publisher:** Delacorte Press, an Imprint of Random House, New York
**Date of Publication:** 1991
**Awards:** None
**Reading Levels:** AR Int. Level Middle Grades, BL 4.4; Lexile Level 790L

## Summary:
Set in England, ten-year-old Tracy has been in two foster homes and in two children's homes. She does not know her birth father and was placed in the first children's home when her mother's boyfriend abused her. She has a vivid imagination and pictures her mom as a busy Hollywood movie star who will someday remember to come for her. She says, ". . . now I'm in a new children's home and they've advertised me in the papers but there weren't any takers and now I think they're getting a bit desperate. I don't care though. I expect my mom will come soon anyway" (p. 10). Tracy's poor self-concept is apparent when she states, "I can't stand fairy tales . . . If you're good and very beautiful . . . this prince comes along . . . But if you're bad and ugly then you've got no chance at all" (p. 16). Tracy makes friends with Petey, a boy she has had to share her birthday cake with and had resented. Tracy is hurt when one foster family that was going to adopt her decides not to when they find they are going to have a baby. She felt they passed her on "like a parcel" (p. 37). When a writer visits the Children's Home, Tracy is fascinated by Camilla Lawson because Tracy also likes to write. Cam and Tracy become friends and Tracy tries to talk Cam into becoming her foster mother. The story ends with Tracy imagining a fairy tale ending to her story and what it will be like when Cam thinks it over and decides she will be Tracy's foster mom.

**Comments and Specific Suggestions:**

The black and white line drawings are engaging because they are drawn as a child would draw. The conversations clearly illustrate Tracy's frustration and hurt. Some of the dialogue is directed toward social workers and is quite humorous. With respect to completing her "life book," Tracy's social worker, Elaine, says, "This is your own special book about you . . . You don't want to spoil it by writing all sorts of silly, smart-alecky, rude things in it, do you?" to which Tracy responds, "It's my life and it hasn't been very special so far, has it, so why shouldn't I write any old rubbish?" (p. 19). In another humorous exchange, Tracy challenges Elaine regarding the meaning of words used in the advertisements about her availability for foster care. Elaine says, "I also say you're lively and chatty" and Tracy replies "Yeah. Well, we all know what that means. Rude. Difficult. Bossy." (p. 51). Teachers might wish to check the BBC television version of Tracy Beaker at the Tracy Beaker Web site (http://www.bbc.co.uk/cbbc/tracybeaker/). Engage children in a discussion about what Tracy really wants (e.g., a mother and a home) and how she feels in this situation. Help children understand how Tracy's imagination, drawings, and "smart-alecky" comments are her survival tools helping her to cope with the events in her life.

**Themes:**

Understanding foster care story
Coping with strong emotions—hurt, anger, abandonment, feeling unloved and unwanted
Longing to belong and be loved by a family

**Title:** *The Whipping Boy*
**Author(s):** Sid Fleischman
**Illustrator:** Peter Sis
**Publisher:** Greenwillow Books, a Division of William Morrow & Company, New York
**Date of Publication:** 1986
**Awards:** Newbery Medal Winner for 1987
**Reading Levels:** AR Int. Level Middle Grades, BL 3.9; Lexile Level 570L

**Summary:**

Jemmy is the son of a rat catcher who has disappeared. Jemmy is taken from the sewers of the city where he lives to serve as the "whipping boy" for Prince "Brat." When Jemmy runs away with the Prince, they are taken hostage by Hold-Your-Nose Bill and Cutthroat. Jemmy uses his wits to help them get free and outsmarts the two highwaymen. Over time, Prince "Brat" learns to be a friend and they both return to the castle as friends.

**Comments and Specific Suggestions:**

This story is an orphan adventure tale. The pictures are interesting in black and white line drawings; however, the book's relevance for adoption and foster care today is limited.

**Themes:**

Learning to be a friend and to trust friends
Survival and using one's wits

**Title:** *Three Names of Me*
**Author(s):** Mary Cummings
**Illustrator:** Lin Wang
**Publisher:** Albert Whitman and Company, Morton Grove, IL
**Date of Publication:** 2006
**Awards:** None
**Reading Levels:** AR Int. Level Lower Grades, BL 3.1; Lexile Level 690L

**Summary:**

Ada Bennett has three names. She knows that she had a first name "whispered" to her by her first mother when she was born in China. Ada wishes she could remember that name when she says, "I am someone I don't even know" (p. 4). She also has a name the orphanage workers gave her at her arrival, Wang Bin, which she loves, because it means "gentle and refined" [Bin] "Princess" [Wang]. Her parents gave her the name "Ada." In Chinese, Ai da means "love arrived." Ada loves all three of her names and all things that are Chinese such as pink flowers, water buffaloes, and rice. She wonders whether or not her "China parents" think of her, and she dislikes when people stare at her family because they do not look alike. She considers herself a Chinese girl as well as an American girl who knows a few words of Chinese. The end of the book contains Chinese words: a thank you to her first mother, a goodbye to China, and a hello full of love to Ada.

**Comments and Specific Suggestions:**
This is an adoption story written by Mary Cunningham about her daughter, Ada. The illustrations are beautiful! The book contains scrap book ideas from Ada to other children and also shares some Chinese characters and information about China. Children might enjoy learning other Chinese characters or creating a scrapbook about a particular event in their lives.

**Themes:**
Comprehending adoption story
Dealing with differences
Intercountry and transracial adoption
Developing an identity—all three names are important to identity

**Title:** *Three's a Crowd*
**Author(s):** Jamie Suzanne and Francine Pascal
**Illustrator:** None
**Publisher:** A Bantam Skylark Book, New York
**Date of Publication:** 1987
**Awards:** None
**Reading Levels:** AR Int. Level Middle Grades, BL 3.6

**Summary:**
The twins, Elizabeth and Jessica, have a friend who lives down the street, Mary, who seems to want to spend a lot of time with their mother. Mary is in foster care but will not allow herself to be adopted by the Allmans. The Allmans are the best foster care family she has ever had and Mary really likes them, but she has always believed her mother would return for her. Mary's mother went to Florida for a funeral when she was younger and never returned. While her mother was gone, Mary was kidnapped and taken to California by one of her mother's co-workers who then later abandoned her. At the end of the story, Mary's mother does return. She had been looking for Mary for years. Mary's name had been changed by the co-worker. Elizabeth and Jessica's mother looked very similar to Mary's mother, explaining Mary's affinity to the twins' mother.

**Comments and Specific Suggestions:**
This is Book #7 in the Sweet Valley Twins Series created by Francine Pascal. The story is not particularly realistic for most children living in foster care, although the jealousy portrayed by the twins is entertaining. The revelation that Mary was kidnapped as a young child by one of her mother's co-workers will need to be handled carefully if this book is chosen for use in the classroom.

**Themes:**
Comprehending foster care story
Coping with strong emotions—longing for return of parents

**Title:** *Touchdown for Tommy*
**Author(s):** Matt Christopher
**Illustrator:** Foster Caddell
**Publisher:** Little, Brown, and Company
**Date of Publication:** 1985 (Originally published in 1959)
**Awards:** None
**Reading Levels:** AR Int. Level Middle Grades, BL 3.3; Lexile Level 570L

**Summary:**

Tommy Fletcher's parents have died and he goes to live with the Powells, his new foster family. Betty and Jimmy are the Powells' children and Mr. Powell is the coach of a football team, the Pirates. Tommy, who loves football, begins to play for the Pirates. During the story, Tommy gets a puppy and he believes that if he plays well the Powells might adopt him. The Powells help Tommy learn about sportsmanship and about how to take responsibility. In the end he finds a family, a home, and love.

**Comments and Specific Suggestions:**

The story is a bit predictable and stereotypical, but it is appropriate for most young children. Matt Christopher is the author of a number of books with football "themes" for young readers. Children may enjoy reading additional books by Mr. Christopher after reading this story.

**Themes:**

Comprehending foster care story

Coping with strong emotions—needing to be wanted, needing to be loved and to belong

**Title:** *Train to Somewhere*
**Author(s):** Eve Bunting
**Illustrator:** Ronald Himler
**Publisher:** Clarion Books, New York
**Date of Publication:** 1996
**Awards:** An American Library Association Notable Children's Book for 1997
**Reading Levels:** AR Int. Level Lower Grades, BL 2.8; Lexile Level 440L

**Summary:**

This is the story of Marianne, who rides the orphan train west in 1878 with Miss Randolph and 13 other children of various ages from St. Christopher's School. Marianne is one of the older children, and she watches from stop to stop as the other children are adopted. Some, like little Nora who wants to stay with Marianne, are adopted by people along the way to become real sons and daughters to their new parents. Others are adopted only to be farmhands or house servants. Marianne clutches a white feather from her mother's hair in her pocket as she travels. Her mother placed her in St. Christopher's, saying she was going west and would return for Marianne someday. Marianne remembers this and looks for her mother with increasing despair at each stop along the way. Finally, she is the last one left on the train and she is feeling unwanted. "I have a terrible hurt inside of me. My mother didn't want me. It looks like nobody wants me. It's not that I'm hoping to be placed, because my mother could be at the very next stop. But what if she isn't?" (p. 23). At the very last stop at the town of Somewhere, is an older couple, Tillie and Roscoe Book, who were looking for a boy. "She looks at me closely and I see a change in her face. A softness. I'd thought my mother would look at me like that. Somehow this woman understands about me, how it felt that nobody wanted me, even though I was waiting inside myself for my mother to come. Somehow she understands the hurt" (p. 28). "I'm not what you wanted, am I? I say. You wanted a boy . . . Mrs. Book squints at me. I expect we're not what you wanted either . . . Sometimes what you get turns out to be better than what you wanted in the first place" (p. 30). They decide to adopt Marianne and she begins to accept her new life. Marianne gives Mrs. Book the feather from her pocket, and she is ready to go with the Books.

**Comments and Specific Suggestions:**

This is a moving orphan train story. Although it is historical fiction, the book certainly personalizes the orphan train experience of so many children. Teachers will want to probe the statement made by Mrs. Book, "I expect we're not what you wanted either . . . Sometimes what you get turns out to be better than what you wanted in the first place." Have children ever wanted something and received something else instead? Did that turn out to be better or worse than what they expected? What does Mrs. Book mean by her statement? Why did Marianne keep the feather for so long? Why did Marianne finally give Mrs. Book the feather from her pocket? After reading *Train to Somewhere*, children may enjoy reading additional stories about the orphan trains (e.g., books in the orphan train series by Joan Lowery Nixon, such as *Lucy's Wish* contained earlier in this chapter, or books by Andrea Warren, such as *We Rode the Orphan Trains* summarized in Chapter 6).

**Themes:**
Coping with strong emotions—Anger, hurt, confusion, abandonment, feeling that nobody wants you
Finding "Somewhere" to call home and family

## SUMMARY

As children in grades 3–5 develop increased social awareness and cognitive ability, they begin to comprehend that adoption and foster care both mean loss. Children in the middle grades want to be accepted and to belong, yet adoption or foster care placement may make them feel different at a time when any difference from their peers may be viewed by them as unacceptable. Important developmental issues for these children, reflected in children's literature, then, include more fully comprehending the adoption and foster care story, dealing with feelings of difference, and coping with strong emotions such as grief, anger, hurt, fear, guilt, shame, or abandonment related to an increased understanding of what it means to be adopted or placed in foster care.

Important literary trends for middle readers include precious child, orphan as worker, and orphan as adventurer/survivor (Nelson, 2006). Works of historical fiction and realistic fiction dominate the literature for children aged eight to ten, although some orphan adventure tales and works of nonfiction are also found. Teachers must carefully select children's literature having adoption and foster care themes for youngsters in grades 3–5. The increasing complexity of the issues emerging in the literature at those grade levels may or may not be appropriate for the developmental level of individual children in the classroom. Helping students understand the relationship between *family* and *biological family* is one important discussion that can be prompted through children's literature at the middle grade levels.

# CHAPTER 6

# Adoption and Foster Care Literature for Older Readers

Thirteen-year-old Marinda enters the classroom loudly complaining to a peer that her parents do not understand her and that they are the source of all of her grief and pain. As a middle school teacher, you have heard many students complaining about their parents' lack of understanding, but a week later when Marinda runs away from home you begin to wonder. Why would Marinda run away from her parents? Marinda has always been an average student and she has always behaved in class, but lately she has become a bit sullen and withdrawn. Nevertheless, her parents obviously love her. They are involved in the school and have provided her with a beautiful home and fashionable clothing. Marinda also has a younger sister at home who, like Marinda, was adopted from a foster care placement when she was about six. Why would Marinda change so dramatically? What has happened to Marinda?

Teachers readily recognize the variability in size and maturity among students in grades 6–8. By ages 11 to 14, most children experience a period of rapid growth and physical development. The tremendous physical changes that take place as the teenager adds height and enters puberty often conflict with the adolescent's need to conform and be accepted by his or her peer group. Changes in bodily shape and size or the clarity of the young person's skin may create great anxiety at a time when he or she is developing sexual curiosity and wanting to "fit in" with the "right" crowd. Simultaneously, the adolescent is experiencing a shift to greater abstract thought. Teenagers are able to examine complicated moral and ethical issues, and they begin to evaluate their own beliefs as well as their place in the world independent of their parents. Adolescents begin to consider questions such as "Who am I?" "What do I believe?" and "What will I become?" In other words, the child develops a sense of self and his or her identity. Such emotional and physical changes can be dramatic and are universally experienced by teens and acknowledged by adults.

As youngsters in grades 6–8 change both physically and emotionally, children who have been adopted or placed into foster care must negotiate additional developmental tasks. Like their peers, they want to belong, "fit in," feel accepted, and be loved. Also like their peers, they are developing a sense of identity; yet, the question of *where* they belong and *whose family identity* becomes increasingly difficult with greater abstract thought. Brodzinsky, Schechter, and Henig (1992), for example, assert that adolescents who have been adopted may enter an identity moratorium, a period of time during which they search in thought or actions for their origins. That is, teenagers who have been adopted or placed into foster care often lack the information they need in order to answer critical questions about themselves necessary to develop their identity. They may feel unable to belong or answer the question "Who am I?" without first considering concrete information about their past. Lacking specific information, these teens may fantasize about their birth families or ask difficult questions such as "Why was I sent to live with someone else?" or "Why did this happen to me?" Lingering uncertainty and confusion may sometimes lead to anger or open rebellion. Conversely, some teens feel guilty for thinking about adoption and worry about disrupting their family and the life they have. They may deny thinking about their birth families or about their adoption and enter "adoption foreclosure," acquiescing, at least temporarily, to the values and beliefs of their family (Brodzinsky, Schechter, & Henig, 1992).

As teenagers grapple with tough questions related to their adoption or foster care placement, some may become angry, oppositional, or withdrawn. Feelings of grief, hurt, rejection, or abandonment may result in teens distrusting any adult or "pushing away" those who care for them. The teen longs to belong and be loved; yet, he or she cannot risk trusting adults to answer difficult questions, and the answers, even if known, are likely to create even more questions and greater uncertainty or confusion. Adolescents also may wonder whether or not their physical characteristics, talents, or personality traits are like those of their birth family and they may resort to concrete thinking more like that of a younger child: One family is "good" and the other is "bad." Perceived disparities are further magnified by any differences in physical appearance from the family. In an attempt to find the "real" family, some teens may run away, as in the opening case of Marinda, or reject any values or life styles perceived to be those of the adults in their daily lives (Brodzinsky, Schechter, & Henig, 1992). Others "act out" the perceived "bad" behaviors or decisions made by members of the birth family. Thinking about the family "lost" and the family "gained," coping with strong emotions, painful memories, or peer reactions, and integrating adoption or foster care placement into one's identity are difficult and additional developmental tasks experienced by teens with complex backgrounds and family histories.

Certainly not all adolescents who have been adopted or placed into foster care will react as noticeably as Marinda. All will, however, consider the deeper meaning of *family* as they attempt to integrate adoption or foster care into their developing identity. Just like other adolescents, they require teachers to provide accurate information in a manner they can understand, and they need support to cope with a range of strong emotions as they change physically and emotionally and search for their identity. Not surprisingly, numerous books are written for adolescents who are "coming of age" and answering the question "Who am I?" In addition, many books relate to feeling different, belonging, or coping with strong emotions related to family. Teachers can help teens focus on the *universality* of these feelings throughout adolescence while sensitively acknowledging that developing one's identity may be more difficult for youngsters living with other than biological family.

Whether used for study in the classroom or recommended for independent reading, all three literary trends regarding adoption and foster care (i.e., Orphan as Worker, Orphan as Adventurer/Survivor, and Precious child) are evident in books written for older readers (Nelson, 2006). While realistic fiction is readily available (e.g., *Pictures of Hollis Woods* written by Patricia Reilly Giff in 2002), other works include historical fiction (e.g., *A Single Shard* by Linda Park), nonfiction (e.g., Andrea Warren's *We Rode the Orphan Trains* and *Orphan Train Rider: One Boy's True Story*), fantasy (e.g., *The Moorchild* by Eloise McGraw), and science fiction (e.g., *The Angel Factory* by Terence Blacker). The prevalent themes in adoption and foster care literature for older readers include coping with strong emotions, past trauma, or painful memories, understanding the full meaning of family, developing an identity, and searching for family. Because of the nature and complexity of these themes and because of the range in reading level for young adolescents, a number of books with estimated reading levels below

**Table 6.1**
**Children's Literature on Adoption and Foster Care for Older Readers**

| Title, Author, Date of Pub. | AR Level and/or Lexile | Genre | Awards | Adoption and Foster Care Themes |
|---|---|---|---|---|
| *A Single Shard*, Linda Park, 2001 | AR Int. Level Middle Grades, BL 6.6; Lexile Level 920L | Historical fiction | Newbery Medal Winner for 2002 | Orphan as worker; Courage and persistence; Coping with strong emotions—longing to be accepted and to belong, wanting to be safe, loved, and important; Search for family; Developing an identity |
| *Crispin: The Cross of Lead*, Avi, 2002 | AR Int. Level Middle Grades, BL 5.0; Lexile Level 780L | Historical fiction | Newbery Honor Book for 2004 | Orphan adventure/survival tale; Developing an identity; Understanding the meaning of family—importance of name and kin |
| *Dave at Night*, Gail Levine, 1999 | AR Int. Level Middle Grades, BL 3.6; Lexile Level 490L | Historical fiction | An ALA Notable Children's Book for 2000 | Orphan adventure/survival tale; Coping with strong emotions—anger, fear, frustration, feeling unwanted and abandoned, wanting to belong; Understanding the meaning of family and kinship |
| *Dicey's Song*, Cynthia Voight, 1982 | AR Int. Level Middle Grades, BL 5.0; Lexile Level 710L | Realistic fiction | Newbery Medal Winner for 1983 | Precious child; Coping with strong emotions—anger, hurt, loss, and pride; Grandmother adopting children; Understanding the meaning of family responsibility; Letting go of the past |
| *Everything on a Waffle*, Polly Horvath, 2001 | AR Int. Level Middle Grades, BL 5.8; Lexile Level 950L | Fiction | Newbery Honor Book for 2002 | Coping with strong emotions; Hope, joy, and finding meaning and importance in one's life |
| *Hattie Big Sky*, Kirby Larson, 2006 | AR Int. Level Middle Grades, BL 4.4; Lexile Level 700L | Historical fiction | Newbery Honor Book for 2007 | Orphan adventure/survival tale; Longing for a place to belong and a home; Search for family; Developing an identity |
| *Heaven*, Angela Johnson, 1998 | AR Int. Level Middle Grades, BL 4.7; Lexile Level 790L | Realistic fiction | Coretta Scott King Author Award Winner for 1999 | Precious child; Understanding the meaning of family; Developing an identity; Trust, honesty, and "family secrets" |

**Table 6.1 (continued)**

| Title, Author, Date of Pub. | AR Level and/or Lexile | Genre | Awards | Adoption and Foster Care Themes |
|---|---|---|---|---|
| *Heaven Eyes*, David Almond, 2000 | AR Int. Level Middle Grades, BL 3.4; Lexile Level 420L | Fantasy | An ALA Notable Children's Book for 2002 | Orphan adventure/survival tale; Coping with strong emotions—loss, death, abandonment; Understanding the meaning of family; Joy and love from friends as "family" |
| *Heck Superhero*, Martine Leavitt, 2004 | AR Int. Level Middle Grades, BL 4.2; Lexile Level 610L | Fiction | None | Orphan adventure/survival tale; Search for family; Longing for a place to belong and a home; Learning to ask for help and trust |
| *Home and Other Big Fat Lies*, Jill Wolfson, 2006 | AR Int. Levels Middle Grades, BL 4.4; Lexile Level 740L | Realistic fiction | None | Longing for a place to belong, a home, and permanence; Wanting to be loved; Coping with feelings of difference |
| *How It Feels to Be Adopted*, Jill Krementz, 1983 | None found | Nonfiction | None | Coping with strong emotions; Comprehending adoption and foster care; Search for family; Search for identity |
| *If It Hadn't Been for Yoon Jun*, Marie Lee, 1993 | AR Int. Level Middle Grades, BL 5.2; Lexile Level 740L | Realistic fiction | None | Coping with feelings of difference; Intercountry and transracial adoption; Search for identity |
| *I'll Sing You One-O*, Nan Gregory, 2006 | AR Int. Level Middle Grades, BL 4.4; Lexile Level 750L | Realistic fiction | None | Coping with strong emotions—abandonment, feeling unloved and worthless, hidden traumas, longing to feel safe and loved; Letting go of the past; Search for family; Coming of age and search for identity |
| *Locomotion*, Jacqueline Woodson, 2003 | AR Int. Level Middle Grades, BL 4.7; Lexile Level NP | Fiction—Nonstandard prose (poetry) | An ALA Notable Children's Book for 2003 | Coping with strong emotions—hurt, grief, rejection, abandonment; Importance of preserving family and memories; Accepting a new home |
| *Maniac Magee*, Jerry Spinelli, 1990 | AR Int. Level Middle Grades, BL 4.7; Lexile Level 820L | Fiction | Newbery Medal Winner for 1991 | Orphan adventure/survival tale; Longing for an address and a home; Wanting to belong and to feel safe; Search for family; Search for identity |

| Title, Author, Date of Pub. | AR Level and/or Lexile | Genre | Awards | Adoption and Foster Care Themes |
| --- | --- | --- | --- | --- |
| *Moccasin Trail*, Eloise McGraw, 1952 | AR Int. Level Middle Grades, BL 5.8; Lexile Level 960L | Historical fiction | Newbery Honor Book for 1953 | Orphan adventure/survival tale; Living between two cultures; Search for family; Developing an identity |
| *Orphan Train Rider: One Boy's True Story*, Andrea Warren, 1996 | AR Int. Level Middle Grades, BL 6.1; Lexile Level 960L | Nonfiction | An ALA Notable Children's Book for 1997 | Orphan train story; Coping with strong emotions—anger, confusion, loss, feeling incomplete and inferior; Search for family |
| *Pictures of Hollis Woods*, Patricia Giff, 2002 | AR Int. Level Middle Grades, BL 4.4; Lexile Level 650L | Realistic fiction | Newbery Honor Book for 2003 | Precious child; Coping with strong emotions—grief, hurt, anger, abandonment; Longing to belong and have a home; Understanding the meaning of family |
| *Raspberry House Blues*, Linda Holeman, 2000 | AR Int. Level Middle Grades, BL 4.2 | Realistic fiction | None | Precious child; Search for identity; Understanding the meaning of family; Search for birth family |
| *Ruby Holler*, Sharon Creech, 2002 | AR Int. Level Middle Grades, BL 4.3; Lexile Level 660L | Realistic fiction | Carnegie Medal for Children's Literature Winner for 2002 (A U.K. award similar to the Newbery) | Precious child; Longing to belong and have a home; Understanding the meaning of family; Coping with strong emotions—abandonment; Learning to trust; Developing an identity |
| *Saffy's Angel*, Hilary McKay, 2001 | AR Int. Level Middle Grades, BL 4.5; Lexile Level 630L | Realistic fiction | An ALA Notable Children's Book for 2003 | Precious child; Comprehending adoption story; Coping with strong emotions—loss, distrust, and anger; Understanding the meaning of family; Belonging and understanding importance of family history |
| *The Angel Factory*, Terence Blacker, 2001 | AR Int. Level Upper Grades, BL 4.9; Lexile Level 700L | Science fiction | None | Search for identity; Need to belong to family; Search for meaning, independence, and control of one's destiny; Choice, free will, and freedom; Need for honesty and trust |
| *The Crying Rocks*, Janet Lisle, 2003 | AR Int. level Middle Grades, BL 4.5; Lexile Level 770L | Realistic fiction | None | Precious child; Coping with strong emotions—hidden traumas, abandonment, and prejudice; Search for identity; Understanding the meaning of family |

**Table 6.1 (continued)**

| Title, Author, Date of Pub. | AR Level and/or Lexile | Genre | Awards | Adoption and Foster Care Themes |
|---|---|---|---|---|
| *The Folk Keeper*, Franny Billingsley, 1999 | AR Int. Level Middle Grades, BL 5.3; Lexile Level 690L | Fantasy | An ALA Notable Children's Book for 2000 | Orphan adventure/survival tale; Search for identity; Living between two cultures; Longing to belong and to be accepted |
| *The Great Gilly Hopkins*, Katherine Paterson, 1978 | AR Int. Level Middle Grades, BL 4.6; Lexile Level 800L | Realistic fiction | Newbery Honor Book for 1979 | Precious child; Coping with strong emotions—abandonment, anger, distrust; Longing to belong, have a permanent home and feel loved; Letting go of past; Searching for identity; Coming of age |
| *The Higher Power of Lucky*, Susan Patron, 2006 | AR Int. Level Middle Grades, BL 5.9; Lexile Level 1010L | Realistic fiction | Newbery Medal Winner for 2007 | Precious child; Coping with strong emotions—abandonment and grief; Letting go of past; Understanding the meaning of family; Searching for identity; Coming of age |
| *The Invention of Hugo Cabret*, Brian Selznick, 2007 | AR Int. Level Middle Grades, BL 5.1; Lexile Level 820L | Historical fiction graphic novel | Caldecott Medal Winner for 2008 | Orphan adventure/survival tale; Coping with strong emotions—fear; Longing to find love and a home; Coming of age; Searching for identity and purpose |
| *The King of Slippery Falls*, Sid Hite, 2004 | AR Int. Level Upper Grades, BL 5.6 | Realistic fiction | None | Precious child; Comprehending adoption story; Searching for one's past and heritage; Understanding the meaning of family; Coping with strong emotions—trust and need to feel secure; Developing an identity and the search for self |
| *The Loner*, Ester Wier, 1963 | AR Int. Level Middle Grades, BL 5.3; Lexile Level 810L | Historical fiction | Newbery Honor Book for 1964 | Orphan as worker; Longing for home and to belong; Learning responsibility and to trust; Learning how to care for others and to be cared for by others; Understanding the meaning of family |

| Title, Author, Date of Pub. | AR Level and/or Lexile | Genre | Awards | Adoption and Foster Care Themes |
|---|---|---|---|---|
| *The Mailbox*, Audrey Shafer, 2006 | AR Int. Level Middle Grades, BL 5.0; Lexile Level 790L | Realistic fiction | None | Orphan adventure/survival tale; Learning to love and need others; Longing for home and to belong; Understanding the meaning of family |
| *The Midnight Diary of Zoya Blume*, Laura Cunningham, 2005 | AR Int. Level Middle Grades, BL 4.8 | Realistic fiction | None | Precious child; Coping with strong emotions—fear, hidden traumas and memories; Letting go of the past; Developing an identity; Intercountry adoption |
| *The Midwife's Apprentice*, Karen Cushman, 1995 | AR Int. Level Middle Grades, BL 6.0; Lexile Level 1240L | Historical fiction | Newbery Medal Winner for 1996 | Orphan as worker; Longing for a place to belong; Learning to care about others; Developing an identity and a place in the world |
| *The Moorchild*, Eloise McGraw, 1996 | AR Int. Level Middle Grades, BL 5.5; Lexile Level 940L | Fantasy | Newbery Honor Book for 1997 | Orphan as worker; Longing for a place to belong; Coping with feelings of difference; Coping with strong emotions—past memories |
| *The Ocean Within*, V. M. Caldwell, 1999 | AR Int. Level Middle Grades, BL 4.5; Lexile Level 500L | Realistic fiction | None | Precious child; Coping with strong emotions—anger, distrust, need for control; Longing to belong and be accepted; Understanding the meaning of family |
| *The Road to Paris*, Nikki Grimes, 2006 | AR Int. Level Middle Grades, BL 4.3; Lexile Level 700L | Realistic fiction | None | Coping with strong emotions—fear, loss, abandonment, and love for a sibling; Understanding the meaning of family; Coming of age; Developing an identity |
| *The Star of Kazan*, Eva Ibbotson, 2004 | AR Int. Level Middle Grades, BL 6.1; Lexile Level 880L | Historical fiction | An ALA Notable Children's Book for 2005 | Orphan adventure/survival tale; Understanding the meaning of family; Longing for a place to belong and a home; Letting go of the past; Searching for identity |
| *The Thief Lord*, Cornelia Funk, 2003 | AR Int. Level Middle Grades, BL 4.8; Lexile Level 640L | Fiction | An ALA Notable Children's Book for 2003 | Orphan adventure/survival tale; Coping with strong emotions—hurt, rejection; Longing to belong and be loved; Understanding the meaning of family |

**Table 6.1 (continued)**

| Title, Author, Date of Pub. | AR Level and/or Lexile | Genre | Awards | Adoption and Foster Care Themes |
|---|---|---|---|---|
| *The Trouble with Skye*, Marsha Huber, 2004 | AR Int. Level Middle Grades, BL 4.7 | Realistic fiction | None | Coping with strong emotions —anger, distrust, need for control, feeling rejected; Comprehending foster care story; Understanding the meaning of family and accepting love |
| *Tides*, V. M. Caldwell, 2001 | AR Int. Level Middle Grades, BL 3.6 | Realistic fiction | None | Precious child; Understanding the meaning of family and learning to accept love; Searching for identity |
| *The Witch's Boy*, Michael Gruber, 2005 | AR Int. Level Middle Grades, BL 6.4; Lexile Level 990L | Fantasy | An ALA Notable Children's Book for 2006 | Searching for identity; Learning to love others |
| *Up a Road Slowly*, Irene Hunt, 1966 | AR Int. Level Middle Grades, BL 6.6; Lexile Level 1130L | Realistic fiction | Newbery Medal Winner for 1967 | Precious child; Coping with strong emotions—loss and feeling insecure; Longing to belong; Developing an identity; Coming of age |
| *We Rode the Orphan Trains*, Andrea Warren, 2001 | AR Int. Level Middle Grades, BL 6.4; Lexile Level 940L | Nonfiction | None | Both precious child and orphan as worker; Developing an identity |
| *Where I'd Like to Be*, Frances Dowell, 2003 | AR Int. Level Middle Grades, BL 5.4; Lexile Level 910L | Realistic fiction | None | Comprehending foster care story; Coping with strong emotions—abandonment and anger; Longing to belong, have a home, and have a family; Understanding the meaning of family |
| *Youn Hee and Me*, C.S. Adler, 1995 | AR Int. Level Middle Grades, BL 4.6; Lexile Level 760L | Realistic fiction | None | Precious child; Dealing with differences; Intercountry and transracial adoption; Sibling adjustment; Understanding the meaning of family |

that of sixth grade are included in this chapter rather than with the books for middle readers described in Chapter 5.

Table 6.1 lists 44 books for older readers containing themes related to adoption or foster care. As in the previous chapters, Table 6.1 organizes the story titles alphabetically, gives estimated reading levels (e.g., Lexile and/or AR levels when known), genre, and any awards received, and lists the relevant developmental themes related to adoption or foster care. Again, the list is not exhaustive, but rather provides *representative* literature related to adoption and foster care that may be appropriate for children in grades 6–8, and as with literature for younger and middle readers, teachers are encouraged to use the guidelines contained in Chapter 3 when considering books appropriate for the maturity level of specific students in their classrooms.

## USING LITERATURE ON ADOPTION AND FOSTER CARE IN THE 6–8 CLASSROOM

Because adolescents have the ability to engage in abstract thought and because the developmental tasks and issues are more complex for adolescents, many books for this age group contain compelling plots and interesting character development. In turn, more books of high quality seem to be available for the older reader than for younger or even middle readers. For example, of the 44 titles included in Table 6.1, 25 (57 percent) have received American Library Association awards and honors! Six of the books received the Newbery Medal based on the author's interpretation of the theme or concept, presentation of information, development of a plot, delineation of characters and setting, and appropriateness of style. In addition, eight more books received a Newbery Honor. One book, *The Invention of Hugo Cabret* (Selznick, 2007), won the Caldecott Medal for 2008, and another, *Heaven*, written by Angela Johnson in 1998, won the Coretta Scott King Award for African American authors in 1999. Finally, nine additional books were named to the American Library Association Notable Children's Books list. Clearly, young adolescents have available to them many books of good quality.

In addition, numerous links to history, science, art, music, and mathematics can also be made for most of the books in order to extend and enrich classroom discussions or activities. When reading nonfiction such as *We Rode the Orphan Trains* (Warren, 2001), for example, students might engage in a Web Quest consulting online sites to locate information about real orphan train riders and their families. The National Orphan Train Complex, a museum and research center in Concordia, Kansas, contains comprehensive records of orphan train riders (http://orphantraindepot.com), and an "American Experience" video, *The Orphan Trains*, along with an educator's guide, is also available for teachers from the Public Broadcasting System (http://www.pbs.org/wgbh/amex/orphan). Older readers should be better able than middle readers to understand and discuss the differing outcomes (e.g., worker or family member) for various individuals who were authentic orphan train riders.

Similarly, students may be challenged to research the specific time period or geographical location contained in a work of historical fiction such as *Crispin: The Cross of Lead* (Avi, 2002), *A Single Shard* (Park, 2001), or *Dave at Night* (Levine, 1999). Adolescents may also enjoy researching background information about the various authors, many of whom, such as Avi and Brian Selznick, have their own quite interesting Web sites. Students may, for example, be interested to find out that Avi has written a sequel to *Crispin: The Cross of Lead* (i.e., *Crispin at the Edge of the World*, Avi, 2006). This sequel is the second book in a planned trilogy. Or, students might enjoy the links provided by Brian Selznick regarding his research trip to Paris and his study of automata.

Throughout classroom reading of any works listed in Table 6.1, teachers will want to help their students examine how the characters have changed from the beginning to the end of the story. Teachers can also lead students to discuss any imagery or symbolism contained in the book. For example, students might discuss the terrifying image of "Red Boy" in *I'll Sing You One-O* (Gregory, 2006), the significance of the pictures in *Pictures of Hollis Woods* (Giff, 2002), or the symbolism of the fish in *King of Slippery Falls* (Hite, 2004), the angel in *Saffy's Angel* (McKay, 2001), or the boat in *Dicey's Song* (Voight, 1982). In addition, teachers can use the following types of generic activities to extend or enrich learning when using books selected from Table 6.1:

- Invite a social worker or counselor to speak to students in the class about foster care, adoption, or other diverse family structures. Guidance counselors or social workers might also guide students during a discussion about coping with strong emotions or the adolescent search for one's "identity."

- Have students write a character description for one of the main characters as that person is depicted at the beginning of a story. Rewrite the character description for the character as he or she is portrayed at the end of the book. For example, students might describe Cynthia Voight's characterization of Dicey at the beginning and ending of *Dicey's Song*. Alternatively, students might depict the selected character and changes in that character through a character talk or through a drawing.

- Compare and contrast a main character from two different novels. Students might compare and contrast Lonnie from *Locomotion* with Jeffrey from *Maniac Magee*, for example.

- Interview someone from an older generation. During the interview, obtain information about that person's adolescence and his or her search for an identity. What major questions or events affected that individual as he or she came of age? Students might also compare and contrast the interviewee's search for identity with that of today's youth. What significant events are universally impacting adolescents as they come of age today?

- Have students keep a daily or weekly diary or log of their "beliefs" or "questions about life." Students can explore how these beliefs or questions impact their daily actions or they can make a list of their "Rules for Living."

- Determine why an author decided to write the particular story being read. Students might locate that information on an author's Web site or they might communicate directly with the author through e-mail or a letter to obtain answers to specific questions they construct about a book as they are reading it.

## AN ANNOTATED BIBLIOGRAPHY OF SELECTED LITERATURE ON ADOPTION AND FOSTER CARE FOR GRADES 6–8

The 44 books for older readers listed in Table 6.1 are arranged in the same alphabetical order by title in the following annotated bibliography. In addition, as in previous chapters, a summary is provided for each book as well as comments containing more information, suggestions, or cautions that may be helpful for teachers when using or recommending the story. Finally, the themes to be emphasized in discussion or extension activities for each title are listed. Given the increased abstract thought of young adolescents and the complexity of the issues contained in children's literature about adoption and foster care for students in grades 6–8, the teacher is encouraged to consult Chapter 5 for additional literature that may be appropriate for some children in the classroom, particularly for those in sixth grade. More mature eighth grade readers may also benefit from reading appropriate young adult literature not reviewed in this book.

## ANNOTATED BIBLIOGRAPHY

**Title:** *A Single Shard*
**Author(s):** Linda Sue Park
**Illustrator:** None
**Publisher:** Clarion Books, New York
**Date of Publication:** 2001
**Awards:** Newbery Medal Winner for 2002
**Reading Levels:** AR Int. Level Middle Grades, BL 6.6; Lexile Level 920L

**Summary:**
Set in Korea in the late 1100s, Tree-ear, an orphan named after a mushroom that grows on a tree without having had a parent seed, lives under a bridge with Crane-man, something he has done as long as he can remember. Crane-man is a wise and loving father figure for Tree-ear who is often shunned as "bad luck" by other children in the village of Ch'ulp'o. Crane-man, however, describes Tree-ear by saying, "...again you see the aptness of your name. You are like the ears of a scrawny little tree, noticed by none, but hearing all" (p. 45). Tree-ear is fascinated by the potter, Min, and his high quality celadon pottery, and he spies on him when he can from the bushes.

Eventually, Tree-ear works for the potter, hoping to learn how to turn a pot on the wheel. Tree-ear is able to provide food and clothing for Crane-man, thanks to the kindness of Min's wife, but Min refuses to teach him how to make pots since that is a skill passed only from father to son. Min and his wife lost their son, Hyung-gu, to illness and Min is bitter over this loss. Min hopes to receive a commission from the emperor to make pottery, and Tree-ear offers to take two vases all the way to the palace. While traveling, he is attacked by bandits and both vases are broken; however, Tree-ear takes the largest shard left and finishes the journey. The Royal Emissary awards Min the commission, and Tree-ear returns to Ch'ulp'o only to find that Crane-ear has died, clutching a little monkey, a pet name for Tree-ear, that Tree-ear had made for him out of clay. Min has seen the fine workmanship in the monkey, and he has noticed all of Tree-ear's hard work over time. Min asks Tree-ear to go cut large logs and then says to a confused Tree-ear, "Do you not understand that I have been assigned a royal commission? Do you not realize how much work it will be?... How am I to do it all myself? How are you to help me if you do not have a wheel of your own and how is the wheel to be made if you do not fetch logs of considerable size? Go!" (p. 146). Min's wife tells Tree-ear to be *home* in time for supper. They ask him to live with them and be called Hyung-pil, an important event because sharing a syllable in a name was an honor bestowed only to siblings. As the book ends, Hyung-pil dreams of making a prunus vase covered with cranes soaring among clouds.

### Comments and Specific Suggestions:

*A Single Shard* is beautifully written and engaging. Students can easily examine how Tree-ear changes over time and takes control of his own destiny. In addition, the author includes in her notes information about celadon pottery and the Thousand-Cranes Vase. All of the pieces of pottery mentioned in the story are real and are in museums or private collections worldwide. As an enrichment activity, students can research the pottery online, make pottery, or read about Korea during the 1100s and the present. Linda Parks can be reached through her Web site at http://www.lindasuepark.com.

### Themes:

Orphan as worker
Courage and persistence
Coping with strong emotions—longing to be accepted and to belong, wanting to be safe, loved, and important
Search for family
Developing an identity

**Title:** *Crispin: The Cross of Lead*
**Author(s):** Avi
**Illustrator:** None
**Publisher:** Hyperion Books for Children, New York
**Date of Publication:** 2002
**Awards:** Newbery Honor Book for 2004
**Reading Levels:** AR Int. Level Middle Grades, BL 5.0; Lexile Level 780L

### Summary:

"Asta's son," a young orphan called only by his mother's name of Asta, lives in England in 1377. He knows very little about his family, other than he and his mother are shunned in their village and his father died in the plague. Asta's son says of himself, "In a world in which one lived by the light of a father's name and rank, that meant— since I had no father—I existed in a shadow" (p. 10). When Asta dies, the boy is marked by John Aycliffe, the Steward for Lord Furnival in the area, as a "wolf's head" to be killed on sight by anyone. On the run, he is hunted and eventually discovers he is the illegitimate son of Lord Furnival. Asta herself was actually of noble birth, born to Lord Douglas, and Asta's son is being hunted to prevent him or Lord Douglas from laying any claim to Lord Furnival's wealth after he dies. The boy discovers his birth name was "Crispin," an inscription on a lead cross owned by his mother that he carries with him as his only possession. When Crispin meets Bear, a large man posing as a juggler but who is really a spy for a movement to give rights to peasants, Bear becomes Crispin's master and later makes him an apprentice. During the story, Bear helps Crispin discover his true identity. Bear becomes a father figure for Crispin, and they eventually gain their freedom and save each other.

**Comments and Specific Suggestions:**
This is the first book in a planned trilogy. The second book in the series, *Crispin at the Edge of the World*, was published in 2006. As students read about Crispin's journey, they can be challenged to research medieval England in the 1300s or to create a map of the area through which Crispin traveled. Comparing Crispin's character traits at the beginning and ending of the story will be an important discussion as he finds his identity. In addition, teachers can help students understand the importance of Bear as a father figure for Crispin. On an additional note, Avi is the pen name of Edward Irving Wortis.

**Themes:**
Orphan adventure/survival tale
Developing an identity
Understanding the meaning of family—importance of name and kin

**Title:** *Dave at Night*
**Author(s):** Gail Carson Levine
**Illustrator:** None
**Publisher:** HarperCollins Publishers, New York
**Date of Publication:** 1999
**Awards:** An ALA Notable Children's Book for 2000
**Reading Levels:** AR Int. Level Middle Grades, BL 3.6; Lexile Level 490L

**Summary:**
Dave's mother died from complications after she gave birth to Dave. When his papa dies, Uncle Jack takes Dave's older brother, the less troublesome Gideon, and his stepmother, Ida, puts Dave in HHB, the Hebrew Home for Boys in New York City, which Dave dubs the "Hell Hole for Boys!" Dave learns he can draw, and he fights to regain his father's Noah's Ark carving from Mr. Bloom (aka Mr. "Doom"), the HHB director who beats the boys and steals their possessions. Dave also finds a way to keep the older bullies from stealing the younger boy's food, which is very bad except on days when visitors are present and Mr. "Doom" attempts to look as though he "loves" the boys. Dave slips out at night to visit Harlem parties with an old man who tells fortunes and pretends to be his Grandpa Solly. He meets a wealthy African American family, the Packers, and their daughter, Irma Lee, who host numerous artists, poets, and musicians at their home. In the end, Dave returns to his "family" at HHB knowing he is protected from the wrath of Mr. Bloom by the power of Mrs. Packer, her wealth, and her acquaintances on the HHB Board of Directors.

**Comments and Specific Suggestions:**
This book is based on the true story of the author's father who grew up in the HOA, the Hebrew Orphan Asylum, which existed on the site of the fictional HHB. Although it closed in 1941, Art Buchwald, the columnist, also grew up there. Discipline and punishment were severe; however, Mr. Bloom and other characters at the orphanage are fictional. The author also includes in an afterword an interesting history of Harlem during the Harlem Renaissance of the 1920s and 1930s. As an enrichment activity, students might research the many African American artists (e.g., Aaron Douglas), poets (e.g., Langston Hughes), or jazz musicians (e.g., Duke Ellington) mentioned in the story who gathered in Harlem during that time period. Students might also enjoy taking a virtual tour of the Tenement Museum to learn about Harlem and the tenements during its Renaissance at www.thirteen.org. Gail Carson Levine is also the author of the acclaimed *Ella Enchanted*, published in 1997 by HarperTrophy Publishers.

**Themes:**
Orphan adventure/survival tale
Coping with strong emotions—anger, fear, frustration, feeling unwanted and abandoned, longing to belong
Understanding the meaning of family and kinship

**Title:** *Dicey's Song*
**Author(s):** Cynthia Voight

**Illustrator:** None
**Publisher:** Atheneum, New York
**Date of Publication:** 1982
**Awards:** Newbery Medal Winner for 1983
**Reading Levels:** AR Int. Level Middle Grades, BL 5.0; Lexile Level 710L

**Summary:**

Dicey Tillerman, an eighth grader, has had to take care of her three younger siblings for a very long time. Dicey was angry and hurt about her absent mother and her responsibilities, and she fought quite a bit when she was younger. Her brother James is extremely intelligent and her other brother Sammy fights like Dicey, particularly when children say things about his mother. The youngest sibling, Maybeth, is gifted at the piano, but she struggles with learning to read or do math. When Momma disappears, and later is identified in a psychiatric hospital, Dicey manages to bring the children from Provincetown, Massachusetts, all the way to Crisfield on the Eastern Shore of Maryland to "Gram's" house. Gram never knew the children, but she cares for them and adopts them. During the course of the story, Dicey discovers that Gram's pride had pushed her husband and her three children, including Dicey's mother, away from their home. Gram tells Dicey, "But I'll tell you something else, too. Something I've learned the hard way. I guess . . . I'm the kind of person who has to learn the hard way. You've got to hold on. Hold on to people. They can get away from you. It's not always going to be fun, but if you don't—hold on—then you lose them" (p. 70). Just like Gram, Dicey learns to be responsible and to reach out, hold on to others, and trust others to help her. She works hard to rebuild a boat and this helps her, and later also Sammy, to be calm when life is difficult and she is angry. When Gram and Dicey go to Boston where Momma's hospital is located, they realize Momma will not survive and they say their "good byes." Finally, they bring her back home to Crisfield in a beautiful wooden box to bury her under the paper mulberry tree at Gram's house.

**Comments and Specific Suggestions:**

Students may enjoy taking the perspective of one of the main characters in this book, Dicey, Gram, James, Sammy, or Maybeth, or of one of Dicey's friends, Mina Smith or Jeff Green, for a book talk. Alternatively, students might write from that character's point of view. The teacher can also help students discuss the symbolism of the boat. As Dicey rebuilds the boat, she is also rebuilding herself. In addition, the symbolism of Dicey's *song* may be of interest. Just after her arrival at Gram's house, Dicey thinks, "What Dicey was used to, she realized, was things being simple, like a song. You sang the words and the melody straight through. That was the way she had brought her family to Crisfield, singing straight through" (p. 18). Yet, Dicey's life, and her *song*, had not been simple and straightforward. Later, as Dicey watches Momma in her hospital bed, she thinks, "All the time Momma had been gone, Dicey had carried around an idea of her. The idea was of Momma sleeping, and behind that were all the ideas of Momma that Dicey had saved up over her life. But idea wasn't the same as real and real hurt. Because she remembered Momma moving around. She remembered Momma's voice singing . . . Momma was tired then, and worried about how to take care of them; but . . . Momma loved her children. You could tell in the way her hands rested on their heads . . . And in her voice when she talked to them. You could tell in how long she tried, how hard she worked. Dicey wondered if Momma had known that she was worked out and tired out. If she had felt herself crumbling at the edges and that was why she had started . . . Trying to get them to a safe place before she crumbled away" (p. 165). Dicey's song had been one of *home was gone* and *family meant loss*. In the end, as Dicey comes of age, she has developed inner strength and a strong sense of the meaning of her family and its *song*. On a final note, *Dicey's Song* is the second in a series of seven books about the Tillerman family. The third book in the series, *A Solitary Blue* (Voight, 1983), about Dicey's friend, Jeff Green, won a Newbery Honor in 1984.

**Themes:**

Precious child
Coping with strong emotions—anger, hurt, loss, pride
Understanding the meaning of family and family responsibility
Letting go of the past
Grandmother adopting children

**Title:** *Everything on a Waffle*
**Author(s):** Polly Horvath
**Illustrator:** None
**Publisher:** Farrar, Straus and Giroux, New York
**Date of Publication:** 2001
**Awards:** Newbery Honor Book for 2002
**Reading Levels:** AR Int. Level Middle Grades, BL 5.8; Lexile Level 950L

**Summary:**
Primrose Squarp, who lives in Coal Harbour, British Columbia, is 11 years old as she tells this story to Bert and Evie, her temporary caregivers. Primrose's parents drowned in a storm at sea, but Primrose never believed her parents to be dead. She believed they were marooned and cold on an island. After the town can no longer afford to pay Miss Perfidy for "baby sitting services," Primrose's Uncle Jack, whom she has never met, comes to take care of her. Miss Honeycutt, the school guidance counselor, has a crush on Uncle Jack and believes Primrose is "disturbed" and "has issues." Primrose finds comfort in the local restaurant, "The Girl on the Red Swing," as Miss Bowzer, who serves everything at the restaurant on a waffle, teaches her how to cook and helps her add recipes to her mother's notepad. In the end, her parents do come back home after having been rescued from an island where they were stranded.

**Comments and Specific Suggestions:**
Although the book is fun to read, caution is advised when using the book with children who have lost both parents. Children in foster or family care may engage in "wishful thinking" or "magical thought" that their parents will return. Hope is important; however, most children will not have parents rescued from an island. The humor in the book is obvious and intriguing. For example, Primrose says about a child who has been adopted, "His name was Spinky Caldwater and he was a Cambodian orphan. His mother was a single woman who wanted a child and flew to Cambodia to get him. Everyone felt sorry for Spinky. Not because he was a Cambodian war orphan or because his foot had been blown off by a land mine, but because his mother was such a twit. She made him wear a necktie everywhere" (p. 86). Teachers might also help students understand the meaning behind the statement, ". . . it is the people who choose to stand by your side [like Uncle Jack who never contradicted her belief that her parents were still alive] who give you the clues. But the important things that happen to you will happen to you even in the smallest places . . ." (p. 147). In addition, teachers can discuss with students the importance of the notepad to Primrose and why she chose to continue to write recipes there. As an extension activity, students might be challenged to research the fishing and whaling industry in British Columbia, to research the history of the waffle, or to bring from home their own favorite recipes for Primrose's notepad.

**Themes:**
Coping with strong emotions—hope, joy, and finding meaning and importance in one's life

**Title:** *Hattie Big Sky*
**Author(s):** Kirby Larson
**Illustrator:** None
**Publisher:** Delacorte Press, a Division of Random House Children's Books, New York
**Date of Publication:** 2006
**Awards:** Newbery Honor Book for 2007
**Reading Levels:** AR Int. level Middle Grades, BL 4.4; Lexile Level 700L

**Summary:**
Hattie Brooks is 16 years old. She has been moved from one relative to another since her parents died, both by the time she was six. Of herself, Hattie said, "My bounce-around life had taught me that dreams were dangerous things—they look solid in your mind, but you just try to reach them. It's like gathering clouds" (p. 3), and "I was simply Hattie Here-and-There with no right to an opinion. I'd been orphaned before I'd lost my baby teeth" (p. 6). When her Uncle Chester, whom she has never met, leaves his claim in Montana to her, Hattie decides to travel west and "prove" the 320 acre claim. Hattie's uncertainty about her identity is evident in her

belief that, "I knew I'd inherited my father's straight nose and my mother's crooked smile. In what other ways they had made their marks upon me, I had no way of knowing" (p. 15). Although in the end Hattie must take a job in order to pay back her debts, and she loses the claim, Hattie learns about herself and the depths of her strength. She also makes deep and lasting friendships and learns the real meaning of home.

**Comments and Specific Suggestions:**
Teachers might help students discuss the meaning of Hattie's statement, "... I was beginning to see there were bigger things in life than proving up on a claim. I was proving up on my life" (p. 146). Interesting enrichment or extension activities include researching Montana and the meaning of "proving up a claim" as well as writing a diary from Hattie's perspective regarding a chosen event from the novel. The search for identity is obvious in this "coming of age" tale.

**Themes:**
Orphan adventure/survival tale
Longing for a place to belong and for a home
Search for family
Developing an identity

**Title:** *Heaven*
**Author(s):** Angela Johnson
**Illustrator:** None
**Publisher:** Simon and Schuster Books for Young Readers, New York
**Date of Publication:** 1998
**Awards:** Coretta Scott King Author Award for 1999
**Reading Levels:** AR Int. Level Middle Grades, BL 4.7; Lexile Level 790L

**Summary:**
Marley, age 14, lives with her parents and brother, Butch, in Heaven, a small town in Ohio where they moved 12 years ago. Marley receives many postcards from her Uncle Jack and his dog named "Boy," and she wires money to her Uncle Jack, her father's twin brother, for her parents at Ma's Superette. When churches are burned in Alabama, the family receives a letter asking for baptismal records for Monna Floyd, and Marley's parents then tell her she was the child of Jack and Christine Floyd. Christine was killed in an automobile accident and "Uncle" Jack could not cope with this, so he and Boy began drifting on the road and writing to Marley. Marley is furious with her parents and with Jack for not telling her the truth. With the help of Bobby and his baby, Feather, for whom Marley babysits, and with the help of Shoogy Maple, Marley's friend who cuts herself and hates her "perfect" family, Marley learns what family really is. "Uncle" Jack finally returns to visit and tells her stories about her biological mother, but Marley's memories of who really cares for her are those of her parents.

**Comments and Specific Suggestions:**
Students can be challenged to discuss how Marley changes over time and how she defines "family" by the end of the story. In addition, students might discuss the meaning of "family" or what makes a family. As an extension activity, students can create a postcard, like Uncle Jack's, from Marley to her family or to her birth mother, Christine, regarding what she has learned about herself and family. Students can also investigate the church burnings in Alabama. Important quotes for discussion throughout this book include:

- "People look for what they think they need, I guess. You find what you think you need and what might make you happy in different places with different people and sometimes it's just waiting in a tiny town in Ohio ... Heaven was waiting for us" (p. 9).

- "The two people I like most—outside my family—have secrets that I don't ask about ... I look at Shoogy and Bobby and think it doesn't matter 'cause the past doesn't always make sense of the future" (pp. 25–26).

- "Pops says, 'Sometimes it's easy to tell where you are. Just look around and notice the people who have always been there for you, and follow them' " (p. 99).

- Marley states what she would want Christine to know, "I love the people who raised me by that river, and that I love the man who finally came back to tell me the stories I needed to hear from so long ago" (p. 138).

**Themes:**
Precious child
Understanding the meaning of family
Developing an identity
Trust, honesty, and "family secrets"

**Title:** *Heaven Eyes*
**Author(s):** David Almond
**Illustrator:** None
**Publisher:** Delacorte Press, an Imprint of Random House, New York
**Date of Publication:** 2000
**Awards:** An ALA Notable Children's Book for 2002
**Reading Levels:** AR Int. Level Middle Grades, BL 3.4; Lexile Level 420L

**Summary:**
Erin Law, January Carr, and Mouse Gullane all live in Whitegates, a home for orphans in St. Gabriels, England. January was named for the month he was left on the steps of Carr Hill Hospital as a baby. He is angry that he has no memory or evidence of his birth family, "I've got nothing, you know . . . No treasures. No photographs. No earrings. No lipsticks. Nothing. Not even a memory. Just dreams and stupid thoughts and stupid hopes . . . Sometimes . . . I want to hate everybody. I want to hate them and hurt them and make them hate me" (p. 151). Mouse carries a mouse named Squeaks. His mother, like Erin's, died and his father simply disappeared. Mouse has tattooed on him the words, "Please look after me," and he has a few pictures and memories of his father. Erin's "mum" was a young, single parent who took good care of Erin until she died when Erin was just ten. Erin has some of her mother's belongings and often talks to her "mum" whose presence she still feels near her. Erin and January dislike Maureen, who runs Whitegates and who calls them all "damaged children." Maureen and the psychiatrists, social workers, and psychologists are always trying to get the children to talk about their issues, problems, and memories and to make Life Books, all of which the children resent. "We always knew that if we cared for each other, we could put up with the psychiatrists who came, the psychologists, the social workers, the caregivers, the play therapists, the drug counselors, the health workers, the welfare workers" (p. 6). Erin, January, and Mouse run away from Whitegates and raft down the River Tyne, where they are stranded in the Black Middens. Heaven Eyes and her "Grandpa," a crazy watchman in an abandoned printing factory, rescue the children. Grandpa had also rescued Heaven Eyes from the black mud and tried to protect her from her life story. Eventually Heaven Eyes learns that she had two brothers and a sister and that her parents and siblings all drowned at sea, but she had washed ashore at the Black Middens. Her name had been Anna May. Heaven Eyes always sees the good in everyone and everything, and she is completely trusting and childlike. In the end, Grandpa dies and Heaven Eyes returns to Whitegates with the other children. January's "mum" returns for him just as he always dreamed and knew she would.

**Comments and Specific Suggestions:**
This is a very unusual and somewhat unsettling orphan adventure/survival tale. Heaven Eyes is quite difficult to understand since she has an odd way of speaking, but she is aptly named since she always feels joy and love in those around her. Her innocence is a symbol for the children's stories despite their difficult situation. The changing relationship among the friends is another important area for discussion. Teachers might, for example, ask children to share how friendships change when new people enter the group and how January's and Erin's friendship changed during the story. As an extension activity, teachers might have students write a letter to one of the children's parents describing the child's life. They might also take the perspective of one of the children and record

their "memories" or emotions in a diary or "life book" during the adventure. Students might also enjoy researching the Black Middens and the River Tyne. Finally, information about the United Kingdom stage production of *Heaven Eyes* is available online.

**Themes:**
Orphan adventure/survival tale
Coping with strong emotions—loss, death, abandonment
Understanding the meaning of family
Joy and love from friends as "family"

**Title:** *Heck Superhero*
**Author(s):** Martine Leavitt
**Illustrator:** None
**Publisher:** Front Street, an Imprint of Boyds Mills Press, Asheville, ND
**Date of Publication:** 2004
**Awards:** None
**Reading Levels:** AR Int. Level Middle Grades, BL 4.2; Lexile Level 610L

**Summary:**
Heck adores comic books and loves to draw and fantasize about superheroes and superpowers. He fantasizes that he lives in a "multiverse" where he can perform "molecular joining" with his friends. Heck's mother lives in "hypertime"; she is mentally ill or on drugs and she disappears for long periods of time. When they are evicted from their apartment for not paying bills, Heck says he will stay with his friend, Spence. His mother then disappears. Heck really lives on the streets and befriends an 18-year-old boy named Marion who is mentally ill. Marion eventually kills himself, and Heck, in the hospital afterward, realizes he needs to be in reality rather than dragged down by his fantasies. He is reunited with his mother who now tries to get help for them both.

**Comments and Specific Suggestions:**
This novel contains many difficult concepts and, therefore, is recommended only for more mature readers despite the estimated reading level. Ultimately, Heck learns to ask for help and learns that even a "superhero" requires assistance. Because Heck "draws" his life as a comic book, students might enjoy finding out about the history and development of the comic book or creating a comic book of one day or one event in their own lives.

**Themes:**
Orphan adventure/survival tale
Search for a family
Longing for a place to belong and a home
Learning to ask for help and trust others

**Title:** *Home, and Other Big Fat Lies*
**Author(s):** Jill Wolfson
**Illustrator:** None
**Publisher:** Henry Holt and Company, New York
**Date of Publication:** 2006
**Awards:** None
**Reading Levels:** AR Int. Level Middle Grades, BL 4.4; Lexile Level 740L

**Summary:**
Whitney, nicknamed Termite because she looks so small and young for her age, is a hyperactive and rude sixth grader who is moved to foster care home number 12 outside of the city of Oakland, California. Her new foster family in Northern California, the McCrays, took her for the income. "I was glad when they were finally done with the dollars-and-cents part because even though I know that I come with a price tag around my neck, I still

get a weird feeling when I hear about the actual ka-ching" (p. 31). Many families in the town of Timberville have taken foster care children since the lumber mill has closed, due to pressure from environmentalists, and put many people out of work. Termite makes friends with other foster children there, and they form a nature and ecology club with their science teacher. Termite learns to love the big woods and in particular a huge tree named "Big Momma." Termite, the nature club, and Striker, the son of Termite's foster parents who does not want to be a logger like his father and see the big forest cut down, team up to save Big Momma, but not the entire forest. Termite finds a sense of belonging with Big Momma, "I wasn't an outsider anymore. There was a place I belonged. I had been to the inside of Big Momma, way up in her branches, surrounded by her smell. I had been to the inside of the tree, and now the tree was inside me" (p. 239). Some of the foster children leave as the local economy improves and others get adopted or stay, like Termite, with their foster families.

## Comments and Specific Suggestions:

Termite is spunky and has a hilarious way of mixing up her words or figures of speech and then making her version "fit" the situation. Students might enjoy tracing how Termite's expressions and misuse of words change from the beginning to the ending of the book. When Termite moves to Northern California, she no longer feels as different since so many foster children live in Timberville. She knows that the others will understand that, ". . . There's something really nice about having my clothes smell like me . . . like I belong somewhere, at least like I belong in my own body. But try explaining that to people who have lived in only one or two houses their entire lives" (p. 19). Termite believes that "Some people act like foster is a dirty word . . . like it's my fault that I had the dumb luck to be born to parents that I never met" (p. 59) and that "No one wanted me or any of us to stay forever. Home! What a big fat lie. It was home just until the turnaround, whatever a turnaround is" (p. 85). Termite begins to sense her first real connection through Big Momma, a symbol of permanence and the mother figure in the forest. As she comes to accept a home, she watches banana slugs hatching and thinks, "Every banana slug mother takes off, not just a few like in the human world. So, there's probably a good reason for why the kids are left on their own. The banana slug kids, I mean, not the human ones. There's no real good reason for that" (p. 249). On a final note, links can easily be made to social studies and economics as students might research the logging and lumber industries' battle with environmentalists and the effect on local economies in the Pacific Northwest.

## Themes:

Longing for a place to belong, a home, and permanence
Wanting to be loved
Coping with feelings of difference

**Title:** *How It Feels to Be Adopted*
**Author(s):** Jill Krementz
**Illustrator:** None
**Publisher:** Alfred A. Knopf, New York
**Date of Publication:** 1983
**Awards:** None
**Reading Levels:** None Found

## Summary:

Nineteen boys and girls, ages 8 through 16, of various ethnic and cultural groups were interviewed regarding their feelings about being adopted. Some of the children were adopted as infants, some through domestic adoption, some through foster care placement, and some through intercountry adoption. The children's feelings range from Jake, age 13, "I don't know anything about my birthfather and I don't wonder about him at all. I think about being adopted, but, you know, I never really think about having another mother. I just consider the mother I have as my mom" (p. 4) to Barbara, age 16, "I just desperately want to have a part of my life that's entirely mine, my own . . . Being adopted can be embarrassing—like when people start talking about their nationalities and you just have to be quiet" (p. 38) to Jack, age 12, whose friends once said, "Let's go over to Jack's house to play. He's adopted and his parents have to be nice to him" (p. 71).

**Comments and Specific Suggestions:**
Students who have been adopted or placed in foster care will see themselves reflected somewhere in this book and their friends may see themselves as well! Teachers can lead students to discuss how adoption does or does not affect a teenager's sense of self. Compare and contrast the adolescents in the book as they search for their identity with other teens as they engage in their search for self.

**Themes:**
Coping with strong emotions
Comprehending adoption and foster care
Search for family
Search for identity

**Title:** *If It Hadn't Been for Yoon Jun*
**Author(s):** Marie G. Lee
**Illustrator:** None
**Publisher:** Houghton Mifflin Company, Boston, MA
**Date of Publication:** 1993
**Awards:** None
**Reading Levels:** AR Int. Level Middle grades, BL 5.2; Lexile Level 740L

**Summary:**
Alice Larsen was adopted from Korea when she was just a baby. She has grown up an American girl in Minnesota with her best friends, Minna and Laura. She even makes the cheerleading squad, along with Minna, as a seventh grader and begins to receive the attention of Troy Hill, a seventh grade football player at their junior high school. When a new boy from Korea, Yoon Jun, moves to town with his mother, Alice is upset that her parents want her to get acquainted with him and that her father is always pushing her to learn about Korean culture. She does not want to be different at a time when she is becoming popular in her school. Through the actions of a bully, Travis, and his father, Alice learns how others in her town hate Asian people and Native Americans. Alice becomes acquainted with Julie Graywolf, an eighth grade cheerleader's friend. At first Alice believes both Yoon Jun and Julie to be strange and "weird," but after completing a project with Yoon Jun, she begins to learn about her Korean heritage. "That's what she would like best, she decided, to be able to blend in completely with her family, to be blond like Mary. But as she thought this, she couldn't ignore the sounds of Korean words beating like far-off drums in her head" (p. 105). Alice starts thinking about someday writing a letter to her birth family through the adoption agency, and she also discovers how similar others like Julie and Yoon Jun are to her.

**Comments and Specific Suggestions:**
The story is a bit stereotypical, particularly when Alice's best friend of many years asks her about her "real" parents. Nevertheless, the story deals with feelings of difference, an area of concern for middle grade students. Teachers might lead a discussion by asking, How would you feel if you were popular and someone new came to the school and took over your place? How would you feel to be new at your school? How are Alice, Yoon Jun, and Julie the same and how are they different?

**Themes:**
Coping with feelings of difference
Intercountry and transracial adoption
Search for identity

**Title:** *I'll Sing You One-O*
**Author(s):** Nan Gregory
**Illustrator:** None
**Date of Publication:** 2006
**Awards:** None
**Reading Levels:** AR Int. Level Middle Grades, BL 4.4; Lexile Level 750L

**Summary:**

Gemma, a 12-year-old girl, is removed from the only home and family she has ever known, the "A's" at the Andersen farm. Gemma loves "Mr." and "Mrs." and the other children in her foster family, Jess, Arlie, Darren, and baby Meg, as well as her hen, Pippi Longstocking. Gemma is to be adopted by her Uncle Dave and her Aunt Moira, who had been looking for Gemma for a long time and had finally located her. She never knew about the Burdettes or about her twin brother Garnet. Ruby, Gemma's mother, was Uncle Dave's older sister through her own adoption into his family. The Andersen farm is up for sale because the "A's" are no longer going to be raising foster care children. Gemma believes that if she does "good things" she can get an angel to notice her and then help save the farm from being sold. She gives her allowance received from the Burdettes away to a homeless woman, Willow, and then to get money for Christmas presents since she has not saved her allowance, she sells what she later finds out to be a priceless family heirloom, a WWI commemorative set of lead soldiers including an angel on horseback, which she keeps as a sign that she is doing the right thing. When she is discovered, Gemma runs away. She finds that the farm has been sold and the "A's" are leaving, taking only Jess with them. She goes to a hotel, followed by Garnet, with a strangely familiar neon sea horse flashing red/pink and green. There, Gemma remembers being abandoned and locked in a room as a four-year-old for several days until the police broke down the door and found her. She had been terrified at night of the flashing sea horse that now haunted her dreams as the nightmare dragon, "Red Boy." Gemma finally discovers the truth about her past. Ruby had always had difficulty, running away and using drugs. Ruby had taken Gemma with her because she had feared that her brother Dave and his wife would take Gemma just as they had taken Garnet. Garnet had been quite ill as an infant, and the childless couple had taken him to the hospital and then refused to return him to Ruby. They gave Ruby money to sign adoption papers and had wanted to adopt Gemma as well. When Ruby ran away again, they had never given up looking for Gemma. In the end, the Burdettes assure Gemma that Ruby had never meant to leave her and that the only way Ruby would not have returned for her was death. Gemma finally begins to open herself to her family.

**Comments and Specific Suggestions:**

The story is a vivid and poignant first person account of Gemma's search for the truth about her life. Teachers can lead students in an interesting discussion regarding how Gemma changes over time and tries to solve her dilemma. Gemma's wishful thinking and thought processes (e.g., selling "old stuff" that nobody cares about, an angel will notice and help) are quite realistic for children in this age group and can easily be compared to characters in other stories such as Galadriel in *The Great Gilly Hopkins* (Paterson, 1978). About Mr. A., Gemma says, "He taught me the thousands when I first came to the farm, back when I was four. I arrived not talking at all, just singing the question song over and over and over as high as I could count and throwing tantrums all over the place" (p. 3). Mr. A. taught Gemma to count when she was angry or upset. Red Boy is quite haunting and terrifying, "Red Boy stands at the top of a rise . . . he crushes the house and the barn together . . . everyone is calling for help, and I'm behind this glass wall and I can't get to them and I can't look away" (p. 189). Students might also enjoy researching the old song "I'll Sing You One-O," the song her mother sang just before she left and the question song she sang over and over upon arrival at the Andersen farm, and its significance as the title for the novel: "Now I know. I'm One is one. I'm all alone and I always will be. I'm not a saint. I'm not special. I'm just another kid abandoned by her mom. A piece of garbage to be tossed away and forgotten. Not worth a mom's going back for. Not worth the A's taking to Mexico . . ." (p. 204).

**Themes:**

Coping with strong emotions—abandonment, feeling unloved and worthless, hidden traumas, longing to feel safe and loved
Letting go of the past
Search for family
Coming of age and search for identity

**Title:** *Locomotion*
**Author(s):** Jacqueline Woodson
**Illustrator:** None
**Publisher:** G. P. Putnam's Sons, a Division of Penguin Group, New York

**Date of Publication:** 2003
**Awards:** An ALA Notable Children's Book for 2003
**Reading Levels:** AR Int. Level Middle Grades, BL 4.7; Lexile Level NP

**Summary:**
Lonnie Collins Motion was so named because his mother loved the song "Locomotion" and would dance to it with Lonnie and his sister, Lili. When Loco was only four, his parents died in a house fire. Loco and Lili were cared for by various church members until finally they were placed in a group home. Lili was adopted quickly, but Loco was placed in a foster home with Miss Edna who has two grown sons, one fighting "far away in a war" and Rodney who comes back from "upstate" and calls Loco "Little Brother." Loco grows fond of Miss Edna and Rodney, but he routinely visits Lili at "her new mama's house" or at the "agency" because he and Lily want to stay together as a family. Loco's memories of his mother are sweet, "You know honeysuckle talc powder? Mama used to smell like that . . . sometimes when the missing gets real bad I go to the drugstore and before the guard starts following me around like I'm gonna steal something I go to the cosmetics lady and ask her if she has it . . . I say can I smell it to see if it's the right one . . . and for those few seconds, Mama's alive again" (p. 7).

**Comments and Specific Suggestions:**
The entire book revealing Lonnie's life story is written as nonstandard prose, including poetry of various forms such as free style, Haiku, and sonnets. Lonnie's fifth-grade teacher, Ms. Marcus, who is later named teacher of the year, encourages Lonnie to write his feelings down as poetry. The novel is believable and moving as Lonnie strives to cope with his feelings of grief and rejection. As students read the book, they might discuss how certain smells trigger strong memories and examine why Lonnie smells the talc powder at the store. Students might also write what they believe Lonnie's life will be like five or ten years from the time of the story. As additional enrichment activities, teachers might encourage students to research the song "Locomotion" or to choose one of their own memories and write it in Haiku or freestyle verse. (See also Chapter 5 for an additional novel, *Coming on Home Soon*, written by Jacquelyn Woodson in 2004.)

**Themes:**
Coping with strong emotions—hurt, grief, rejection, abandonment
Importance of preserving family and memories
Accepting a new home

**Title:** *Maniac Magee*
**Author(s):** Jerry Spinelli
**Illustrator:** None
**Publisher:** Little, Brown, and Company, Boston, MA
**Date of Publication:** 1990
**Awards:** Newbery Medal Winner for 1991
**Reading Levels:** AR Int. Level Middle Grades, BL 4.7; Lexile Level 820L

**Summary:**
Jeffrey Lionel Magee was three when his parents were killed in an accident after a trolley plunged off a trestle bridge. Jeffrey no longer allows himself to look at the bridge. He lives with his Aunt Dot and Uncle Dan who feud constantly but who will not divorce because they are Catholic. Finally, Jeffrey runs away to Two Mills, a town just across the river from Bridgeport where he was born. Through the growth of numerous street legends, he earns the name "Maniac Magee" and begins to live in both the "black" and the "white" sides of town. Jeffrey does not understand the differences of "color" until he sees Mrs. Beale and her family become the target of someone in the East End. Once again, Jeffrey runs away and stays with Mr. Grayson, a park keeper, at "101 Band Shell Boulevard." Mr. Grayson loves Jeffrey and Jeffrey teaches Mr. Grayson how to read, but when Mr. Grayson dies, Jeffrey runs away once more and stays with the McNabs, a West End family that believes the East Enders will riot and come to their side of town someday. Jeffrey tries to help the East Enders and West Enders realize that they are only different from each other by their "colors." When Jeffrey rescues a child from the trestle bridge, his enemy,

Mars Bar, finally becomes his friend and Jeffrey returns to live with the Beales. He has always yearned for an address and to be a face at a window looking out! "It had to do with homes and families and schools, and how a school seems sort of like a big home, but only a day home, because then it empties out; and you can't stay there at night because it's not really a home, and you could never use it as your address, because an address is where you stay at night, where you walk right in the front door without knocking . . . School. Home. No, he was not going to have one without the other" (p. 86).

**Comments and Specific Suggestions:**
The novel is an entertaining, inner city, "street legend" or "urban tall tale." Students might make a list of exaggerations from the story or list the parts of Maniac's life that are fact and those that are fiction/legend. Teachers might also help children examine why having an address meant so much to Maniac. As an extension activity, students can research the history of segregation in urban areas such as Bridgeport.

**Themes:**
Orphan adventure/survival tale
Longing for an address and a home
Wanting to belong and to feel safe
Search for family
Search for identity

**Title:** *Moccasin Trail*
**Author(s):** Eloise Jarvis McGraw
**Illustrator:** None
**Publisher:** Coward-McCann, Inc., New York
**Date of Publication:** 1952
**Awards:** A Newbery Honor Book for 1953
**Reading Levels:** AR Int. Level Middle Grades, BL 5.8; Lexile Level 960L

**Summary:**
Jim Keath ran away from home as a boy. After being attacked by a grizzly bear and killing it, he was rescued by Crow Indians who raised him as their own "Son of Scalp Necklace," "Talks Alone." As a wagon train moves west, Jim finds out his mother and father have died, but his two younger brothers, Jonathan and Daniel, and his younger sister, Sally, are with the wagon train. He helps them west to Oregon and helps them settle the land, but his Crow "medicine," years of "counting coup," and years of beaver trapping with his old friend, Tom Russell, haunt him and call him back. He finally reconciles his past, decides to stay with his siblings, and understands the old ways are fading as the land is changing with the coming of the settlers. As Jim returns to his family, he thinks, "My valley . . . my people. Home" (p. 224). Jim and his siblings place his braids and bear claws in a leather box so they would always remember his "other family," and they place his coup feather with their Pa's medal in a place of honor under the family clock.

**Comments and Specific Suggestions:**
If teachers recommend this book, they should realize that the language of the 1950s is not as "politically correct" as the language of today, particularly with respect to Native Americans. The grammar and Native American vocabulary may also be a bit difficult for some students to read. Nevertheless, this is an adventure tale that might appeal to some children in grades 6–8. Parallels can be drawn between the two worlds of "Talks Alone" and Jim Keath and the cross-cultural adjustments of children of intercountry or transracial adoption. Children might also research the Crow Indians or read other books by Eloise Jarvis McGraw such as *The Moorchild*, written in 1996.

**Themes:**
Orphan adventure/survival tale
Living between two cultures

Search for family
Developing an identity

**Title:** *Orphan Train Rider: One Boy's True Story*
**Author(s):** Andrea Warren
**Illustrator:** None
**Publisher:** Houghton Mifflin Company, Boston, MA
**Date of Publication:** 1996
**Awards:** An ALA Notable Children's Book for 1997
**Reading Levels:** AR Int. Level Middle Grades, BL 6.1; Lexile Level 960L

**Summary:**

Lee Nailling, born as Alton Lou Clement, was only seven when his mother died. His father was unable to cope with his grief or with seven children, so he sent Lee's two older brothers and older sister out to take care of themselves on the streets. The new baby, Gregory, and his youngest brother, Gerald, were taken by others. Lee and his next oldest brother, Leo, were finally taken to the Jefferson County Orphan Asylum in New York. Lee says, "The adults in charge did not beat the children as they did at some orphanages, but they never showed the children any affection either... What I learned was that all adults lied to you... Our father had deserted us; our relatives didn't care about us; the people running the orphanage did only what they had to for us. I came to distrust anything an adult said to me" (p. 19). Two years later Lee and Leo rode the orphan trains, ultimately adopted by two neighboring families, as was Gerald who was brought to the train station by their father just as their train left. Lee finally grew to love his new family, the Naillings, although he was affected by the experience his entire life. "For years I felt like something was missing in my life" (p. 64). He reunited at age 67 with his oldest brother, Ross, and youngest brother, George. The book alternates between Lee telling his own stories as one of the remaining orphan train riders still alive and chapters giving history about orphanages, the orphan trains, and Charles Loring Brace's "placing out" of homeless children through founding the Children's Aid Society.

**Comments and Specific Suggestions:**

Pictures of some of the original advertisements for "placing" out orphans are shown in the book. These, and the stories of what happened to some of the children, could be disturbing for less mature students. Lee Nailling won an award in 1994 from the Orphan Train Society for helping the public learn about the orphan trains.

**Themes:**

Orphan train story
Coping with strong emotions—anger, confusion, loss, feeling incomplete and inferior
Search for family

**Title:** *Pictures of Hollis Woods*
**Author(s):** Patricia Reilly Giff
**Illustrator:** None
**Publisher:** Wendy Lamb Books, a Trademark of Random House, New York
**Date of Publication:** 2002
**Awards:** A Newbery Honor Book for 2003
**Reading Levels:** AR Int. Level Middle Grades, BL 4.4; Lexile Level 650L

**Summary:**

Hollis Woods is 12 years old, a gifted artist who is named after the place where she was found abandoned as a baby. Hollis considers herself to be a "mountain of trouble" who frequently runs away from the many foster homes in which she has been placed. When Hollis is placed with the Regans (i.e., Izzy, the "Old Man," and their son, 13-year-old Steven) in their summer place at Branches, she feels at home and as though she belongs. She is happy and the Regans want to adopt her, but Hollis believes she is creating a problem for the family because

Steven and the "Old Man" are always arguing. After an accident on the "Old Man's mountain" where Steven gets hurt, Hollis runs away back to a previous foster home because she considers the accident to be her fault. She hopes the social worker, the "Mustard Lady," will have to place her again. She is then placed with Josie, an eccentric artist who is quickly losing her memory. Hollis likes Josie and realizes after Josie's sister, Beatrice, also an artist, leaves to paint out west that Josie cannot take care of herself. Hollis does not want to be taken away from Josie so she takes Josie to Branches in the depths of the winter. At Christmas time, Hollis recognizes that Josie misses her home on the ocean and that she belongs in Long Island rather than in the mountains. She also realizes that Steven must know she is at Branches and that he has been leaving supplies, riding in on his snowmobile. Josie sets out to find Steven. With Steven's help, she calls Beatrice, who is delighted to return home to care for Josie, and then calls Izzy to ask if she can come home.

**Comments and Specific Suggestions:**
The story is told alternately between the present with Josie and recollections of her time with the Regans illustrated through pictures that Hollis has drawn of the events. As Hollis examines the pictures, she realizes the truth in what Beatrice once told her: "Drawing is what you see of the world, truly see . . . and sometimes what you see is so deep in your head you're not even sure of what you're seeing. But when it's down on paper, and you look at it, really look, you'll see the way things are" (p. 45). As Hollis looks at the pictures, she realizes that Steven and his dad do fight because that is the way they are, but that they love each other completely. Teachers might have students depict the many characters in the book through a portrait of Hollis's family. The book was also made into a Hallmark Hall of Fame television movie which aired on CBS in December 2007.

**Themes:**
Precious child
Coping with strong emotions—grief, hurt, anger, abandonment
Longing to belong and have a home
Understanding the meaning of family

**Title:** *Raspberry House Blues*
**Author(s):** Linda Holeman
**Illustrator:** None
**Publisher:** Tundra Books, Plattsburgh, NY
**Date of Publication:** 2000
**Awards:** None
**Reading Levels:** AR Int. Level Middle Grades, BL 4.2

**Summary:**
Poppy lives with her mother, with whom she does not "get along." Poppy was adopted by her parents and then her mother and father divorced. Her father has remarried, and he and his new wife are having a baby. Poppy's mother is going to Greece with her boyfriend, and Poppy is to spend the summer at her father's house. Poppy has always spent her time cutting out pictures of mothers and placing them into her "Mother's Book." When intending to hurt her mother, she says, "Some mother you are . . . but then you aren't a real mother . . . you're just a pretend mother" (p. 13), and "I'm talking about my real mother, not an adopted one or a stepmother. I'm talking about the connection of blood. The way that connection is so special, so huge that it can make you finally feel that you know who you are" (p. 188). Because her father lives in the town where she was born, Poppy decides to search for her birth mother. She thinks she has discovered her birth mother in an eccentric woman who has red hair like Poppy's and who also placed a child for adoption. In the end, Poppy is disappointed to find that the woman is not her birth mother, but rather was simply lying to her. Poppy comes to accept her father, stepmother, and mother as her parents and family.

**Comments and Specific Suggestions:**
Some of the conversation is a bit stereotypical, but the book is easy to read. Teachers can lead students in a discussion about how Poppy sees only what she wants to see, at home with her family and with the eccentric woman

with red hair. In addition, following research on blues music, students might talk about how "Raspberry House" is like a "Blues" song.

**Themes:**
Precious child
Search for identity
Understanding the meaning of family
Search for birth family

**Title:** *Ruby Holler*
**Author(s):** Sharon Creech
**Illustrator:** None
**Publisher:** Harper Trophy/Joanna Cotter Books, an Imprint of HarperCollins Publishers, New York
**Date of Publication:** 2002
**Awards:** A Carnegie Medal Winner for Children's Literature for 2002
**Reading Levels:** AR Int. Level Middle Grades, BL 4.3; Lexile Level 660L

**Summary:**
Thirteen-year-old twins, Dallas and Florida, were named for two tourist pamphlets the boy and girl were laying on in a box when they were found by the Trepids at the Boxton Creek Home for Children. Dallas and Florida consider themselves to be trouble. They have been placed in a number of different foster homes, most of which were very bad (e.g., they were locked in a cellar), and they have always been returned to the Boxton Creek Home. When Tiller and Sairy Morey take them, they travel to Ruby Holler, a beautiful spot for children to grow up. Tiller and Sairy are planning separate trips. Tiller plans to take Florida down the Rutabago River on a boat he is building, and Sairy wants to take Dallas hiking on Kangadoon to see a special bird. They "try out" the boat and camping gear on a smaller trip and Tiller and Florida almost drown. Tiller has a heart attack and is saved by Florida. The four decide it would be better to stay in Ruby Holler, and the twins finally feel free and wanted. They start to run away again, but Tiller and Sairy come with their "welcome-home" bacon.

**Comments and Specific Suggestions:**
Sharon Creech has written a number of wonderful books for the middle grades. Students can be asked to compare and contrast the twins and to compare and contrast Tiller and Sairy Morey. Dallas and Florida obviously do not trust adults or understand the concept of a family. For example, when Dallas looks at family pictures of Sairy and Tiller, he asks, "How do we know who we are? How will we know what we'll be?" (p. 44), and later he remembers hearing the Trepids say they had "listed their birth date as the day they arrived at the orphanage. So Dallas thought, their real birthday must have been several months before that . . . It made him mad. A person ought to know when his birthday was" (p. 219). Students can engage in a discussion of trust: Who do we trust and how do we develop trust? In addition, students might describe a "holler" by writing using adjectives, by constructing a diorama, or by drawing a picture.

**Themes:**
Precious child
Longing to belong and have a home
Understanding the meaning of family
Coping with strong emotions—abandonment
Learning to trust
Developing an identity

**Title:** *Saffy's Angel*
**Author(s):** Hilary McKay
**Illustrator:** None
**Publisher:** Aladdin Paperbacks, an Imprint of Simon and Schuster, New York

**Date of Publication:** 2001
**Awards:** An ALA Notable Children's Book for 2003
**Reading Levels:** AR Int. Level Middle Grades, BL 4.5; Lexile Level 630L

**Summary:**
In this odd, chaotic family, Eve, the mother, paints, and Bill, the father, lives his own life as a painter in London. Caddy, Saffron (i.e., Saffy), Indigo, and Rose live with Eve in the "Banana House." Saffy found out at age eight that she was adopted by Eve and Bill when Eve's twin sister, Linda, was killed in a car crash in Siena, Italy, when Saffy was only three years old. "Everything seemed to change for Saffron after the day she deciphered the color chart and discovered that her name was not on there and found out why this was. She never felt the same again. She felt lost" (p. 9). Her grandfather had brought her to Eve and returned to get a stone angel from the garden of their home in Siena, but he had a heart attack before he could tell the family about it. He never spoke again except to say "Saffron" one time. With the help of her siblings and her friend, Sarah, who uses a wheelchair, Saffy goes to Italy and finds her angel again. The angel was left to her in her grandfather's will, and to Saffy was "... proof that she mattered as much as anyone else" (p. 116). Saffy comes to accept that this is her family and she loves them just as they love her. "Then it was time to go home, and Saffron was still all right. Happy even. How strange it was, she thought, to have come so far and found so little and feel so contented" (p. 122).

**Comments and Specific Suggestions:**
Although the events are quite funny, teachers will certainly want to help children understand that the characters in this story use poor judgment. For example, Saffy hides in her friend's car to go to Europe without telling her parents, and her sister, Rose, eats paint! Children might discuss how we all sometimes lack judgment and make poor choices. In addition, students can describe or illustrate the "odd ball" characters in this family or they might illustrate the "Banana House." One important question, of course, is, What does the angel represent to Saffy?

**Themes:**
Precious child
Comprehending adoption story
Coping with strong emotions—loss, distrust, and anger
Understanding the meaning of family
Belonging and understanding importance of family history

**Title:** *The Angel Factory*
**Author(s):** Terence Blacker
**Illustrator:** None
**Publisher:** Simon and Schuster, New York
**Date of Publication:** 2001
**Awards:** None
**Reading Levels:** AR Int. Level Upper Grades, BL 4.9; Lexile Level 700L

**Summary:**
Thomas Wisdom, age 12, with the help of his best friend, Gip, "hacks" his father's computer. He discovers he was adopted as an infant. Thomas is furious with his parents about their lie, but then he uncovers an even greater secret. His parents, his sister, Amy, his dog, Dougal, and even his best friend, Gip, are "angels" created at an "Angel Factory" in California. They are controlled by the Presence, a society or being in a universe far beyond ours. The angels are on Earth to help humankind from destroying itself. They are placed in positions of power serving as police, teachers, media workers, and so forth. Even the president of the United States, President Foxx, is an angel. Angels cannot reproduce themselves and, therefore, many angels have adopted humans to participate in Phase II of the "Project," humans helping the angels to save humankind. Ultimately, Thomas finds his birth mother, comes to appreciate his parents, and shuts down the Project. He wonders if the Presence is watching and perhaps respecting the free will and need for freedom of humans. The angels on Earth now become human to live out the rest of their lives before returning to the Presence.

## Comments and Specific Suggestions:

Although the stated interest level is upper grades, the estimated reading level is fourth grade; therefore, the novel is included with literature for older readers. Nevertheless, this is a strange science fiction story that may not be appropriate for all children in grades 6–8. The notion that "angels" are adopting children is somewhat stereotypical; however, parallels can also easily be made with religious philosophy and with the battle between "good" and "evil" forces. Thomas's anger, hurt, and distrust over having not been told of his adoption by the age of 12 are quite realistic, though. The story takes place in and around London, England.

## Themes:

Search for identity
Need to belong to family
Search for meaning, independence, and control of one's destiny
Choice, free will, and freedom
Need for honesty and trust

**Title:** *The Crying Rocks*
**Author(s):** Janet Taylor Lisle
**Illustrator:** None
**Publisher:** A Richard Jackson Book, Atheneum Books for Young Readers, an Imprint of Simon and Schuster, New York
**Date of Publication:** 2003
**Awards:** None
**Reading Levels:** AR Int. Level Middle Grades, BL 4.5; Lexile Level 770L

## Summary:

Joelle has only fleeting memories of her trip from Chicago on a freight train and only conflicting stories about her past, such as that she was thrown from a third floor window and lived in a box at the railway depot. Her parents, "Aunt Mary Louise" and "Uncle Vernon," have told her very little about her life story. Joelle, who is very tall, has never felt that she fit in with others at her school or in her town. She befriends Carlos, a boy in her Spanish class, who is fascinated by the Narragansett Indians who once occupied their part of Rhode Island. He tells Joelle that she looks like one of the Narragansett Indians in a mural at the library. Joelle discovers that she is of Narragansett descent. Her mother, Sylvie, had twins. Joelle was named Sissie, and her twin, Sylvia, had physical and cognitive challenges. When Sissie was only five, Sylvie jumped off the third floor balcony of their Chicago apartment, taking Sylvia with her in order to keep her from having to go back into the hospital as the social workers wanted. Sylvie's brothers arrived too late for Sylvie and Sylvia, but they rescued Sissie from entering the foster care system. As railroad workers, they managed to get Sissie from Chicago to Rhode Island where she stayed at the railroad depot with Queenie, Sylvie's aunt and a woman of Narragansett heritage. Uncle Vernon and Mary Louise adopted her, but Uncle Vernon was actually Joelle's birth father. He had discovered this, but never let Mary Louise know because he loved her and did not want to lose her. Vernon had only let others know that he "had been married before and had a child who died or something" (p. 36). Even the "adoption agency" was arranged by Vernon and Sylvie's brothers who had always been close. Mary Louise died never knowing that Vernon was Joelle's biological father. In the end, Joelle helps Carlos accept that it was not his fault that his older brother had fallen and died at the Crying Rocks.

## Comments and Specific Suggestions:

This is a beautiful and haunting tale full of interesting legends. Supposedly, Native American women would toss their children off the Crying Rocks if they were weak or disabled, and sometimes the women jumped taking their children with them. Legend has it that sometimes one can hear the cries of the mothers at the rocks. The similarity to Joelle's life is obvious when she says, "There's nothing more pathetic than a little child asking 'Do I get my own pillow?' as if she'd never been anything to anybody her whole life, as if she were a throw-out who needs to be reminded of that?" (p. 28), and when she states, "No mother on Earth would cast her child to the wind" (p. 8). Students might enjoy researching the Narragansett Indians or other Native American legends.

**Themes:**
Precious child
Coping with strong emotions—hidden traumas, abandonment, and prejudice
Search for identity
Understanding the meaning of family

**Title:** *The Folk Keeper*
**Author(s):** Franny Billingsley
**Illustrator:** None
**Publisher:** Atheneum Books for Young Readers, an Imprint of Simon and Schuster, New York
**Date of Publication:** 1999
**Awards:** An ALA Notable Children's Book for 2000
**Reading Levels:** AR Int. Level Middle Grades, BL 5.3; Lexile Level 690L

**Summary:**
Corinna lives in the Rhysbridge Foundling Home. When she is transported from another orphanage to Rhysbridge, in order to survive and escape the drudgery of carrying water buckets and scrubbing floors, she changes herself from Corinna to Corin and becomes the "Folk Keeper" at Rhysbridge, a post held only by boys. The Folk Keeper must stay in the cellar and keep the "Folk," all mouths and teeth that become harmful energy in the dark, from making mischief. Corinna has never felt she belonged in this world. She is sent for by Lord Merton on his deathbed to be the Cliffsend Folk Keeper and a family member. After a clue from Lord Merton as he dies, "Remember that, The Lady Rona" (p. 11), Corinna finds out she was the daughter of Lord Merton and Lady Rona, a "Sealfolk" maiden who went "mad" after Lord Merton destroyed her Sealskin. At her birth, Lord Merton took Corinna's Sealskin and put it on his trophy wall where it continued to grow and stretch as Corinna grew, but he told everyone that the baby had died. Lord Merton placed Corinna in a foundling home because she would not be an appropriate heir to the estate. At the end, when Corinna finds out all the secrets of her birth, she puts on her Sealskin and returns to the water where her long hair becomes her eyes and she does not need lungs. Corinna almost lets her skin become permanently attached so that she would become a Sealfolk, but then she decides she can be part of both worlds. She returns to Cliffsend, where Finian, Lord Merton's stepson by his most recent marriage to Lady Alicia, loves her and where she can be "human" and also return to the sea when she wants to, something Lady Rona never was able to discover.

**Comments and Specific Suggestions:**
This is an interesting fantasy novel in the tradition of orphan adventure and survival tales. Students can be asked to write in the form of a journal as Corinna does. In addition, students who enjoy fantasy may also like *The Moorchild* (McGraw, 1996).

**Themes:**
Orphan adventure/survival tale
Search for identity
Living between two cultures
Longing to belong and to be accepted

**Title:** *The Great Gilly Hopkins*
**Author(s):** Katherine Paterson
**Illustrator:** None
**Publisher:** Thomas Y. Crowell Company, New York
**Date of Publication:** 1978
**Awards:** A Newbery Honor Book for 1979
**Reading Levels:** AR Int. Level Middle Grades, BL 4.6; Lexile Level 800L

**Summary:**
A sixth grader, Galadriel, the name of the queen in J. R. R. Tolkien's book, has been shuttled from foster care home to foster care home ever since her first foster care family, the Dixons, moved to Florida and left her behind

like "the rest of the trash" in Washington, D.C. Angry and hurt, Gilly Hopkins gets into fights at school and creates trouble in each foster home placement until she is moved again. "The trick was in knowing how to dispose of people when you were through with them, and Gilly had had plenty of practice performing that trick" (p. 43). When Gilly is placed in another home with Mrs. Trotter, another foster child, William Ernest, and their next door neighbor, Mr. Randolph, the three capture Gilly's heart and teach her how to love no matter how hard she tries to push them away. "She'd spent all her life—at least all of it since the Dixons went to Florida and left her behind—making sure she didn't care about anyone but Courtney. She had known it never pays to attach yourself to something that is likely to blow away . . ." (p. 131). All of her life Gilly has believed that her mother, Courtney Hopkins, would come back from California for her. Gilly, desperate to meet her mother, sends Courtney a letter, lying about her "horrible" foster care placement. Courtney's mother, "Nonnie," who had not heard from Courtney for many years and who had not known about Gilly, comes to retrieve Gilly from Mrs. Trotter's home. After finally meeting Courtney, Gilly is disappointed to find that her mother does not really want her. Gilly then wants to go back home to Mrs. Trotter, where she is loved, but now she must stay with her grandmother who has been all alone for a long time. "I just wanted—what had she wanted? A home—but Trotter had tried to give her that. Permanence—Trotter had wanted to give her that as well. No, what she wanted was something Trotter had no power over. To stop being a 'foster child,' . . . to be real without any quotation marks. To belong and to possess . . ." (p. 124).

**Comments and Specific Suggestions:**
Students can certainly describe the changes in Gilly from the beginning of the story to its ending. Teachers can help students discuss how Gilly might feel about the unexpected results of her actions, living with "Nonnie" rather than with the people she has grown to love. Students might also be challenged to research Gilly's name, Galadriel, and if possible to compare and contrast Gilly's character with that of Tolkien's queen.

**Themes:**
Precious child
Coping with strong emotions—abandonment, anger, distrust
Longing to belong, have a permanent home, and feel loved
Letting go of the past
Searching for identity
Coming of age

**Title:** *The Higher Power of Lucky*
**Author(s):** Susan Patron
**Illustrator:** Matt Phelan
**Publisher:** Atheneum Books for Young Readers, an Imprint of Simon and Schuster, New York
**Date of Publication:** 2006
**Awards:** Newbery Medal Winner for 2007
**Reading Levels:** AR Int. Level Middle Grades, BL 5.9; Lexile Level 1010L

**Summary:**
Lucky carries her "survival backpack" to collect bugs and scientific specimens for her "museum" in Hard Pan, California. When her mother died in an accident by electrocution, her father called his first wife, Brigitte, who lived in France and never wanted children, to be Lucky's guardian. Lucky fears that Brigitte will miss France, return there, and place Lucky in a foster home or orphanage in Los Angeles. Lucky has two friends, Lincoln, who does nothing but tie knots, and five-year-old Miles, who lives with his grandmother, tells everyone that his mother is in Florida caring for a sick friend, and always carries around his favorite book, "Are You My Mother?" Lucky also enjoys hiding and listening to the "Twelve-Step People" at their meetings as they describe how they have hit "rock bottom" and then found their "higher power." Fearful that she will be sent away, Lucky runs into the desert, followed by Miles. "It's almost impossible to get control of your life when you're only ten. It's other people, adults, who have control of your life, because they can abandon you. They can die like Lucky's mother. They can decide they don't even want you, like Lucky's father" (p. 80). They stay sheltered during a dust storm

and Lucky tells Miles that his mother is not caring for a friend in Florida but instead is in jail. Miles finds it easier to know that his mother is in jail rather than continuing to believe that she is in Florida and simply does not want to come to visit him. When the town comes to rescue them, Lucky is finally ready to let go of her mother. She spreads her mother's ashes to the desert wind as she was unable to do two years ago at the memorial service. Later, Lucky finds out from Brigitte that she was planning to adopt Lucky all along. Lucky finds her "higher power" after hitting "rock bottom" just like the "Twelve Step People."

**Comments and Specific Suggestions:**
This novel is quite humorous, but it does deal with difficult themes. Both Miles and Lucky have suffered significant losses in their lives and both are searching for their mothers. Students may generate a list of what they believe to be in Lucky's "survival backpack" and give reasons why these items are of importance to Lucky. If they were to have a "survival backpack," what would it contain? Students can also discuss Lucky's "survival strategies" and the meaning of her "higher power." As an additional note, Susan Patron has recently released a sequel to this novel, *Lucky Breaks*, published in 2009.

**Themes:**
Precious child
Coping with strong emotions—abandonment and grief
Letting go of the past
Understanding the meaning of family
Searching for identity
Coming of age

**Title:** *The Invention of Hugo Cabret*
**Author(s):** Brian Selznick
**Illustrator:** Brian Selznick
**Publisher:** Scholastic Press, New York
**Date of Publication:** 2007
**Awards:** Caldecott Medal Winner for 2008
**Reading Levels:** AR Int. Level Middle Grades, BL 5.1; Lexile Level 820L

**Summary:**
Hugo Cabret, age 12, is like his father, very good with mechanical objects and tools. His father, a clock maker, finds an automaton, a mechanical man, in the attic of a museum and draws many sketches of it and its inner workings in order to repair it someday. Hugo's father, however, dies in a fire in the museum attic. Hugo is taken by his father's brother, Uncle Claude, to be a secret apprentice to him as the "clock keeper" for the train station in Paris, France. When Uncle Claude does not return one day and is later found dead because of his drinking problem, Hugo continues to tend the clocks and live secretly in the hidden apartments over the train station. He steals food from nearby merchants to survive, and he also steals mechanical parts from an elderly toy maker to repair the automaton he found in the ashes of the museum fire. Hugo is convinced that if he can repair the automaton the mechanical man will write him a message from his father that will help him out of his predicament. Hugo fears being caught by the Station Inspector or police because he does not want to be put in an orphanage. When the toy maker catches Hugo stealing from him and takes the notebook from him that contains drawings of the automaton made by his father, the toy maker demands to know where Hugo got the notebook. Through the help of Isabelle, the toy maker's goddaughter whom he and his wife are raising, he obtains a heart-shaped key Isabelle takes from "Papa George's" wife. Hugo gets the automaton working, and it draws a scene from an early movie that Hugo's father once told him about. It signs the name George Méliès, a famous early filmmaker in Paris. Isabelle and Hugo discover that Papa George, the toymaker, was once a famous magician who became a film-maker because he thought films were like magical dreams. They help him heal and accept movies back into his life again. Hugo is also "mended" as he indicated in his conversation with Isabelle, "Did you ever notice that all machines are made for some reason? . . . They are built to make you laugh, like the mouse here, or to tell the time, like clocks, or to fill you with wonder, like the automaton. Maybe that's why a broken machine always

makes me a little sad, because it isn't able to do what it was meant to do . . . Maybe it's the same with people . . . If you lose your purpose . . . it's like you're broken" (p. 374). Hugo finally enters the family with "Mama Jeanne," Isabelle, and Papa George, and he ultimately finds his purpose, using his mechanical talents to become a magician himself.

## Comments and Specific Suggestions:
This is a fascinating book! The black and white drawings are much like slides from an old movie. They are integrated so completely that they tell important parts of the story on their own. In addition, black and white "still" photographs from early movies are included. The entire novel is an intriguing blend of story text, "movie," and illustrations, which all contribute equally to the telling of this orphan adventure/survival tale. The title of the story is significant. Teachers can help students understand the nature of the time period in Paris and that Hugo had a family who loved him. Through unfortunate circumstances, Hugo was in a bad situation; however, he used his talents to "invent" himself again. Students may enjoy discovering that George Méliès was a famous filmmaker in Paris in the early 1900s and that the automata existed in the 1800s and were often made and used by magicians in France. Although the events in the novel are all fictional, Brian Selznick's Web site (http://Theinventionofhugocabret.com) contains wonderful links to the history of automata and a slide show of Paris. Students can also learn about the filmmaker George Méliès.

## Themes:
Orphan adventure/survival tale
Coping with strong emotions—fear
Longing to find love and a home
Coming of age
Searching for identity and purpose

**Title:** *The King of Slippery Falls*
**Author(s):** Sid Hite
**Illustrator:** None
**Publisher:** Scholastic Press, New York
**Date of Publication:** 2004
**Awards:** None
**Reading Levels:** AR Int. Level Upper Grades, BL 5.6

## Summary:
Lewis Hinton, a high school student, just found out a year ago that he was adopted. A French speaking woman had handed him as a baby in a basket to Avery Hinton. Avery and Martha Hinton were married immediately and then adopted Lewis. Lewis discovers that his name was Louis Poisson (i.e., the name on his birth note was J. A. Poisson or "fish" in French), and he believes that he might have been related to French nobility through Madame de Pompadour. Meanwhile, Lewis is teased because he spends his time trying to catch a huge trout living behind Slippery Falls. No one else has ever seen the trout and Lewis saw it only once as a large shadow behind the falls. In his confusion, Lewis spends much time at Slippery Falls watching for the trout and listening to the water as it falls, which says "Who are you?" to Lewis but says "You r you" to his friend Sophie (pp. 108–109). Eventually Lewis finds the big fish trapped in a hidden pool below the falls. Instead of catching the fish, he frees it from the pool, but falls as he does so. The fish supports Lewis until he gets to shore, unconscious from his fall over the rocks. The other older fishermen see, but do not understand what has happened. Lewis finally sets off to find out about his heritage in France, but he tells his mother, "We're family. If I searched for J. A. Poisson, and if by chance I found her, she would be a stranger I was meeting for the first time. I'd still be your son, Lewis Hinton. That will never change" (p. 128).

## Comments and Specific Suggestions:
Although the interest level is designated for the upper grades, the estimated reading level of the book is 5.9. No event or theme in the story is particularly difficult; therefore, the novel is included here as appropriate for most

students in grades 6–8. The message regarding one's search for self and the power of those beliefs we have about ourselves and our experiences is evident throughout the story. In addition, students might discuss the symbolism of the fish. Lewis, carrying the name Poisson, saves the fish, which in turn saves him. Lewis sets the fish free and finding the truth about his identity finally sets Lewis free.

**Themes:**
Precious child
Comprehending adoption story
Searching for one's past and heritage
Understanding the meaning of family
Coping with strong emotions—trust and need to feel secure
Developing an identity and the search for self

**Title:** *The Loner*
**Author(s):** Ester Wier
**Illustrator:** Christine Price
**Publisher:** David McKay Company, Inc., New York
**Date of Publication:** 1963
**Awards:** A Newbery Honor Book for 1964
**Reading Levels:** AR Int. Level Middle Grades, BL 5.3; Lexile Level 810L

**Summary:**
Probably set in the 1930s, a young boy travels with one group of crop pickers after another picking crops throughout the country until he meets Raidy, a young girl who is the first person ever to seem to care about him. The boy has no name and no memories of anything except for crop picking. He says, "Nobody ever called me anything that I can remember, 'cept Boy or Hey, You" and "Raidy explained to him how important a name was. It gave you a feeling of being someone, not just a stray" (p. 12). Unfortunately, Raidy dies in a picking accident before she tells him the name she has chosen for him. After Raidy's death, the boy goes to California where he is rescued from near death from starvation and the cold by Boss, a large woman who is a sheepherder who lost her only son, Ben. Through Boss's care, the boy gets the name David, a sheepherder in the Bible. He learns how to sheep herd and how to care for others, including Ben's widow, Angie, and Boss's hand, Tex. David now knows "... next week he would be going home, home to the ranch. Home was a special word to a loner, to a bum lamb ... It said, 'This is where you belong' " (p. 153).

**Comments and Specific Suggestions:**
Although teachers may need to help students understand the historical context and some of the expressions (e.g., "stray" and "bum lamb") used in the novel, the book is appropriate for most older readers. Students may need some discussion regarding the 1930s, the Depression, and crop picking. Researching sheepherding during that time period may also be of interest.

**Themes:**
Orphan as worker
Longing for home and to belong
Learning responsibility and to trust
Learning how to care for others and to be cared for by others
Understanding the meaning of family

**Title:** *The Mailbox*
**Author(s):** Audrey Shafer
**Illustrator:** None
**Publisher:** Delacorte Press, a Division of Random House Books, New York
**Date of Publication:** 2006

**Awards:** None
**Reading Levels:** AR Int. Level Middle Grades, BL 5.0; Lexile Level 790L

## Summary:

Twelve-year-old Gabe was adopted two and one-half years ago by his Uncle Vernon after some time in foster care. Uncle Vernon was "crusty" and a recluse. When Gabe comes home from his first day in sixth grade, he finds Uncle Vernon dead. Fearful that he will be taken away and placed back in foster care, he tells no one about Uncle Vernon's death. Mysterious notes begin to appear in the mailbox from an old friend of Vernon's named Smitty. Smitty even leaves a dog, Guppy, for Gabe to care for and to keep him company. Gabe misses the love of family, evident as he thinks at a sleepover at his best friend Webber's house, "But what really filled Gabe with the yellow and gold shine of contentment was the tuck-in after the stories. Mrs. Pickering pulled the covers snug around him then kissed him on the check. 'You sleep tight, Gabe. I love you, honey' " (p. 63). When it is finally discovered that Uncle Vernon is dead, Gabe realizes how many people at his school really care for him. Webber and his mother, Mrs. Pickering, a teacher named Mrs. Garvey and her husband who is a judge, and Gabe's English teacher, Mr. Boehm, all do love him. In the end, Mr. Boehm decides to adopt Gabe and Gabe agrees that he needs Mr. Boehm. The funeral for Uncle Vernon is attended by many Vietnam War veterans who were all touched by Vernon or saved by Vernon during the war. Through Captain Tarkenton, Gabe learns the truth about Vernon and Smitty. Smitty had mental illness ever since he shot a ten-year-old boy by mistake in a tent that he was to "clear of snipers" during the war. Vernon brought him out of shock, but Smitty shot part of his own face off as punishment for killing the boy. Smitty had communicated with Vernon through notes for many years, just as he had done with Gabe. Smitty now feels better about himself after having helped save a boy, Gabe, who had accepted him and Guppy without question. The final note left to Gabe by Smitty stated, "A life marked only by secrets is of no consequence. If I have helped one child toward happiness in helping you, then my life has, after all, been worth living. With deepest gratitude, Paul" (p. 178).

## Comments and Specific Suggestions:

The horrors of the Vietnam War, its impact on the soldiers for many years after, and Smitty's painful memory of killing a child by mistake may require some interpretation by teachers. Students might be encouraged to write a letter to Smitty just as Gabe left letters for him in the mailbox. Alternatively, students might interview a Vietnam War veteran. The theme of needing others is obvious throughout the story.

## Themes:

Orphan adventure/survival tale
Learning to love and need others
Longing for home and to belong
Understanding the meaning of family

**Title:** *The Midnight Diary of Zoya Blume*
**Author(s):** Laura Shaine Cunningham
**Illustrator:** None
**Publisher:** Laura Geringer Books, an Imprint of HarperCollins Publishers, New York
**Date of Publication:** 2005
**Awards:** None
**Reading Levels:** AR Int. Level Middle Grades, BL 4.8

## Summary:

Zoya, 12 years old, was adopted by her single mother, Mimi, when she was only four. Zoya was adopted from an orphanage in Russia. When her mother leaves for an operation, her mother's former "love" and partner in a magic act, Leon, comes to take care of Zoya. Other characters in the story include Zoya's friend, Flynn, as well as Zoya's grumpy grandmother, Gramma, who changed after the death of her first daughter, Shirley, and who is now starting to become "senile." Zoya's mother tells her "Your first memory is your point of view" (p. 5), but Zoya is fearful of her memories and what she might find. During her mother's ten-day absence, Zoya writes in a diary, watches the Stone Girl, and faces her fears and memories from Russia. Zoya has night terrors and she "sleepwalks." She had terrible, unexplainable temper tantrums when she first arrived. Zoya has always been curious about the plaid suitcase she carried home from the orphanage, but she has been afraid to open it. When she finally opens it to see its contents, her memories return. She has been haunted in her dreams by fear of the "Buka," a shadowy old woman who waits to snatch children. Zoya remembers her birth mother taking her to the orphanage and hearing herself screaming and kicking as an older woman, her Buka, pulled her inside. In the end when her mother returns from the hospital, Zoya says, "I know some secrets, too . . . I know sometimes you love someone and cannot stay . . ." (p. 156) and she realizes that ". . . .maybe that is the Secret of Life—that love is something bigger and finer than the shadow witch!" (p. 148).

**Comments and Specific Suggestions:**
This book does deal with frightening reminders for older-adopted children, particularly those adopted from orphanages in Eastern Europe; however, it is a realistic portrayal of the painful memories and the night traumas experienced by many children of intercountry adoption. Zoya states, "I come from a country that I cannot remember and whose name even now makes me shiver. Is this a memory or a bad dream? Do I remember Russia? I remember flashes . . . Even the name—Russia—comes in as an ice blast . . . I hear the ssssh, the hush of falling snow, the whisper of sleet, needling. Sssssh, the Russian wind hisses. Keep the secrets" (p. 28). Included in the book are memories of green painted cribs with flaked paint, holes in shoes, a milk bottle with the milk thickened by ice crystals, the smell of cleaning liquid, and the fear of having to use the bathroom and not being permitted to do so at night while also fearing to "let go" because the sheets would become colder and freeze. The fear of losing her mother, understandable due to the way she lost her first mother, is clear, and the final message is of love from her mother. "I can hear my mother think, and she can hear me too, and we both are thinking 'I love you' as the clock strikes twelve" (p. 163). A poignant and startling book, teachers might help students discuss nightmares or "scary dreams" they have had. In addition, Leon, the magician, helps Zoya remember her past. Students could suggest people who have produced "magic" or a positive impact on their lives. Additional questions for discussion include: Why is the Stone Girl important to Zoya? and, What does her mother mean when she tells Zoya her "first memory" is her "point of view"? For enrichment, children might also research Russian legends and tales (e.g., the Buka) or conduct research on orphanages in Russia.

**Themes:**
Precious child
Coping with strong emotions—fear, hidden traumas, and painful memories
Letting go of the past
Developing an identity
Intercountry adoption

**Title:** *The Midwife's Apprentice*
**Author(s):** Karen Cushman
**Illustrator:** None
**Publisher:** Clarion Books, New York
**Date of Publication:** 1995
**Awards:** Newbery Medal Winner for 1996
**Reading Levels:** AR Int. Level Middle Grades, BL 6.0; Lexile Level 1240L

**Summary:**
A young girl has no notion of her age and is called simply "Brat" or "Beetle" by others because she is filthy and sleeps in a dung heap. She works as an apprentice to a midwife who is harsh with the girl. Lacking confidence, she sets off to work at an inn. When Magister Reese asks her at the inn, "And what, inn girl, do you want?" she thinks carefully and later responds, "No one had ever asked her that . . . I know what I want, but it is my misfortune instead to be hungry, out of humor, and too stupid to be a midwife's apprentice" (p. 80). The girl, who takes the name of Alyce, eventually finds that she is "worth something." She finds her place as the midwife's apprentice and knows that she can try and try again until she succeeds. She also comes to learn how to care for others

such as Cat, an orphan named Edward for whom she finds work at the manor house, and women giving birth who are in pain.

**Comments and Specific Suggestions:**
Teachers can help students research the historical context of this novel and its setting in medieval England in order to understand the need for a midwife and to comprehend some of the expressions used in the books (e.g., "dung beetle"). During that time period, orphans may indeed have served as apprentices to masters who provided them with some degree of care. Similar to Tree-ear in *A Single Shard* (Park, 2001), Alyce is an apprentice; therefore, students might compare and contrast Alyce's life and living conditions with those of Tree-ear. In addition, children might discuss why Alyce thinks she is a failure and how she changes her opinion of herself in the story. Illustrating Alyce's house in medieval England or learning about the herbs and flowers used by the midwife might also provide interesting extension activities.

**Themes:**
Orphan as worker
Longing for a place to belong
Learning to care about others
Developing an identity and a sense of one's place in the world

**Title:** *The Moorchild*
**Author(s):** Eloise McGraw
**Illustrator:** None
**Publisher:** Margaret K. McElderry Books, an Imprint of Simon and Schuster Children's Publishing Division, New York
**Date of Publication:** 1996
**Awards:** A Newbery Honor Book for 1997
**Reading Levels:** AR Int. Level Middle Grades, BL 5.5; Lexile Level 940L

**Summary:**
Born Moql, one of the "Folk" who live in the "Mound" on the moor, the young fairy is half human (i.e., the fisherman, Fergil, was her father and was lured into the Mound by Talabar) and half "Folk." Because she cannot hide from humans, the Prince has her sent out of the Mound and she becomes a "changeling," exchanged for the baby of Yanno and Anwara who becomes a servant in the Mound. Moql's new name is Saaski, but because she looks and behaves so differently than the others she is never accepted by the children or the townspeople. Saaski befriends an orphan boy, Tam, on the moors. Over time, she realizes she can see the Folk and she remembers her true identity. In the end, she knows the townspeople are so afraid of her that they plan to burn her at the Mid Summer Night festival and that they will shun her parents if they try to keep her or protect her. She gives Anwara the only gift she can think of. She tricks one of the Folk so that she and Tam can enter the Mound. They rescue the child of Anwara and Yanno, Leoran (i.e., Lekka in the Mound), and return her to her home. Saaski sets out with Tam because she knows she does not belong anywhere else, "But she was sure she belonged with Tam" (p. 238). As the Prince told Saaski, "Aye, you're neither one thing nor yet quite t'other . . . Pity, but there 'tis" (p. 31).

**Comments and Specific Suggestions:**
The novel presents a sad tale of loneliness because Saaski never quite grasps emotions. She learns about love and hate, but she never really feels the emotions herself. She also never ends up with a family. At the end of the story, the reader has the sense that Yanno, Anwara, and Old Bess, the grandmother, think fondly of Saaski and miss her occasionally, but are happy to have their "real" daughter back. Students can be challenged to find out about the Moors and British legends about the Moors. Students might also enjoy creating pictures of Torskaal and of the Mound. Eloise McGraw is also the author of *Moccasin Trail*, published in 1952.

**Themes:**
Orphan as worker
Longing for a place to belong

Coping with feelings of difference
Coping with strong emotions—past memories

**Title:** *The Ocean Within*
**Author(s):** V. M. Caldwell
**Illustrator:** Erica Magnus
**Publisher:** Milkweed Editions, Minneapolis, MN
**Date of Publication:** 1999
**Awards:** None
**Reading Levels:** AR Int. Level Middle Grades, BL 4.5; Lexile Level 500L

**Summary:**
Eleven-year-old Elizabeth has been passed among various foster homes since her parents died when she was only five. She has learned to be silent and sullen. Now Elizabeth is a member of the Sheridan clan, a large, noisy, extended family. Kevin and Karen Sheridan plan to adopt Elizabeth as their third child, in between Caroline, age 13, and Paul, age 9. The extended family, nine cousins and their respective parents, spends time at the ocean with the matriarch of the family, Martha Sheridan, or Grandma. Elizabeth reluctantly agrees to go with the Sheridans because she has always wanted to see the ocean. It terrifies her but draws her to it at the same time. Elizabeth does not understand the noise, the rules, the love, or the forgiveness of the family. She does not understand Grandma, whom she dubs "Iron Woman" in her mind because no one "crosses" Grandma but everyone obviously respects and adores her. Elizabeth remains silent and afraid of going in the ocean throughout the summer. Petey, the youngest cousin at age four, and Grandma eventually help Elizabeth understand what the family means to each member and to learn about loving, apologizing, and accepting apologies while really meaning it. Finally, Elizabeth is helped to say she wants to belong to this family.

**Comments and Specific Suggestions:**
The title of the novel obviously suggests a major theme. The symbolism of the ocean and its terrifying depths and crashing turmoil mirror Elizabeth's own inner emotions. Like the ocean, she is drawn to the Sheridan family while she is simultaneously terrified of it. Students might discuss this symbolism as well as the changes in Elizabeth during the story. She originally recites her litany, "Do as you're told. Say as little as possible. Tell them what they want to hear and they'll leave you alone. Never let them see you cry. Never let them know what's important to you" (p. 69). She refuses to let anyone in the family know how important the ocean is to her. Later, she thinks, "Dinner had come to represent everything Elizabeth hated about family life in general, and family life at the Sheridan's in particular . . . She hated bests . . . She hated family jokes . . . What she hated was not understanding things, not knowing what everyone else knew" (p. 87). Finally, Adam, the oldest cousin, says to Elizabeth, "Belonging to my family is so much a part of who I am that I don't have any way to begin to understand what your life's been like" to which Elizabeth answers, "I don't know what it's like to be you . . . I don't know how it feels to belong" (p. 271).

**Themes:**
Precious child
Coping with strong emotions—anger, distrust, need for control
Longing to belong and be accepted
Understanding the meaning of family

**Title:** *The Road to Paris*
**Author(s):** Nikki Grimes
**Illustrator:** None
**Publisher:** G. P. Putnam's Sons, a Division of Penguin Group, New York
**Date of Publication:** 2006
**Awards:** None
**Reading Levels:** AR Int. Level Middle Grades, BL 4.3; Lexile Level 700L

**Summary:**

Paris is a biracial child. Her mother, Viola, was African American and her father, who "ran off" when she was four years old, was Caucasian. Viola left Paris, age eight, and her half-brother Malcolm, age ten, after her most recent husband left her and she began drinking and staying away from home for several days at a time. When their grandmother came one day and found their mother gone, the children were placed in foster homes. At one, Paris was constantly beaten, so Malcolm took her back to their grandmother's home. The grandmother again called Social Services. Malcolm was placed in a group home and Paris was placed with a family she grew to love. The family wanted to adopt Paris, but before the adoption could take place her mother called and said she wanted Paris to come back. Viola told Paris she had stopped drinking, been remarried, and would bring Malcolm back home too. Paris had to make a difficult decision and decided ultimately to give her mother another chance because she desperately missed Malcolm. "She still loved her mother. She just didn't want to. Loving her meant getting hurt, and Paris had had enough of hurting" (p. 95).

**Comments and Specific Suggestions:**

Teachers might lead children in a discussion about times they have been away from their family for a period of time and how that made them feel. Paris had a very hard decision to make, staying with people she had come to love and trust, but people she did not "look like," or returning to Viola. Students might also share times when they had to make a difficult decision or they could think about what they might have done if they had been in Paris's shoes. In addition, students might compare and contrast Paris and Malcolm. How have their lives changed over the course of a year? How have the students' lives changed?

**Themes:**

Coping with strong emotions—fear, loss, abandonment, and love for a sibling
Understanding the meaning of family
Coming of age
Developing an identity

**Title:** *The Star of Kazan*
**Author(s):** Eve Ibbotson
**Illustrator:** Kevin Hawkes
**Publisher:** Dalton Children's Books, a Division of Penguin Group, New York
**Date of Publication:** 2004
**Awards:** An ALA Notable Children's Book for 2005
**Reading Levels:** AR Int. Level Middle Grades, BL 6.1; Lexile Level 880L

**Summary:**

This story, set in Vienna, Austria, and also in Germany, in the early 1900s just before World War I, is an adventure story of "rags to riches." Annika was left as a baby in a church and found by Ellie, who adopts her. She is cared for by Ellie, the cook, and Sigrid, the house servant to three professors, two brothers, Professor Emil and Professor Julius, and their sister, Professor Gertrude. When Annika begins to "tell stories" with an elderly woman across the square, the woman shares her story of being La Rondine, an actress who was given many jewels such as the Star of Kazan, an emerald from Russia, by an admirer. After her admirer died, she took the jewels one at a time to Fabrice, a famous jeweler in Paris, who made her "paste" copies of each and gave her the money from the sale of the original jewel. Upon her death, the old woman left Annika her trunk containing her stage clothes and jewels, but Annika never knew about the woman's will. As she has always dreamed, her mother, Frau Edeltraut Von Tannenberg, returns for her and takes her back to Spittal, a run-down castle in Germany. Frau Edeltraut sends Annika to a boarding school. While at Spittal, Annika meets Zed, an orphan boy descended from gypsies whose deceased father had worked the "Stallion Farm" for the Lipizzaner Stallions. Zed has a three-legged dog named Hector and has his father's talent with the stallions. Zed and Annika's old friends, Pauline and Stefan, find out that Annika has inherited the jewels and that they are actually the real ones and not copies. The French jeweler, Fabrice, had so admired La Rondine that he gave her the money himself and gave her back her real jewels, something she had never known. Frau Edelhart had found out about the jewels and had only pretended to be Annika's mother to get the money and keep Spittal in the von Tannenberg family. Annika literally jumps off the ship as it departs from Vienna and returns to her family, Ellie, Sigrid, Julius, Emil, Gertrude, Zed, Stephan, and Pauline. Zed and his stallion, Rocco, get to join the Lipizzaner Stallions, with Rocco chosen as the "dark" (i.e., "Good luck") or Emperor's horse, an honor bestowed on only one stallion in the group at a time.

## Comments and Specific Suggestions:
This is an engaging adventure story despite some references to "strays" and "foundlings." Kazan is a city in Russia that students may wish to research. In addition, locating information about the Lipizzaner Stallions and the expression "dark horse" might be of interest to older readers. Numerous opportunities for enrichment exist as well by researching Vienna.

## Themes:
Orphan adventure/survival tale
Understanding the meaning of family
Longing for a place to belong and a home
Letting go of the past
Searching for identity

**Title:** *The Thief Lord*
**Author(s):** Cornelia Funke
**Illustrator:** Cornelia Funke
**Publisher:** Scholastic, Inc., New York
**Date of Publication:** 2003
**Awards:** An ALA Notable Children's Book for 2003
**Reading Levels:** AR Int. Level Middle Grades, BL 4.8; Lexile Level 640L

## Summary:
Prosper, age 12, and Bo, age 5, ran away from their Aunt Esther and her husband after the death of their mother because Aunt Esther only wanted to adopt young Bo with the "angelic blonde" hair. The boys go to Venice because their mother always told them stories about the beautiful city. In Venice, Prosper and Bo meet and are taken in by other "street children" including Riccio, Mosca, Hornet, and the mysterious Scipio, the "Thief Lord," who finds shelter for the boys in an abandoned movie theater but who does not live there with them. Aunt Esther hires a detective, Victor, to hunt for Bo. Scipio turns out to be the son of a wealthy nobleman in Venice, but his father is not kind to him. At the end of the story, Scipio rides a magical merry-go-round and becomes a young adult while Ernesto Barbarossa, a "crooked" antiques dealer, becomes a little boy who is adopted by Aunt Esther. Scipio goes to work for Victor as a detective. Hornet, Prosper, and Bo go to live with a wealthy lady, Ida Spavento, who grew up in a nearby orphanage run by the Merciful Sisters. Ida befriends and helps the boys, but Riccio and Mosca go back to the streets in another section of town.

## Comments and Specific Suggestions:
The first edition of this book was published in German in 2000. The parallels to street children today are obvious, although the magical merry-go-round is every child's fantasy. Children are often in a hurry to grow up and have control of their lives while the adults around them would like to become children again! Students might discuss how the siblings desired to stay together and how they became a family with the other boys. In addition, they can discuss why the boys were hurt by Scipio despite his kindness to them. The novel was made into a Warner Brothers movie released in 2006 and directed by Richard Claus. It is available for viewing on DVD.

## Themes:
Orphan adventure/survival tale
Coping with strong emotions—hurt, rejection
Longing to belong and be loved
Understanding the meaning of family

**Title:** *The Trouble with Skye*
**Author(s):** Marsha Huber
**Illustrator:** None
**Publisher:** Zonderkidz, Grand Rapids, MI
**Date of Publication:** 2004
**Awards:** None
**Reading Levels:** AR Int. Level Middle Grades, BL 4.7

**Summary:**
Skye knows nothing about her birth parents, except that they were involved in drugs and that she had been removed from them when she was only three years old. Now at age 13, Skye has been in many different foster homes, never staying in any of them for more than six months. Skye does everything she can to stay in trouble, and she does not believe that anyone has ever loved her. A judge gives Skye a long sentence to a detention center, but Eileen Chambers and her husband take the rebellious Skye to a ranch they operate for teens with various disabilities and difficulties. Eileen becomes Skye's foster mother as well as her counselor at Maranatha Treatment Center. Eileen tells Skye, "Although you are totally responsible for your own actions, there's a reason behind it. You are so full of hate for your parents that you can't see straight" (p. 80). Eileen and her husband give Skye a horse and teach her to ride and "show." After she wins a horse show, she tries to "show off" and jump the horse, creating a bad accident for Mr. Chambers who is trying to stop her. Skye finally discovers the love of her foster parents and the love of God.

**Comments and Specific Suggestions:**
The novel is Book Number One in the Keystone Stables Series, a series of Christian stories. The plot and characters are a bit stereotypical and predictable, but students who "show" horses may enjoy the story.

**Themes:**
Coping with strong emotions—anger, distrust, need for control, feeling rejected
Comprehending foster care story
Understanding the meaning of family and accepting love

**Title:** *Tides*
**Author(s):** V. M. Caldwell
**Illustrator:** Erica Magnus
**Publisher:** Milkweed Editions, Minneapolis, MN
**Date of Publication:** 2001
**Awards:** None
**Reading Levels:** AR Int. Level Middle Grades, BL 3.6

**Summary:**
In this sequel to *The Ocean Within* (Caldwell, 1999), Elizabeth returns one year later to "Grandma's" house at the ocean. She has taken swimming lessons and she knows she is loved by her parents, Kevin and Karen. She has been looking forward to her summer with her cousins and hopes it will be the same as the previous year, but her oldest cousin, Adam, is sullen and withdrawn because his two best friends were killed in an automobile accident while drinking. Adam is hurt and believes that nothing he has been told as a Sheridan is true. He leaves Grandma's house to work all summer. Elizabeth finds she is still fearful of going in the ocean, and this makes her feel that she is not really a Sheridan. She does not swim and play sports, and she is still quiet and observant, unlike the others in the family. "Alone in her room, Elizabeth contemplated the family portraits that stood on her desk . . . Elizabeth looked nothing like any of them . . . Being part of a family wasn't about physical resemblance, but did she have to look so horribly pasted on?" (p. 9). While the others swim, Elizabeth spends time with Pap, an "Ocean Minder" who collects data on the contents of the ocean water for an environmental group. Petey, Elizabeth's youngest cousin, now five, almost drowns and Elizabeth goes into the ocean to save him. Like Elizabeth, Petey is very hurt by Adam's distance and coldness, and he tries to destroy a painting Elizabeth made for Grandma. In the end, Adam returns to the family at Christmas, now planning to major in forestry after working

in Montana and Maine. Adam, who always called Elizabeth "Turtle," tells her how he felt about his friends' deaths and that he has learned he *is* a Sheridan. Adam carved Elizabeth a snake as a Christmas gift and told Elizabeth, "Snakes are quiet creatures. Hard to appreciate, at first . . . But they play a critical role in an ecosystem" (p. 308). Elizabeth repairs the damaged painting and begins to feel that she really is a member of the family too, even if she does not swim like the others.

## Comments and Specific Suggestions:

As with the first book in the sequel, a major theme for the novel is captured in the title. As the tides ebb and flow in the ocean, family life and the lives of individual family members ebb and flow as well. Elizabeth wanted her extended family to stay the same as the previous summer, but Adam changed. Even Grandma changed as a result of Adam's behavior. Elizabeth came to understand that family members and situations can change, but the family still belongs together and draws support from its members. In addition to this theme, students might also discuss how Adam might have felt when Petey, whom Adam had always taken care of, almost drowned. Why did Adam choose to call Elizabeth "Turtle" and why would he choose to carve her a snake for a Christmas present? In what way does this present help Elizabeth realize that she is a critical member of the family?

## Themes:

Precious child
Understanding the meaning of family and learning to accept love
Searching for identity

**Title:** *The Witch's Boy*
**Author(s):** Michael Gruber
**Illustrator:** None
**Publisher:** HarperTempest, an Imprint of HarperCollins, New York
**Date of Publication:** 2005
**Awards:** An ALA Notable Children's Book for 2006
**Reading Levels:** AR Int. Level Middle Grades, BL 6.4; Lexile Level 990L

## Summary:

This is an unusual fantasy about an abandoned boy found as a baby by a witch. This witch keeps the patterns of the world running. The baby is very ugly and the witch calls him "Lump." She, her cat, Falance, and a bear, Ysul, raise Lump. Lump and the witch can converse with animals. The witch loves Lump even though he becomes self-centered and interferes with her work. After being tortured by humans, he seeks revenge, putting the witch and the patterns of the world in danger. Ultimately, Lump learns about himself and learns to love others more than himself.

## Comments and Specific Suggestions:

Although an ALA Notable Children's Book, the novel is a bit difficult to understand. The themes regarding self-discovery and learning to love, however, are appropriate for children in grades 6–8. The novel may also be appropriate for young adults.

## Themes:

Searching for identity
Learning to love others

**Title:** *Up a Road Slowly*
**Author(s):** Irene Hunt
**Illustrator:** None
**Publisher:** Follett Publishing Company, Chicago, IL
**Date of Publication:** 1966
**Awards:** Newbery Medal Winner for 1967
**Reading Levels:** AR Int. Level Middle Grades, BL 6.6; Lexile Level 1130L

**Summary:**
Julie was only seven when her mother died. Her grieving father moved her to live with her stern, "school teacher" aunt, Aunt Cordelia, and her mother's brother, Uncle Haskell, a man who drinks and has never succeeded at anything in life. The story spans Julie's life from age seven until her graduation from high school and preparation to enter college. Over time, Julie falls in love with Danny, a boy she played with as a child, and she comes to love Aunt Cordelia. Julie's father also remarries, a woman Julies grows to like, and her older sister, Laura, who stayed with their father and to whom she is quite attached, marries and has a baby girl she names Julie. By the end of the story, Julie realizes that Aunt Cordelia was really more her parent than her father ever was.

**Comments and Specific Suggestions:**
Because the writing style is a bit complex and "old fashioned," the book may be difficult for some children in grades 6–8 to read. The old philosophy that children have no real feelings and should be "seen and not heard" is evident when Julie's brother, Chris, moves back with their father. Julie thinks, "Once again, both Chris and I were manipulated like small puppets in our world of adults. We didn't like it, and we suffered, but the tall ones around us said that we would soon get over our sadness, that we would 'adapt' in a matter of weeks" (p. 22). Students can discuss whether or not adolescents have any control over their lives. In addition, the teacher can help students determine how Aunt Cordelia's character traits made her a good mother for Julie.

**Themes:**
Precious child
Coping with strong emotions—loss and feeling insecure
Longing to belong
Developing an identity
Coming of age

**Title:** *We Rode the Orphan Trains*
**Author(s):** Andrea Warren
**Illustrator:** None
**Publisher:** Houghton Mifflin Company, Boston, MA
**Date of Publication:** 2001
**Awards:** None
**Reading Levels:** AR Int. Level Middle Grades, BL 6.4; Lexile Level 940L

**Summary:**
Andrea Warren, also the author of the 1996 book *Orphan Train Rider: One Boy's True Story*, interviewed living orphan train riders. Through historical pictures and through the interviews, she makes the point that most found good homes and were loved and happy. Some, however, were emotionally, physically, or sexually abused or used as child labor, becoming house servants or farmhands rather than family members. The difficulty of developing one's identity when information was withheld from them is obvious for most of the individuals who were interviewed. For example, Ruth Jensen speaks of the prejudice aimed at the orphan train riders when she says she was viewed by others as "That orphan girl, or nasty girl, a troublemaker who couldn't be trusted and other children were not allowed to associate with her" (p. 62). Betty sadly states that the earliest photograph she has of herself is her high school graduation picture. On the other hand, Art comes to the conclusion in his seventies that his birth mother leaving him in a department store where he would be found was an act of love.

**Comments and Specific Suggestions:**
Teachers will need to provide accurate information to accompany any reading of this nonfiction book, particularly since several stories depict abuse and unfortunate outcomes. With assistance, however, the text is an excellent document regarding a little known event in the history of the United States. Not only are true stories included, but also facts regarding the early history of "Foundling homes," orphanages, and the Children's Aid Society established by Charles Brace. Advanced students may be able to draw parallels between the economic difficulties experienced in the big cities in the late 1800s and early 1900s and the economic circumstances in countries such as Russia or China today.

**Themes:**
Both precious child and orphan as worker
Developing an identity

**Title:** *Where I'd Like to Be*
**Author(s):** Frances O'Roark Dowell
**Illustrator:** None
**Publisher:** Atheneum Books for Young Readers, an Imprint of Simon and Schuster Publishing, New York
**Date of Publication:** 2003
**Awards:** None
**Reading Levels:** AR Int. Level Middle Grades, BL 5.4; Lexile Level 910L

**Summary:**
Maddie is 11 years old and has been in several foster homes after being removed from Granny when Granny was losing her eyesight. Now, Maddie lives at the East Tennessee Children's Home. Maddie befriends a new girl, Murphy, as well as a six-year-old boy, Ricky Ray. She also becomes friends with Donita and with Logan Parrish, who is not at the Home, who is considered "weird" by the kids at their school, and whose mother never seems to approve of him. The group builds a fort in Logan's yard where they meet and make books (e.g., The Book of People, The Book of Houses) together by cutting and pasting pictures from magazines. As they make their books, they tell stories to accompany the pictures. When Murphy's mother comes for her, the group finds out that Murphy has lied to them about the whole story of her life. In the end, Maddie is about to be adopted, but she has decided she will not go unless the single woman, an artist like Maddie, also takes Ricky Ray. Ricky Ray always hoped his mother, Crystal, would come back for him; however, she returned only long enough to tell him she wanted him to be adopted. She did not even remember his age. Donita returns to her mother as the other children are adopted.

**Comments and Specific Suggestions:**
Students can easily discuss the meaning of the "books" made by Maddie and the other children. The books and the stories represent how the children wanted their lives to be, the title of the novel. Although Murphy lied about herself, she also obviously told a story about how she "wanted her life to be." As an extension activity, students might make a "book" or a collage from pictures cut from magazines. They can entitle their books appropriately, The Book of (*Chosen Topic*), and create their own "story."

**Themes:**
Comprehending foster care story
Coping with strong emotions—abandonment and anger
Longing to belong, have a home, and have a family
Understanding the meaning of family

**Title:** *Youn Hee and Me*
**Author(s):** C. S. Adler
**Illustrator:** None
**Publisher:** Harcourt Brace and Company, New York
**Date of Publication:** 1995
**Awards:** None
**Reading Levels:** AR Int. Level Middle Grades, BL 4.6; Lexile Level 760L

**Summary:**
Caitlin is 11 and her little brother, Simon, now 5, was adopted from Korea. Caitlin and Simon find out from their mother that Simon had an older sister in Korea. Youn Hee is Caitlin's age and has been living in an orphanage in Korea. The family adopts Youn Hee, but Youn Hee dislikes how Caitlin gets into trouble and is a poor role model for Si Won (i.e., Simon) who is also now starting to misbehave. Their single-parent mother is a working woman

who does not cook well or discipline properly according to Youn Hee. Youn Hee wants to return to Korea, but eventually Caitlin and Youn Hee learn to be sisters and to share Simon. They decide to be a family. "We are different, like most people in a family are different, but our hearts are bound up together. We belong to each other, Youn Hee and Simon and Mom and me. We're a family. You can just look at us and tell" (p. 183).

**Comments and Specific Suggestions:**
The book contains some prejudicial references from Caitlin's schoolmates that Youn Hee and Simon are "different." The language of adoption is also a bit dated (e.g., "natural father," "just adopted"). Nevertheless, the themes of dealing with difference and understanding the meaning of family are evident. In addition, students might have an interesting discussion regarding "culture" and "heritage." When children are from an intercountry or transracial adoption, they may have difficulty reconciling "which" culture or heritage they will integrate into their identities.

**Themes:**
Precious child
Dealing with differences
Intercountry and transracial adoption
Sibling adjustment
Understanding the meaning of family

## SUMMARY

Older readers in grades 6–8 have the abstract thought and cognitive ability to attack difficult ethical and moral questions and themes in children's literature. While children at these grade levels are experiencing rapid physical changes and attempting to be accepted and to "fit in," they are simultaneously searching for their sense of self in the world. The child who has been adopted or placed into foster care may have more difficulty establishing his or her identity. Coping with strong emotions related to "family," dealing with peer reactions, learning to let go of the past, and searching for family may be additional developmental tasks for these youngsters. Adoption and foster care placement must eventually become integrated into the adolescent's identity, and some must also adjust to their place in a cross-cultural family.

Children's literature for older readers in grades 6–8 is rich and complex. Much quality literature is available to help adolescents comprehend the meaning of family despite adoption or foster care placement. Teachers can provide accurate information and lead sensitive discussions to help adolescents discover the universality of the search to answer the question "Who am I?"

# References

Adler, C. S. (1995). *Youn Hee and me.* New York: Harcourt Brace and Company.

AFCARS. (2008). Trends in foster care and adoption—FY 2002–FY 2007. U.S. Department of Health and Human Services Administration for Children and Families. Retrieved January 9, 2009, from http://www .acf.hhs.gov/programs/cb/stats_research/afcars/trends.htm.

Almond, D. (2000). *Heaven eyes.* New York: Delacorte Press, an Imprint of Random House.

American Association of Retired Persons (AARP). (2000). *Help for grandparents raising grandchildren.* Retrieved January 9, 2009, from http://www.aarp.org/families/grandparents/raising_grandchild/a2004-01-16-findinghelp.html.

Askeland, L. (2006). Informal adoption, apprentices, and indentured children in the Colonial Era and the New Republic, 1605–1850. In L. Askeland (Ed.), *Children and youth in adoption, orphanages, and foster care: A historical handbook and guide* (pp. 3–16). Westport, CT: Greenwood.

Avi. (2002). *Crispin: The cross of lead.* New York: Hyperion Books for Children.

Avi. (2006). *Crispin at the edge of the world.* New York: Hyperion Books for Children.

Banks, K. (2002). *Dillon Dillon.* New York: Farrar, Straus and Giroux.

Bartholet, E. (2006). International adoption. In L. Askeland (Ed.), *Children and youth in adoption, orphanages, and foster care: A historical handbook and guide* (pp. 63–77). Westport, CT: Greenwood.

Bawden, N. (1987). *The finding.* New York: Puffin Books, an Imprint of Penguin Group.

Bemelman, L. (1939). *Madeline.* New York: Simon and Schuster.

Bemelman, L. (1953). *Madeline's rescue.* New York: Viking Press.

Billingsley, F. (1999). *The folk keeper.* New York: Atheneum Books for Young Readers, an Imprint of Simon and Schuster.

Blacker, T. (2001). *The angel factory.* New York: Simon and Schuster.

Boyd, B. (2000). *When you were born in Korea: A memory book for children adopted from Korea.* St. Paul, MN: Yeong & Yeong Book Company.

Brodzinsky, A. B. (1996). *The mulberry bird: An adoption story (Revised).* Indianapolis, IN: Perspectives Press.

Brodzinsky, D. M., Schechter, M. D., & Henig, R. M. (1992). *Being adopted: The lifelong search for self.* New York: Anchor Books.

Brodzinsky, D. M., Smith, D. W., & Brodzinsky, A. B. (1998). *Children's adjustment to adoption: Developmental and clinical issues.* Developmental Clinical Psychology and Psychiatry Series, Vol. 38. Thousand Oaks, CA: Sage Publications.

Brooke, P. (2000). *Jake's orphan.* New York: D.K. Publishing.

Bunin, C., & Bunin, S. (1992). *Is that your sister? A true story of adoption.* Wayne, PA: Our Child Press.

Bunting, E. (1996). *Train to Somewhere.* New York: Clarion Books.

Bunting, E. (2001). *Jin Woo.* New York: Clarion Books.

Byars, B. (1977). *The pinballs.* New York: Harper & Row Junior Books, a division of HarperCollins Publishers.

Caldwell, V. M. (1999). *The ocean within.* Minneapolis, MN: Milkweed Editions.

Caldwell, V. M. (2001). *Tides.* Minneapolis, MN: Milkweed Editions.

Cannon, J. (1993). *Stellaluna.* New York: Harcourt Brace and Company.

Carp, E. W. (1998). *Family matters: Secrecy and disclosure in the history of adoption.* Cambridge, MA: Harvard University Press.

Caseley, J. (2004). *Sisters.* New York: Greenwillow Books, an Imprint of HarperCollins Publishers.

Chen, C. Y. (2004). *Guji Guji.* La Jolla, CA: Keane/Miller Book Publishers.

Child Welfare Information Gateway. (2009). *Foster care statistics.* Washington, DC: The Adoption and Foster Care Analysis and Reporting System. http://www.childwelfare.gov/pubs/factsheets/foster.cfm.

Christopher, M. (1985). *A touchdown for Tommy.* New York: Little, Brown & Company.

Clymer, S. (1994). *There's a hamster in my lunch box.* New York: Scholastic Inc.

Cole, J. (1995). *How I was adopted: Samantha's story.* New York: William Morrow & Company.

Cosby, E. I. (2000). *"A" is for adopted.* Tempe, AZ: Swak-Pak Books.

Coste, M. (2006). *Finding Joy.* Honesdale, PA: Boyds Mills Press.

Creagh, D. (2006). Science, social work, and bureaucracy: Cautious developments in adoption and foster care, 1930–1969. In L. Askeland (Ed.), *Children and youth in adoption, orphanages, and foster care: A historical handbook and guide* (pp. 31–44). Westport, CT: Greenwood.

Creech, S. (2002). *Ruby Holler.* New York: Harper Trophy/Joanna Cotter Books, an Imprint of HarperCollins Publishers.

Cummings, M. (2006). *The three names of me.* Morton Grove, IL: Albert Whitman and Company.

Cunningham, L. S. (2005). *The midnight diary of Zoya Blume.* New York: Laura Geringer Books, an Imprint of HarperCollins Publishers.

Curtis, C. P. (1999). *Bud, not Buddy.* New York: Delacorte Press, a division of Random House.

Curtis, J. L. (1996). *Tell me again about the night I was born.* New York: HarperCollins Publishers.

Cushman, K. (1995). *The midwife's apprentice.* New York: Clarion Books.

Czech, J. M. (2002). *The coffee can kid.* Arlington, VA: CWLA Press, an Imprint of Child Welfare League of America.

D'Antonio, N. (1997). *Our baby from China: An adoption story.* Morton Grove, IL: Albert Whitman and Company.

DePaola, T. (2002). *A new Barker in the house.* New York: G. P. Putnam's Sons, a division of the Putnam and Grosset Book Group.

DiCamillo, K. (2000). *Because of Winn-Dixie.* Somerville, MA: Candlewick Press.

Dorow, S. (1997). *When you were born in China: A memory book for children adopted from China.* St. Paul, MN: Yeong & Yeong Book Company.

Dowell, F. O. (2003). *Where I'd like to be.* New York: Atheneum Books for Young Readers, an Imprint of Simon and Schuster.

Durrant, J. (1999). *Never never never will she stop loving you: The adoption love story of Angel Annie.* St. George, UT: JoBiz! Books.

Edwards, T. (2008). *50 million children lived with married parents in 2007.* Washington, DC: U.S. Census Bureau New Press Release.

Evans, K. (2000). *The lost daughters of China: Abandoned girls, their journey to America, and the search for a missing past.* New York: Jeremy P. Tarcher/Putnam.

Fleischman, S. (1986). *The whipping boy.* New York: Greenwillow Books, a Division of William Morrow & Company.

Fowler, S. G. (1993). *When Joel comes home.* New York: Greenwillow Books, a Division of William Morrow & Company.

Friedrich, M. (2004). *You're not my real mother.* New York: Little, Brown and Company.

Funke, C. (2003). *The thief lord.* New York: Scholastic, Inc.

Ga'g, W. (1941). *Nothing at all.* New York: Coward McCann, Inc.

Giff, P. R. (2002). *Pictures of Hollis Woods.* New York: Wendy Lamb Books.

Gilmore, D. P., & Bell, K. We are family: Using diverse family structure literature with children. *Reading Horizons, 46*(4), 279–299.

Girard, L. W. (1986). *Adoption is for always.* Morton Grove, IL: Albert Whitman and Company.

Gray, K. (2003). *Our Twitchy.* New York: Henry Holt & Company.

Gregory, N. (2006). *I'll sing you one-o.* New York: Clarion Books.

Grimes, N. (2006). *The road to Paris.* New York: G. P. Putnam's Sons, a Division of Penguin Group.

Gruber, M. *The witch's boy.* New York: HarperTempest, an Imprint of HarperCollins Publishers.

Hamilton, B. E., Ventura, S. J., Martin, J. A., & Sutton, P. D. (2004). *Preliminary births for 2004.* National Center for Health Statistics, Centers for Disease Control and Prevention. Retrieved January 9, 2009, from http://www.cdc.gov/nchs/products/pubs/pubd/hestats/prelim_births04.htm.

Harrar, G. (2001). *Parents wanted.* Minneapolis, MN: Milkweed Editions.

Harris Interactive. (2002). *National adoption attitudes survey research report.* Sponsored by the Dave Thomas Foundation for Adoption, Dublin, OH, & The Evan B. Donaldson Adoption Institute. New York.

Hite, S. (2004). *The king of Slippery Falls.* New York: Scholastic Press.

Holeman, L. (2000). *Raspberry house blues.* Plattsburgh: Tundra Books.

Holt, M. I. (2006). Adoption reform, orphan trains, and child-saving, 1851–1929. In L. Askeland (Ed.), *Children and youth in adoption, orphanages, and foster care: A historical handbook and guide* (pp. 17–29). Westport, CT: Greenwood.

Horvath, P. (2001). *Everything on a waffle.* New York: Farrar, Straus and Giroux.

Huber, M. (2004). *The trouble with Skye.* Grand Rapids, MI: Zonderkidz.

Hunt, I. (1966). *Up a road slowly.* Chicago, IL: Follett Publishing Company.

Ibbotson, E. (2004). *The star of Kazan.* New York: Dulton Children's Books, a Division of Penguin Group.

Johnson, A. (1998). *Heaven.* New York: Simon and Schuster Books for Young Readers.

Joose, B. (2005). *Nikolai, the only bear.* New York: Philomel Books, a Division of Penguin Group.

Kasza, K. (1992). *A mother for Choco.* New York: G. P. Putnam's Sons, a Division of Putnam and Grosset Book Group.

Keller, H. (1991). *Horace.* New York, NY Greenwillow Books, an Imprint of William Morrow Company.

Kreider, R. M. (2007). *Living arrangements of children: 2004.* Current Population Reports (pp. 70–114). Washington, DC: U.S. Census Bureau.

Krementz, J. (1983). *How it feels to be adopted.* New York: Alfred A. Knopf.

Krishnaswami, U. (2006). *Bringing Asha home.* New York: Lee and Low Books.

Kroll, V. (1994). *Beginnings: How families come to be.* Morton Grove, IL: Albert Whitman and Company.

Larson, K. (2006). *Hattie big sky.* New York: Delacorte Press, a Division of Random House.

Lears, L. (2005). *Megan's birthday tree: A story about open adoption.* Morton Grove, IL: Albert Whitman and Company.

Leavitt, M. (2004). *Heck superhero.* Asheville, NC: Front Street.

Lee, M. G. (1993). *If it hadn't been for Yoon Jun.* Boston, MA: Houghton Mifflin Company.

Levine, G. C. (1999). *Dave at night.* New York: HarperCollins Publishers.

Levy, J. (2004). *Finding the right Spot.* Washington, DC: Magination Press, an Imprint of the American Psychological Association.

Lewis, R. (2000). *I love you like crazy cakes.* Boston, MA: Little, Brown & Company.

Lewis, R. (2007). *Every year on your birthday.* Boston, MA: Little, Brown & Company.

Lisle, J. T. (2003). *The crying rocks.* New York: Atheneum Books for Young Readers, an Imprint of Simon and Schuster.

Little, J. (2001). *Emma's yucky brother.* New York: HarperCollins Publishers.

London, J. (1993). *A koala for Katie: An adoption story.* Morton Grove, IL: Albert Whitman and Company.

Markle, S. (2006). *Little lost bat.* Watertown, MA: Charlesbridge.

Martin, A. M. (1989). *Karen's little sister.* New York: Scholastic Inc.

McGraw, E. (1996). *The moorchild.* New York: Margaret K. McElderry Books, an Imprint of Simon and Schuster.

McGraw, E. J. (1952). *Moccasin Trail.* New York: Coward-McCann, Inc.

McIntyre, J. (1989). *The common loon, Spirit of northern lakes.* Minneapolis, MN: University of Minnesota Press.

McKay, H. (2001). *Saffy's angel.* New York: Aladdin Paperbacks, an Imprint of Simon and Schuster.

McMahon, P., & McCarthy, C. C. (2005). *Just add one Chinese sister: An adoption story.* Honesdale, PA: Boyds Mills Press.

Meese, R. L. (1999). Teaching adopted children with disabilities: What teachers need to know. *Intervention in School and Clinic, 34*(4), 232–235.

Meese, R. L. (2002). *Children of intercountry adoptions in school: A primer for parents and professionals.* Westport, CT: Bergin & Garvey.

Melosh, B. (2002). *Strangers and kin: The American way of adoption.* Cambridge, MA: Harvard University Press.

MetaMetrics, Inc. (2009). *The Lexile Framework for reading.* Available at http://www.lexile.com.

Miller, K. A. (1994). *Did my first mother love me? A story for an adopted child.* Buena Park, CA: Morning Glory Press.

Myers, W. D. (1988). *Me, Mop, and the Moondance Kid.* New York: Dell Publishing, a Division of Bantam Doubleday Dell Publications.

Nelson, C. (2006). The orphan in American children's literature. In L. Askeland (Ed.), *Children and youth in adoption, orphanages, and foster care: A historical handbook and guide* (pp. 79–91). Westport, CT: Greenwood.

Neufield, J. (2002). *The handle and the key.* New York: Dial Publishing.

Nisse, A. (2008). *Do you see what I see? Portrayals of diversity in Newbery Medal-Winning children's literature.* Paper presented at the annual meeting of the Association for Education in Journalism and Mass Communication, Chicago, IL.

Nixon, J. L. (1998). *Lucy's wish.* New York: Delacorte Press, a Division of Random House.

Okimoto, J. D. (1990). *Molly by any other name.* New York: Scholastic, Inc.

Okimoto, J. D., & Aoki, E. M. (2002). *The white swan express: A story about adoption.* New York: Clarion Books.

O'Malley, B. (2000). *Lifebooks: Creating a treasure for the adopted child.* Winthrop, MA: Adoption Works.

O'Malley, B. (2006a). *For when I'm famous.* Winthrop, MA: Adoption Works.

O'Malley, B. (2006b). *My foster care journey.* Winthrop, MA: Adoption Works.

Park, L. S. (2001). *A single shard.* New York: Clarion Books.

Parr, T. (2003). *The family book.* New York: Little, Brown and Company.

Paterson, K. (1978). *The great Gilly Hopkins.* New York: Thomas Y. Crowell Company.

Patron, S. (2006). *The higher power of Lucky.* New York: Atheneum Books for Young Readers, an Imprint of Simon and Schuster.

Peacock, C. A. (2000). *Mommy far, mommy near: An adoption story.* Morton Grove, IL: Albert Whitman and Company.

Pellegrini, N. (1991). *Families are different.* New York: Holiday House.

Pertman, A. (2000). *Adoption nation: How the adoption revolution is transforming America.* New York: Basic Books.

Prater, M. A., and Dyches, T. T. (2008). Books that portray characters with disabilities: A top 25 list for children and young adults. *Teaching Exceptional Children, 40*(4), 32–38.

Renaissance Learning (2009). *Accelerated Reader.* Available at http://www.renlearn.com.

Rhodes, S. (1999). *Adoption is okay.* Garland, TX: Key to the Heart Publications.

Richardson, J., & Parnell, P. (2005). *And Tango makes three.* New York: Simon and Schuster Books for Young Readers.

Rodowsky, C. (2007). *Ben and the sudden too-big family.* New York: Farrar, Straus and Giroux.

Rogers, F. (1994). *Let's talk about it: Adoption.* New York: The Putnam and Grosset Group.

Rosen, M. (1995). *Bonesy and Isabel.* New York: Harcourt Children's Books.

Rosenberg, L. (2002). *We wanted you.* Brookfield, CT: Roaring Brook Press, a Division of the Millbrook Press.

Satz, M., & Askeland, L. (2006). Civil rights, adoption rights: Domestic adoption and foster care, 1970 to the present. In L. Askeland (Ed.), *Children and youth in adoption, orphanages, and foster care: A historical handbook and guide* (pp. 45–61). Westport, CT: Greenwood.

Say, A. (1997). *Allison.* Boston, MA: Houghton Mifflin Company.

Schoettle, M. (2000). *W.I.S.E. up powerbook.* Silver Spring, MD: The Center for Adoption Support and Education, Inc. (C.A.S.E.).

Schoettle, M. (2003). *S.A.F.E. at school: A manual for teachers and counselors.* Fairfax, VA: The Center for Adoption Support and Education, Inc. (C.A.S.E.).

Schreck, K. H. (2001). *Lucy's family tree.* Gardiner, ME: Tilbury House.

Selznick, B. (2007). *The invention of Hugo Cabret.* New York: Scholastic Press.

Shafer, A. (2006). *The mailbox.* New York: Delacorte Press, a Division of Random House.

Smith, S. L., & Riley, D. (2006). *Adoption in the schools: A lot to learn.* New York: The Evan B. Donaldson Adoption Institute.

Spinelli, J. (1990). *Maniac Magee.* Boston, MA: Little, Brown and Company.

Stoeke, J. M. (2005). *Waiting for May.* New York: Dutton Children's Books, a Division of Penguin Young Reader's Group.

Sugarman, B. O. (2006). *Rebecca's journey home.* Minneapolis, MN: Kar-Ben Publishing.

Suzanne, J. (1987). *Three's a crowd.* New York: Bantam Skylark Books.

Thomas, E. (2004). *The red blanket.* New York: Scholastic Press.

Turner, A. (1990). *Through moon and stars and night skies.* New York: A Charlotte Zolotow Book, an Imprint of HarperCollins Publishers.

U.S. Citizenship and Immigration Services. (2008). *Intercountry adoptions.* Retrieved January 9, 2009, from http://www.uscis.gov/portal/site/uscis/menuitem.eb1d4c2a3e5b9ac89243c6a7543f6d1a/?vgnextoid=063807b03d92b010VgnVCM10000045f3d6a1RCRD&vgnextchannel=063807b03d92b010VgnVCM10000045f3d6a1RCRD.

Voight, C. (1982). *Dicey's song.* New York: Atheneum.

Voight, C. (1983). *A solitary blue.* New York: Atheneum.

Warner, G. C. (1989). *The box car children, Book #1.* Morton Grove, IL: Albert Whitman and Company.

Warren, A. (1996). *Orphan train rider: One boy's true story.* Boston, MA: Houghton Mifflin Company.

Warren, A. (2001). *We rode the orphan trains.* Boston, MA: Houghton Mifflin Company.

Wier, E. (1963). *The loner.* New York: David McKay Company, Inc.

Wilson, J. (1991). *The story of Tracy Beaker.* New York: Delacorte Press, an Imprint of Random House.

Wolfson, J. (2006). *Home and other big fat lies.* New York: Henry Holt and Company.

Wood, L., & Ng, N. S. (2001). *Adoption and the schools.* Palo Alto, CA: Families Adopting in Response (FAIR).

Woodson, J. (2003). *Locomotion.* New York: G. P. Putnam's Sons, a Division of Penguin Group.

Woodson, J. (2004). *Coming on home soon.* New York: G. P. Putnam's Sons, a Division of Penguin Group.

Young, E. (2006). *My Mei Mei.* New York: Philomel Books, a division of Penguin Group.

Zisk, M. (2001). *The best single mom in the world: How I was adopted.* Morton Grove, IL: Albert Whitman and Company.

# Appendix: Additional K–8 Children's Literature Having Adoption or Foster Care Themes

## LITERATURE FOR YOUNGER READERS IN GRADES K–2

Aubrey, A. (2008). *Flora's family*. London, England: QED Publishers.

Ballengee, F. (2008). *Sara Elizabeth: An adoption story*. Frederick, MD: PublishAmerica.

Bashista, A. E. (2007). *Mishka: An adoption tale*. Pittsboro, NC: DRT Press.

Bemelman, L. (1939). *Madeline*. New York: Simon and Schuster.

Bemelman, L. (1953). *Madeline's rescue*. New York: Viking Press.

Carlson, N. (2004). *My family is forever*. New York: Viking Press, an Imprint of Penguin Group.

Czech, J. M. (2000). *An American face*. Arlington, VA: Child and Family Press, and imprint of Child Welfare League of America.

Dellinger, A. E. (1987). *Adopted and loved forever*. St. Louis, MO: Concordia Publishing House.

Drew, Y. (2007). *Today I was adopted*. Mustang, OK: Tate Publishing and Enterprises.

Eldridge, S. (2007). *Forever fingerprints: An amazing discovery for adopted children*. Warren, NJ: EMK Press.

Friedman, D., & Roth, R. (2009). *Star of the week: A story of love, adoption, and brownies with sprinkles*. New York: HarperCollins.

Gabbin, J. V. (2004). *I bet she called me Sugar Plum*. Harrisonburg, VA: Franklin Street Gallery Productions.

Gaynor, K. (2008). *Joe's special story*. Dublin, Ireland: Special Stories Publishing.

Gordon, S. (2000). *All families are different*. Amherst, NY: Prometheus Books.

Gormally, E. (2008). *Little Lucy's family: A story about adoption*. Skokie, IL: ACTA Publications.

Heath, K., & Martin, K. (2007). *Logan's journey*. Chesapeake, VA: Bplus Books, a Division of Bumble Bee Productions.

Hodge, D. (2003). *Emma's story*. Plattsburgh, NY: Tundra Books.

Howe, J. (1993). *Pinky and Rex and the new baby*. New York: Aladdin, an Imprint of Simon and Schuster.

Katz, K. (2001). *Over the moon: An adoption tale*. New York: Henry Holt and Company.

Kennedy, P. (2006). *A sister for Matthew: A story about adoption*. Cumming, GA: Ideals Publications.

Kitz, C. A. (2003). *I don't have your eyes*. Warren, NJ: EMK Press.

Kitz, C. A. (2003). *We see the moon*. Warren, NJ: EMK Press.

Klein, A. F. (2007). *Max and the adoption day party*. Mankato, MN: Picture Window Books. (Also available in Spanish.)

Lewis, R. (2007). *Every year on your birthday*. Boston, MA: Little, Brown & Company.

Lin, G. (2007). *The red thread: An adoption fairy tale*. Morton Grove, IL: Albert Whitman and Company.

Madrid-Branch, M. (2004). *The tummy mummy*. Santa Fe, NM: Adoption Tribe Publishing.

McCutcheon, J. (1996). *Happy adoption day*. New York: Little, Brown and Company.

McNamara, J. (2005). *Borya and the burps: An Eastern European adoption story*. Indianapolis, IN: Perspectives Press.

Meissner, J. (2009). *Why am I brown? A child's view of multi-cultural adoption*. Frederick, MD: PublishAmerica.

Moore-Mallinos, J. (2007). *We are adopted (Let's talk about it books)*. Hauppauge, NY: Barrons Educational Books.

Mora, P. (1994). *Pablo's tree*. New York: Simon and Schuster.

Nelson, J. (2006). *Families change: A book for children experiencing termination of parental rights (Kids Are Important Series)*. Minneapolis, MN: Free Spirit Publishing.

Oelschlager, V. (2008). *Made in China: A story of adoption*. Akron, OH: Vanita Books.

Parr, T. (2007). *We belong together: A book about adoption and families*. Boston, MA: Little, Brown and Company.

Rankin, J. (1999). *You're somebody special, Walliwigs!* New York: Margaret K. McElderry Books, an imprint of Simon and Schuster.

Rice, B. (2008). *I'm adopted, I'm special*. Sarasota, FL: The Peppertree Press.

Richmond, M. R. (2008). *I wished for you: An adoption story*. Minneapolis, MN: Marianne Richmond Studios.

Rosenberg, L. (2002). *We wanted you*. New York: Roaring Brook Press, an Imprint of Macmillan.

Rounce, R. B. (2008). *The magical friendship garden*. Bloomington, IN: Xlibris Book Publishing Company.

Sansone, A. (1999). *The little green goose*. Chambersburg, PA: North-South Books.

Schaumberg, R. (2007). *Three blessings from China adopted*. Bloomington, IN: AuthorHouse.

Schwartz, C. P. (1996). *Carolyn's story: A book about an adopted girl*. Minneapolis, MN: Lerner Publishing.

Shermin, C., & Capone, D. (2003). *Families are forever*. Southampton, NY: As Simple as That.

Simon, N. (1976). *All kinds of families*. Morton Grove, IL: Albert Whitman and Company.

Simon, N. (2003). *All families are special*. Morton Grove, IL: Albert Whitman and Company.

Stinson, K. (1992). *Steven's baseball mitt*. New York: Firefly Books.

Valeri, A. (2006). *Mother's day in March: A story of adoption*. Bloomington, IN: AuthorHouse.

Werner, T. O. (2005). *Quilt of wishes*. Centennial, CO: LifeVest Publishing.

Wilgocki, J., Wright, M. K., & Geis, A. I. (2002). *Maybe days: A book for children in foster care*. Washington, DC: American Psychological Association.

Willis, W. (2000). *This is how we became a family: An adoption story*. Washington, DC: Magination Press, American Psychological Association.

Wynne-Jones, T. (2007). *The boat in the tree*. Honesdale, PA: Front Street, an Imprint of Boyds Mills Press.

Xinran. (2007). *Motherbridge of love*. Cambridge, MA: Barefoot Books.

## LITERATURE FOR MIDDLE READERS IN GRADES 3–5

Alston, D. (2008). *All about Aisha*. Raleigh, NC: Sweetie's Books.

Byng, G. (2003). *Molly Moon's incredible book of hypnotism*. New York: HarperCollins.

Creech, S. (2007). *The castle Corona*. New York: Joanna Cotler Books, an Imprint of HarperCollins.

Downing, W. (2001). *Leonardo's hand*. Boston, MA: Houghton Mifflin Company.

Ellis, S. (2003). *The several lives of orphan Jack*. Toronto, Canada: Groundwood Books.

Garden, N. (2004). *Molly's family*. New York: Farrar, Straus and Giroux.

Girard, L. W. (1989). *We adopted you, Benjamin Koo*. Morton Grove, IL: Albert Whitman and Company.

Godden, R. (2002). *Gypsy girl*. New York: HarperTrophy, an Imprint of HarperCollins.

Harlow, J. H. (2005). *Thunder from the sea*. New York: McElderry Books, an imprint of Simon and Schuster.

Kraus, J. H. (1993). *Tall boy's journey*. Minneapolis, MH: Carolrhoda Books/Lerner Publishing.

Lupica, M. (2008). *Safe at home: A comeback kids novel*. New York: Philomel, a Division of Penguin Group.

MacLeod, J. (2003). *At home in this world: A China adoption story*. Warren, NJ: EMK Press.

Mitchell, C. (2009). *Family day: Celebrating Ethan's adoption anniversary*. Bloomington, IN: AuthorHouse.

Mollel, T. M. (1990). *The orphan boy*. New York: Clarion Books.

Muldoon, K. M. (2003). *The copper king.* Logan, IA: Perfection Learning.

Muldoon, K. M. (2003). *The real Hannah Green.* Logan, IA: Perfection Learning.

Nepa, A. (2008). *Red in the flower bed: An illustrated children's story about interracial adoption.* Archbald, PA: Tribute Books.

Nixon, J. L. (1998). *Aggie's home.* New York: Delacorte Press, a Division of Random House.

Polacco, P. (2009). *In our mothers' house.* New York: Philomel, a Division of Penguin Group.

Quattlebaum, M. (2003). *Grover, Graham and me.* New York: Yearling, a Division of Random House.

Remza, F. (2007). *The journey to Mei.* Parker, CO: Outskirts Press.

Shreve, S. R. (1995). *Zoe and Columbo.* New York: Tambourine Books.

Sibley, L. (2003). *My brother, Javier.* Logan, IA: Perfection Learning.

Stanley, D. (1999). *Raising sweetness.* New York: Putnam and Grosset, a Division of Penguin Group.

Timberlake, S. (2007). *A family for Leanne.* Bloomington, IN: AuthorHouse.

Umansky, K. (2005). *The silver spoon of Solomon Snow.* Cambridge, MA: Candlewick Press.

Weitzman, E. (1996). *Let's talk about foster homes.* New York: Rosen Publishing Group.

Welch, S. K. (1990). *Don't call me Marda.* Philadelphia, PA: Our Child Press.

Woodson, J. (2002). *Our Gracie aunt.* New York: Hyperion Books.

## LITERATURE FOR OLDER READERS IN GRADES 6–8

Alma, A. (2002). *Summer of adventures.* Winlaw, B.C.: Sono Nis Press.

Atinsky, S. (2008). *Trophy kid: Or, how I was adopted by the rich and famous.* New York: Delacorte Press, an imprint of Random House.

Avi. (2006). *Crispin at the edge of the world.* New York: Hyperion Books for Children.

Casselman, G. (2005). *A walk in the park.* Toronto, Canada: Napoleon Publishing.

De Guzman, M. (2007). *Finding stinko.* New York: Farrar, Straus and Giroux.

Golding, T. M. (2008). *Niner.* Honesdale, PA: Front Street, an Imprint of Boyds Mills Press.

Hansen, J. (2001). *One true friend.* New York: Clarion Books.

Harrison, M. I. (2003). *The monster in me.* New York: Holiday House.

Haugaard, E. C. (1985). *The Samurai's tale.* Boston, MA: Houghton.

Hicks, B. (2006). *Get real.* New York: Roaring Brook Press, an Imprint of Macmillan.

Horowitz, A. (2005). *Raven's gate.* New York: Scholastic Press.

Huser, G. (2006). *Skinnybones and the wrinkle queen.* Toronto, Canada: Groundwood Books.

Jones, D. W. (2003). *Archer's goon.* New York: HarperTrophy, an Imprint of HarperCollins.

Kearney, M. (2005). *The secret of me: A novel in verse.* New York: Persea Books.

Kent, R. (2007). *Kimchi and calamari.* New York: HarperCollins.

Kolosov, J. A. (2004). *Grace from China.* St. Paul, MN: Yeong and Yeong Book Company.

Lewis, B. (1998). *Only the best.* Grand Rapids, MI: Bethany House Publishers.

Miner, C. (1998). *Rain forest girl: More than an adoption story.* Hockessin, DE: Mitchell Lane Publishers.

Murphy, R. (2005). *Looking for Lucy Buick.* New York: Delacorte Press, a Division of Random House.

Okimoto, J. D. (1990). *Molly by any other name.* New York: Scholastic, Inc.

Parks, M. A. (2006). *They called me Bunny.* Livingston AL: Livingston Press.

Patron, S. (2009). *Lucky breaks.* New York: Ginee Seo Books, an Imprint of Simon and Schuster.

Perkins, M. (2008). *First daughter: Extreme American makeover.* New York: Puffin Books, an imprint of Penguin Group.

Sleator, W. (1999). *Rewind.* New York: Puffin Books, an imprint of Penguin Group.

Sparks, B. (2005). *Finding Katie: The diary of anonymous, a teenager in foster care.* New York: HarperCollins.

Sylvia, C. (1985). *Behind the attic wall.* New York: HarperCollins.

Warren, A. (2004). *Escape from Saigon: How a Vietnam War orphan became an American boy.* New York: Farrar, Straus, and Giroux.

White, R. (2007). *Way down deep, West Virginia.* New York: Farrar, Straus and Giroux.

Williams, L. (2008). *Slant.* Minneapolis, MN: Milkweed Editions.

Wolfson, J. (2005). *What I call life.* New York: Henry Holt and Company.

# Index

# About the Author

**RUTH LYN MEESE** is a Professor of Special Education at Longwood University in Central Virginia. She has been a special educator for over 30 years, publishing three books for special education teachers and one book about children of intercountry adoption. Dr. Meese is the proud parent of a daughter adopted at age 4-1/2 from Russia in 1997. She lives with her husband, now 16-year-old daughter, and three cats in Buckingham, Virginia.